What people a

Seeds of Silence

This book is destined to be a classic of Quaker theology and spirituality. A deep dive into the roots, coherence, and originality of Quaker living, this text is a stunning articulation of *what* and *how* Quakers believe. Keiser draws on recent philosophers and early Quaker authors to articulate the contemporary vitality of Quaker insights regarding issues such as equality, interrelation, and mending creation. However, the brilliance of the book is not ultimately educational but invitational. Every page emerges from the depths of Keiser's own mature spirituality, shaped by a lifetime of Quaker commitment, experience, and practice. The reader is carried into a particularly Quaker way of being in the world. Like the works of Kelly or Thurman, the book leaves one both satisfied and longing, comforted and unsettled, encouraged and challenged to live more deeply in this strange and sacred world.

Rev. Dr. Shannon Craigo-Snell, Professor of Theology, Louisville Presbyterian Theological Seminary, author of *Silence, Love, and Death: Saying "Yes" to God in the Theology of Karl Rahner; The Empty Church: Theater, Theology, and Bodily Hope*

This is the fruit of a life's work reflecting on the basic questions of life and death. Such directness and honesty as we find here is not usual, even among philosophers and theologians. These basic questions are raw and imponderable. But Keiser is not trying to think his way through them, as many would expect a philosopher to, but is opening himself up to the experience of wonder and puzzlement that made him ask these questions in the first place. This leads into exploration of silence. This is not to say that he gives up thinking. Finding commonalities with the philosophies of Wittgenstein, Polanyi, and Merleau-Ponty, and the poetry of T.S. Eliot and Wallace Stevens, Keiser discovers how attending to silence yields a sense of reality which opens the possibility of us moderns perceiving answers to questions that most concern us. Much of the book is devoted to recovering the vision of early Quakers who articulated this response to the mysteries of life.

Rex Ambler, Senior Lecturer in Theology, Birmingham University, author of *The Quaker Way: A Rediscovery; Truth of the Heart: An Anthology of George Fox 1624–1691; Light To Live By: An Exploration in Quaker Spirituality*

Mel Keiser's work draws deeply on Quaker tradition and experience to bring fresh perspectives on contemporary philosophical, theological spiritual and ethical questions. His essays — accessible, scholarly and profound — reveal the richness of Quaker theology, and invite the reader into further dialogue and reflection.

Rachel Muers, Professor of Theology, School of Philosophy, Religion and the History of Science, University of Leeds, author of *Keeping God's Silence: Towards a Theological Ethics of Communication; Testimony: Quakerism and Theological Ethics*

In this book Mel Keiser has gathered the distilled results of several decades of deep theological and philosophical study and probing reflection on some issues long held to be basic for Quaker religious thought and witness. For those with ears to hear, there is much to be gained from these pages.

Chuck Fager, Quaker writer and retired activist; editor of the journal *Quaker Theology*; author of *Indiana Trainwreck: the Schism in Indiana Yearly Meeting over Abuse of Church Governance and Exclusion of LGBT Persons; Passing the Torch: When Quaker Elders' Lives Speak* (Co-author with Steve Angell); member of Spring Friends Meeting, Snow Camp, North Carolina; lives in Durham, North Carolina

Seeds of Silence

Essays in Quaker Spirituality and
Philosophical Theology

Seeds of Silence

Essays in Quaker Spirituality and Philosophical Theology

R. Melvin Keiser

CHRISTIAN ALTERNATIVE
BOOKS

Winchester, UK
Washington, USA

JOHN HUNT PUBLISHING

First published by Christian Alternative Books, 2021
Christian Alternative Books is an imprint of John Hunt Publishing Ltd.,
No. 3 East St., Alresford, Hampshire SO24 9EE, UK
office@jhpbooks.com
www.johnhuntpublishing.com
www.christian-alternative.com

For distributor details and how to order please visit the 'Ordering' section on our website.

Text copyright: R. Melvin Keiser 2020

ISBN: 978 1 78904 549 9
978 1 78904 550 5 (ebook)
Library of Congress Control Number: 2020933707

A CIP catalogue record for this book is available from the British Library.

Design: Stuart Davies

UK: Printed and bound by CPI Group (UK) Ltd, Croydon, CR0 4YY
Printed in North America by CPI GPS partners

We operate a distinctive and ethical publishing philosophy in all areas of our business, from our global network of authors to production and worldwide distribution.

Contents

Previous Titles

Recovering the Personal: Religious Language and the Postcritical Quest of H. Richard Niebuhr (Atlanta: Scholars Press, 1988)
ISBN 1-55540-185-6, & 1-55540-186-4 (pk)
The Way of Transfiguration: Religious Imagination as Theopoiesis (Louisville: Westminster Press, 1992; selected essays of Stanley Romaine Hopper, eds. R. Melvin Keiser and Tony Stoneburner)
ISBN 0-664-21936-5
Roots of Relational Ethics: Responsibility in Origin and Maturity in H. Richard Niebuhr (Scholars Press, 1996)
ISBN 0-7885-0211-5, & 0-7885-0212-3
Knowing the Mystery of Life Within: Selected Writings of Isaac Penington in Their Historical and Theological Context (London: Quaker Books, 2005; eds. R. Melvin Keiser and Rosemary Moore) ISBN 0 85245 378 7

Introduction

I have been seeking throughout my life to make sense of my and our existence in this world of ours. I am exploring how to live with and to respond to the deeper questions about my being in the world—Who am I; What is death and is there eternal life; Why is there something rather than nothing; How should I relate to suffering and oppression; What is it that matters most? My life is a Friends journey: raised in a Quaker Meeting, attending Quaker schools, teaching in a Quaker college, writing in Quaker thought. Throughout, Silence has been the undergirding reality. As I began to write Quaker essays, wanting to get at the essence of the Quaker Way in my experience and in my understanding of the beginnings of Quakerism, Silence became a conscious theme. What I have written over many years about Quaker spirituality and the philosophical and theological insights engendered within it, I am gathering here.

Silence is the basis of the Quaker way of being—underlying, sustaining, creating our many ways of relating in word and act to the world, other persons, our own selves, and our efforts at mending the world. By *waiting in silence*, alone and in communal worship, we receive insight into our condition and the condition of the world, guidance into action that is justice-seeking and whole-making, a sense of divine presence in daily living and worship, and a taste of the love that engenders and pervades being.

We find arising from the Silence, as well, words that bear meaning of our lives, and thoughts that seek to say what is ultimately unsayable about the Silence in which we dwell. These essays explore spiritual, theological, and philosophical aspects in the Quaker way.

I draw upon writings of some leading Friends in its beginnings in England in the latter half of the seventeenth century as they arise from and manifest the encompassing Silence. You will meet various early Friends—George Fox, Robert Barclay, Isaac and Mary Penington, James Nayler, Margaret Fell, Thomas Lurting.

My search for understanding the reality I, and we, inhabit— what sense the world makes, and how to dwell responsibly in it—and how Quaker spirituality and thought engage and express it has taken me, as well, into many areas outside of traditional Quaker thought. In the philosophical writings of major twentieth-century thinkers—Michael Polanyi, Maurice Merleau-Ponty, Ludwig Wittgenstein—and theological writings—of H. Richard Niebuhr, Stanley Romaine Hopper, Paul Tillich—I find explorations of the creative dimension in our being beneath words, reason, and explicit consciousness. No doubt expressed in very different words from Quaker language, and from each other, they have been important, because of their insights and differences, in broadening and deepening my understanding of meaning in our Silence-encompassed life. Through them I see more of the richness of my own Quaker tradition and its relevance to our contemporary situation.

My underlying theme is the nature and practice of Silence at the roots of our living, thinking, and speaking. I explore how they are related to Silence; how they emerge from or defend against Silence. The inquiry takes us into questions of how words work in relation to Silence. The faith and practice of Friends, especially in its inaugural period, is a densely woven fabric of metaphor and symbol. How do Friends relate to modernity's dualisms of self/world, mind/body, subject/object, established at the same time as Quakerism's divergent beginnings? What difference, what new insight and relatedness, can come using the lens of Silence—a Quaker perspective on self, world, language, meaning—on traditional theological issues such as Christ and God language, the historical Jesus, the resurrection, and release from oppression?

I am particularly interested to sketch out what I see as the distinctive nature of Quaker thinking. What is Quaker theology embedded as it is in a mesh of metaphor? For this I use Hopper's word "theopoetic" to distinguish Friends' creative use of figural language and participation in experience of divinity they evoke, from theology as usual devoted to making logical connections between concepts which define divinity. How then do we speak as Friends in the intertwinings of metaphors, symbols, and ideas emergent from the depths of Silence? How does such experiential thought handle philosophical issues, and therefore what is Quaker philosophical theology? How does it relate to ethics, historical meaning, and scriptural interpretation? How do we seek to live in the world and deal with oppressions?

I have been exploring from my adolescence the meaning of Silence in my own life and thought, in my Quaker communities of Germantown (Coulter Street, Philadelphia, Pennsylvania), Friendship Friends Meeting (Greensboro, North Carolina), and Swannanoa Valley Friends Meeting (Black Mountain, North Carolina), as a student at Westtown Friends Boarding School (West Chester, Pennsylvania) and Earlham College (Richmond, Indiana), as a teacher of Religious and Interdisciplinary Studies at Guilford College (Greensboro, North Carolina), and as Co-Director of Common Light Meetingplace in Black Mountain at the beginning of our refirement after Guilford.

For over forty years I have been writing, as a way of understanding and sharing, about aspects of our lives in this world environed by Silence. Before being published, most were read at conferences. Many of these were presented over ten years at the Quaker Theological Seminar at Woodbrooke in Birmingham, England. Others were presented at The Quaker Theology Roundtable at Pendle Hill (Wallingford, Pennsylvania), Friends Association in Higher Education (George Fox College, Newberg, Oregon), The Coolidge Research Colloquium (Episcopal Divinity School, Cambridge, Massachusetts), Guilford College's Faculty Colloquium (Greensboro, North Carolina),

Swannanoa Valley Friends Meeting (Black Mountain, North Carolina), and in various periodicals: *Friends Journal, Pendle Hill, Quaker History, Quaker Religious Thought, Quaker Studies, Quaker Theology, Guilford Review, Cross Currents.*

Evoking real-life situations, I have retained the particularities of my addressing certain groups on their defined themes. While essays overlap in the telling of anecdotes and exploring the thought of various figures, I hope different angles and contexts will elicit a richness of insight and imaginative reflection.

I dedicate this book to my children—Megan and Christopher Keiser—and grandchildren—Jahniya and Ondessa Kiliru-Liontree, and Sophia and Sam Fairbairn. May the Seeds of Silence fructify in their lives and the lives they touch.

I. Silence as Origin

The lives of Friends are embodied in and shaped by our words. Much of early Friends language, spoken and written, is metaphoric, creating a dense weave of dynamic meanings. This mesh of metaphors as the home of our being arises from "waiting in silence" and seeks to evoke awareness of Silence as it becomes present in the depths of hearer and reader. Friends' response to the world, to war and other forms of oppression, and to theological thinking as well are activated and sustained in the waiting and Silence-bearing metaphors. Our understanding of God and Christ, our approach to history and scripture, and our spiritual way is within this web of waiting and word.

In stories from the beginnings of Quakerism in England in the second half of the seventeenth century, we can see how Silence is origin of word and action. Thomas Lurting, an officer on a British warship, was convinced of the Quaker way of nonviolence by observing sailors, waiting in Quaker silence, joining them, and then refusing to fight as his ship moved towards a military engagement. The young George Fox was convinced in the solitude of silence of the presence of God in his inward depths as he, at the edge of despair, let go of finding any outward help.

Waiting in silence, our center is the Light (or other metaphors for the divine—Seed, Inward Teacher, That of God in Everyone, the eternal Christ) which fills us with Presence, illumines our condition, and guides us into transformative action. The circumference is the New Creation, the whole world as originally created hidden now in the depths of our being in the world. Descending into silence we can live in and from its unfractured wholeness, in unity with persons and nature.

The philosophical implications of waiting in the silence, centered in the Light, environed by the New Creation, the wholeness of being, are an emergent way of knowing and being.

As an alternative to the Cartesian dualisms of modern life and thought, which separate the mind and body, self and world, me and others, Quaker thought seeks to integrate disparate aspects of our existence emerging from Silence, meeting and greeting, transforming and mending, self and world, and to evoke mystery in silence.

While doubt was central to Descartes' dualistic approach to reality, Friends embrace doubt and critical reason from within silence. A year later after his convincement, the young Fox found himself sitting in silence, overwhelmed with doubt about the existence of God. His response to this experience of doubt was to wait in a deeper Silence for an answer to arise. What this means in his life and thought can be clearly seen by comparing his response to doubt with a seminal moment in the formation of the modern world when René Descartes earlier encountered doubt. Descartes' dualistic response separated mind and body, self and world, by appropriating intellectual doubt as his method to achieve conceptual certainty. As this definition of critical reason as active doubting was becoming the springboard for modern thinking, Fox and other early Friends turned to the "inaction" of waiting in silence to discover what is real through words that arise, especially in metaphor and story, eliciting an existential confidence rather than an intellectual certainty.

While Cartesian mind/body dualism and advocacy of critical reason was fundamental to the basis of the burgeoning Enlightenment, freeing science from ecclesiastical hegemony, and resulting in the affirmation of natural rights and impulse to achieve justice and to establish democracy, Friends' efforts to mend the world arose from non-dualistic waiting in Silence. The basis is a unity of spirituality and ethics, rather than making ethics an application of reason. Being led from waiting in Silence, Friends challenged the injustice of the British social, gender, and religious hierarchy, participated in the rise of modern science, provided a template for the formation of American democracy, and became much involved, though in no way ideal, in the work of abolition of slavery, racial justice, Native rights, sexual equality, business integrity, political and socio-economic equity. The origin of the Quaker way of thinking, acting, worshiping is in the Silence surrounding and pervading our being in the world.

Waiting in Silence: The Metaphoric Matrix of Quakerism

The vitality and potency of Quakerism is borne in the lives of Friends but also in words which sustain and shape those lives. I want to explore a cluster of such words that have been central since its beginning in order to grasp what is essential to the Quaker way of being. "Seed" and "light" are admittedly crucial metaphors but I want to show that they take on their characteristically Quaker meanings in the context of "waiting in silence." This is both something we do and also the way in which we understand what that is—both act and word. In fact, it is an excellent example of how a word is a form of life—something that expresses and shapes an aspect of our lives. Moreover, I want to show how Friends encounter God within these forms of life; our religious words are not only freighted with the spiritual substance of our lives, they are bearers of divine reality. Within such words we not only encounter ourselves and are transformed, we encounter ultimate reality which transforms us.

If these words are forms of life, and not merely signs, ideas, or rhetorical embellishments, separable from and unessential to the shape of our lives, then we need to catch their meaning as they are being enacted in actual living. To do this we will need to tell some stories. We are seeking, therefore, to get at the nature of Quakerism by exploring certain religious expressions as they come to life in narrative.

One cold morning in Nottinghamshire while sitting in front of a fire, George Fox, at the very beginning of his career in 1648, was overwhelmed with a profound doubt about the existence of God in the face of modern science. As he was sitting by the fire, he says, a great cloud came over him and he felt a voice rise within that tempted him to believe that "'All things come by nature'; and the elements and stars came over me so that I was in a manner quite clouded with it."[1] The way he dealt with this was characteristic of his handling of both ideas and situations, and has shaped the Society of Friends throughout its history. While so commonplace for being so central among Quakers, we should, nevertheless, not miss the extraordinariness, indeed the unprecedentedness within religious history, of his response. Not appealing to some authority, such as Bible, ecclesiastical figure, or religious thinker; not arguing on the basis of reason; not setting out to study the issue or to explore it in conversation; neither disregarding it nor succumbing to it—Fox *sat still and silent*. He puts it in this way:

> But inasmuch as I sat, still and silent, the people of the house perceived nothing. And as I sat still under it and let it alone, a living hope arose in me, and a true voice, which said, "There is a living God who made all things." And immediately the cloud and temptation vanished away, and life rose over it all, and my heart was glad, and I praised the living God.[2]

While there are some peculiar things here, such as speaking of the stars and elements coming over him, and more so in hearing voices declaring and responding within himself—although I suspect we "hear" more "voices" within than we would admit— the strangest thing is this action of inaction, this waiting in silence.

A novel approach to doubt, to be sure: Fox allows an answer to rise from the depths rather than dealing with it through any powers under his control, such as intellect or will. As he sat with the challenge and "let it alone," refusing to cope with it but allowing it to be, he found a hope rising and a voice articulating his theological commitment. It is to experience rather than to external authority or autonomous reason that he turns, but experience of a particular kind: it is an encounter with the transcendent depths within. Waiting in silence is an expectant inaction that is a hope for what one does not yet know how to name nor how to think about and work for. To sit under the weight of such a doubt, which threatened the core of his vocational and personal identity just beginning to form, and to wait for the silence to become articulate requires a significant degree of trust in the helpfulness of those depths. In the face of doubt Fox is exhibiting a hope and faith, yet not directed to any object, but rather an openness at a deep level to what will emerge in his being.

It is fascinating to realize that only a few decades earlier on the continent another young man had been sitting in front of another fire thinking about doubt. This man was not, however, overcome by doubt but was very deliberately working out a method of thinking that employed it. He was of course Descartes. Systematically he set out to doubt everything in order to arrive at a point of absolute certainty. What he arrived at was *Cogito ergo sum* — I think therefore I am. The certainty was of his own existence and from that he went on to prove, at least so he thought, the existence of God and of the perceptible world. It is interesting that, while he meant to doubt everything, he did not in fact doubt God's existence, even though he tried to prove it, whereas Fox had no intention of doubting; it simply came upon him, and he did in fact doubt God's existence.

The methods they developed, formative of modern philosophy and of Quakerism, are direct antitheses. Descartes wants a rational certitude and seeks for it through the act of doubting, believing it will bring him to that which is indubitable and certain. Fox wants an existential certitude and seeks it, not in doubting the existence of something, but in opening to it, embracing it within the context of his own depths. The judgmental act versus the accepting act: in the face of the first, the world of our ordinary experience withers; in the face of the second, a deeper meaning emerges from beyond our ken and control. It is as though Descartes clung to the *Cogito*, the "I think," wanting to erect a life of thought upon this rational act, whereas Fox adhered to the *sum*, finding in his own "I am," his own being, as it speaks out of the depths, a meaning for his life.

It is perhaps a failing in our eyes that Fox was so successful, that he eradicated all doubt from his life and presents himself as always right and good, even in his morally questionable handling of James Nayler. If not a failing in Fox, it is, nevertheless, a difficulty for many today that he is unable to speak to this aspect of our condition—that doubt and faith, cognitive uncertainty and existential commitment, are intertwined for us, that being religious involves living intimately in touch with the unknown. There are the beginnings in Fox of coping with doubt which can help us, but we do not find ourselves able or willing summarily and definitively to dispose of it. There is a strength there in the midst of the pain of unknowing that we need.

We have known much about doubt in our day. The three hundred-year search for Cartesian certainty has led us to the despair and alienation of the twentieth century. We have seen the objects of belief, whether God or absolute values, dissolve under the acid of Cartesian doubt, and have found some thinkers picking up the notion of waiting—waiting for Godot, waiting for what will come after the twilight of the gods. Tillich talks about the anxiety of meaninglessness and suggests there comes in the midst of the loss of the objects of belief and of our spiritual center a sense of meaning. Camus says, although Sisyphus is enmeshed in the absurdity in being, that we should, nevertheless, imagine him happy. Neither speaks of waiting, yet what they speak of does not come as a result of any action on our part nor by a theistic God but in an attentiveness. Eliot, however, does name it as waiting:

> I said to my soul, be still, and wait without hope
> For hope would be hope for the wrong thing; wait without
>   love

For love would be love of the wrong thing; there is yet faith
But the faith and the love and the hope are all in the waiting.
Wait without thought, for you are not ready for thought:
So the darkness shall be the light, and the stillness the
  dancing.[3]

In the face of modernity's profound doubt and sense of
nothingness, Eliot is unwittingly recommending what Fox
developed as his method for coping with every sort of problem.
It is not only to an intellectual problem, but to every situation—a
personal attack, an injustice, a political event, a decision to be
made, the restraints of imprisonment, social needs—that Fox
responds with this initial waiting. It is perhaps ironic that
Quakers who are best known around the world for performing
certain deeds—feeding the starving in post-war Europe,
carrying medical supplies to North Vietnam, participating in
the underground railroad in nineteenth-century America or
twentieth-century Nazi controlled France, working for sexual
and social equality from its beginnings—should arrive at these
actions by the initial inaction of waiting.

In order to understand this better and to show the centrally
formative effect of religious language upon it, we turn to another
story, little known but extraordinary, of Thomas Lurting who
became a Quaker in the 1650s while serving as an officer on a
British man-of-war. While his convincement was dramatic, as
we shall see, what is especially interesting is that it occurred
out of the most minimal amount of knowledge about Quakers
imaginable; he found his own way towards a Quakerly manner
of responding to others and eventually to a rejection of all
fighting with no knowledge that this was characteristic of
Friends. I want to suggest that under such circumstances we can
see the formative power of "waiting in silence" as both word and
deed, and thereby gain a better understanding of the nature of
Quakerism.

In 1653 Thomas Lurting, then Boatswain of the British frigate, Bristol, narrowly escaped death four times while participating courageously in an engagement in the Canary Islands with Spanish ships in which all sixteen Galleons, heavily laden with silver and men, were sunk. Shortly after this battle their ship took on several British soldiers for a brief time. Among them, in Lurting's own words, was a man "who had been at a Meeting in Scotland of the people called Quaker."[4] Before being placed on shore this soldier had "some converse" with two sailors.

Six months later these two began to exhibit characteristics peculiar to Quakers: they refused to take their hats off to the Captain; they refused to attend the ship's church service; they met often in silence.

In the face of this insubordination the Captain told the Boatswain to beat them back to order. Lurting set about it with a will but found their silence and the remembrance of his recent four deliverances unnerving. For six months he struggled within himself and finally went and sat in silence with the Friends, now grown to six. The Captain was furious but did not punish him. Shortly thereafter, a sickness swept across the ship killing some forty people. The Quakers showed themselves diligent in caring for all on board. Temporarily, Lurting regained the respect of the Captain. But he was to enrage him once again when he realized he must never again fight.

It was in the midst of getting ready to bombard a coastal fort that it came to him he should not kill. And so he stopped in the midst of the preparations. Later that evening he shared what had happened with his now ten Friends. The next time they faced a battle situation, they all met in silent worship on deck within view of the Captain. Furious, the Captain drew his sword and Lurting approached to within a few paces confronting him out of the inner stillness. The Captain hesitated and then withdrew.

This is truly an extraordinary account of a religious conversion, but what I find most incredible is how little Lurting knew about

Quakerism with yet such momentous effects. Lurting did not know what the soldier had told the two sailors; he was not even a Friend. But we can assume he told them that Quakers wait in silence since the sailors much later began to meet in silence. A word is communicated; for six months it worked on them until it issued in their waiting in silence. Lurting, after six months more, is overwhelmed by the quality of being of those waiting in silence and joins them. Not only does this conversion alter his understanding of God and his religious practice, it changes his entire demeanor; he meets the threat of violence with few words while caring for the others, with a stillness fostered in silence. He says of this himself: "I was very quiet and still in my Mind; for I found, therein was my Strength."[5] Finally, out of the silent waiting emerges a testimony against all fighting.

The words of the soldier engendered an action and a whole way of being; they evoked a form of life lived in the presence of God. It is out of this matrix of meaning that the metaphors of seed and light have come. To see their emerging within this context, we turn back to the early life of Fox to find the first Quaker appearance of waiting in silence, for it is here that we shall find the origins of the Quaker use of these metaphors.

In 1647, the year before his experience of doubt, we find the first injunction to wait in silence in his convincement. Fox presents this as occurring just after that turning point of his youthful, anguished search:

[W]hen all my hopes in them [all ministers] and in all men were gone, so that I had nothing outwardly to help me, nor could tell what to do, then, Oh then, I heard a voice which said, "There is one, even Christ Jesus, that can speak to thy condition," and when I heard it my heart did leap for joy.[6]

Throughout his youth he had sought out ministers and religious thinkers near and far in order to find answers to the religious questions that were continually brimming over. This time of search was much filled with anguish and despair, although there were moments of release and joy. He spent much time in solitary places inquiring of God and reading the Bible. He had already understood in the Bible that "the Lord would teach his people himself";[7] the power of this realization that only divine resources within could speak to his condition was not in the idea, which he already had from scriptures, but in the depth of the experience. At the moment of despair, as later with doubt, he found something arising from within himself that could respond to his situation. He became committed to what he had already understood: "For though I read the Scriptures that spoke of Christ and of God, yet I knew him not but by revelation...." By revelation he means he came to this through direct experience of God within, as he says: "And this I knew experimentally."[8]

While he speaks once earlier of his solitariness as a waiting upon the Lord,[9] he urges waiting as a religious way for the first time just after this experience: "Therefore, all wait patiently upon the Lord, whatsoever condition you be in...."[10] It is within this context after his "conversion" that he begins to speak of light and seed (with one earlier exception, a reference to his father as having had "a Seed of God in him"[11]). Prior to this experience he speaks of his search as a looking for wisdom[12] and describes his experiences of God as being taught[13] and commanded by God,[14] as a consideration arising or an opening occurring,[15] as being moved,[16] being inclined,[17] or being gently led by God.[18] But it is only after this experience that he begins to use these metaphors of seed and light, and to advocate waiting in silence.

There is a continuity between "before" and "after"; what is different is that he discovers that what he has in fact been doing can become the "method" to experience divine reality speaking to one's condition both for himself and for others. And he realizes this way of waiting in silence can be powerfully borne by the metaphors seed and light. Immediately after enjoining waiting,

15

Fox speaks of "the unchangeable truth in the inward parts, the light of Jesus Christ" and of "my inward mind being joined to his good Seed."[19] If we will look closely at how he uses these two metaphors, we can see how they arise out of waiting in silence and are able to engender this experience of the inward teacher.

There is a gentle and gradualistic quality in Fox's use of both metaphors—an opening of the light and a springing forth of new life from the seed.[20] They embody what Fox tells us in the initial paragraph of his *Journal* he is intending to do, to say "how the work of the Lord was begun and gradually carried on in me."[21] Waiting in silence allows the gradual illumination of light and growing of the seed. There is a peacefulness in these, yet there is as well a vigor and even a violence. The light not only illumines the infinite love and goodness of God,[22] it "let me see myself as I was without him,"[23] Fox says, and it made possible that "all appeared that is out of the Light, darkness, death, temptations, the unrighteousness, the ungodly; all was manifest and seen in the Light."[24] Following this he says: "I saw how he sat as a refiner's fire."[25] The pain of self-discovery and knowledge of the evil of the world and the cleansing force of God's refining fire is exceeded by the violence of the seed which "bruised the head of this Serpent the destroyer."[26] Indeed, the love of God present in seed and light can bring about a reversal, destroying and creating: "Thou, Lord, makest a fruitful field a barren wilderness, and a barren wilderness a fruitful field...."[27] There is then in these metaphors as used by Fox a coincidence of opposites—the gentle and gradually emergent is also overwhelmingly powerful and destroying.

As Fox indicates several pages later, the fruitful field being made barren is "that which is pleasant to the outward eye and fleshly mind."[28] He employs a typical Christian opposition between spirit and flesh, but, like St. Paul, he does not equate flesh with the physical world. Rather flesh is the self which cannot let go of its ego-control in order to be responsive to the transcendent depths that would lead us beyond the narrow confines of our self-serving, outward-turned desires. Immediately after speaking of "flesh (that could not give up to the will of God),"[29] he goes on, like St. Paul, to affirm "the redemption of the body and of the whole creation."[30] The natural world in fact figures prominently in his experience from early on. On the second page of the *Journal*, he speaks of a "unity with creation," and curiously of God's covenant with all creatures, not just certain humans, which he has come up into.[31] Later Fox speaks of this unity in a mystical ascent, as he says, up "through the flaming sword into the paradise of God [where] [a]ll things were new, and all the creation gave another smell...."[32] Light and seed as natural images are confirmatory of our being in this world.

The darkness the light overcomes, as when he speaks of "an ocean of darkness and death" being overwhelmed by "an infinite ocean of light and love,"[33] is the same as the flesh—life lived on the surface adhering to its own ego possessions. There is, however, presumably a different kind of darkness implied in the use of the seed, for it grows in the darkness of the soil. Fox does not, however, draw out such an implication. Nevertheless, the light metaphor is not rational cognition, as it is for Thomas Aquinas, who uses it to speak of the intellectual vision of God, but involves, if not the darkness at least unknowing, non-rational feelings.

In a remarkable passage that shows how intertwined are illuming light, gradually growing seed, and waiting, Fox says "by the light you will come to see through and feel over winter storms."[34] Through this light feelings come; moreover, the light is something that can be felt—there are those who have "been convinced and have felt the light."[35] This mixing of the senses shows that light for Fox is different from the clear light of grace-perfected reason of St. Thomas. It is not rational clarity simply seen with the spiritual eye, but is a feeling-ful experience in which having felt the light, one may later "feel winter storms, tempests, and hail, and be frozen, in frost and cold and a wilderness and temptations."[36] In this obscuring of the felt light by feelings of spiritual winter, he recommends waiting in silence in which the light and summer will again gradually emerge:

> Be patient and still in the power and still in the light that doth convince you, to keep your minds to God; in that be quiet, that you may come to the summer, that your flight be not in the winter. For if you sit still in the patience which overcomes in the power of God, there will be no flying. For the husbandman after he hath sown his seed he is patient.[37]

The life nurtured by these metaphors is non-authoritarian. There is no law, principle, command, or goal that is the basis of Fox's ethics. Rather, there is that in waiting in silence which emerges from the depths within. While such a leading of light or seed comes from the universal God, it has a particular appropriateness to the concrete situation. A leading always occurs in a specific context as an inclining towards a particular action in this time and place. It is not a specific application of a general principle. Nor is it the product of thought. There is the implication that every situation transcends our ability to understand and to control it. The leading emerges out of our unconscious depths through which we are relating to the ingredients in the given situation. What arises is also appropriate to the measure of spiritual maturity maintained by the individual.[38]

Seed and light, born out of and carrying the message of waiting in silence, rather than denying our humanity, confirm it and fulfill it. As a particular leading of light and seed emerges out of the darkness of our being, it exists in a divinely established fittingness that includes feelings not denied but rising from the depths, the measure of our individual humanity, and our relations beneath consciousness to the unknown complexity of the context.

Waiting in silence as word and act is a vehicle of virtue, in the etymological sense of power and excellence. In Lurting's life, word has led to act and act has led to the transformation of behavior and belief. In Fox's life, word has named the already existent act and provided a form of life that bears both self-knowledge and divine awareness, and becomes, as we have seen with seed and light, the metaphoric matrix of Quakerism.

Inward Light and the New Creation: A Theological Meditation on the Center and Circumference of Quakerism

Preface

Once there was a ten-day gathering of Friends at Pendle Hill who called themselves, somewhat pretentiously, "The Working Party for the Future of the Quaker Movement." The two characteristics possessed by all thirty participants were that each felt him or herself to be on the edge of Quakerism and sought some sort of renewal—for ourselves and Quakerism—from this place of marginality. What follows is an interim report from one on the edges of Quakerism and the modern world.

That I have located myself in the context of the whole world, and worse yet at its center, you may take as a sign that the margins of a group already on the edges of modernity are desperate indeed for a place to be. Nevertheless, whether aware of mythic understandings of the world or not, we all seek for a context and a center of reality. Invariably we interpret context and center from our own perspective which casts light on certain aspects of reality while leaving other areas obscure and unnoticed. Hence the need for dialogue.

What I have been doing in the intervening twenty years since our "Party" is exploring our own tradition and the modern world. While I write with the intention of historical accuracy and even with the hope of insight, I am unconscionably probing my own roots to see what stands out and speaks in our modern day, or better what stands under with which I can understand. Rather than an antiquated body of writing and practices, I am finding in Quakerism resources for spiritual maturing, thought, and action, and a vitality resonant with current radical movements, such as certain types of feminism and "postcritical" or "phenomenological" (i.e. non- or trans-dualistic) philosophies.

It is the mutuality of critique and constructive proposal in feminism and Quakerism that I explore here. If the main substance of modernity is fixed upon an objectifying domination that is propelling us ever more clearly towards environmental and nuclear disaster, then it is incumbent upon us all to use what wits we have, even theological wit, to allow the edges to speak — which speak to me of a center and context, beyond the alienating and isolating dichotomies of modernity, of Light and the New Creation.

Introduction

The center of Quakerism is the Inward Light, its circumference the New Creation. To open to the Light—or Seed, Truth, Life, Inward Teacher, Christ within (we have used many metaphors for the indwelling presence of God)—is to live within the world as originally created. Seventeenth-century Friends were not only responsive to the Light but related to a context, and this context was the world as the divinely created original matrix of being. From this underlying center and circumference flows early Friends' way of being in the world, the peculiar nature of their spirituality, theology, and ethics.

What follows is a theological meditation upon history, drawing from Quaker origins to clarify and enrich contemporary Quaker spirituality and engagement in theology and ethics today. In sharing this theological meditation, I want to make explicit what every historian and theologian does implicitly: to share not only what I see, but also the perspective from which I am looking.

The spirituality of Inward Light and New Creation that I see manifest in early Friends can help us address contemporary issues as fruitfully as they did. That spirituality affirms that God and world are inseparable because we relate inherently both to divine presence as acting on each of us and to the web of interrelations as the world within which we dwell. Our radical affirmation of individuality is therefore inseparable from our radical affirmation of relatedness; our sense of the immediate presence of God inseparable from our motivation to transform an oppressive social order; our theological thought inseparable from our ethical action.

Nature of the New Creation

To discover and open to the Light at our center is to dwell within the total world as originally created. "World" here is not the corrupt state of the carnal mind, as Friends following the Johannine writer speak of in various places, but the created context of our being. While sin obscures it, distorts and fragments it, the Light awakens us to our participation in this divinely undergirded unity of creation. In *Love to the Lost* (1656), one of the major Quaker books of the 1650s, James Nayler characterizes the New Creation in this manner:

> And as man beholds the seed growing, so he comes to see the new creation, and what he lost in the fall, and so is restored by the power of the word, the son of God, into his dominion, power and purity, made able to resist the devil, to choose the thing that is good, and delight in it, as before he delighted in the contrary: so comes man to be reconciled to his maker in the eternal unity, beyond what is to be expressed.[1]

The world is the context for convincement. The Light convinces us to open to this whole world. To respond to the Light is to come into unity not only with God but with the world. But this is not the world at the surface; the New Creation is the world in its depths. Beneath our surface life the world exists in our depths as originally created. While obscured in the Fall, it has not been obliterated. The Light opens us to our depths and there we are brought into touch with the original matrix of our being.

While Nayler uses the exact phrase, George Fox, the founder

of the Society of Friends, speaks of it as the "new world": "And if ever your eyes come to see repentance and own the light of Jesus Christ in you, you will witness me a friend of your souls and eternal good. Then will you own your condemnation; and that you must all own before you come into the new world here there is no end."[2] Even though the New Creation was not a watch-word of early Quakers, its meaning permeates their experience and thought. Coming soon after his convincement, Fox makes explicit that the context of his conversion is the creation. In the midst of his youthful search for a grounding and direction for his life that took him to the religious authorities of his day, he despaired of any help and only then discovered the divine resources within. He writes of this:

> And when all my hopes in them and in all men were gone, so that I had nothing outwardly to help me, nor could tell what to do, then, Oh then, I heard a voice which said, "There is one, even Christ Jesus, that can speak to thy condition," and when I heard it my heart did leap for joy.[3]

During the next year the cosmic significance of this discovery of Christ within is revealed in his visionary experience of returning to Eden:

> Now was I come up in spirit through the flaming sword into the paradise of God. All things were new, and all the creation gave another smell unto me than before, beyond what words can utter. I knew nothing but pureness, and innocency, and righteousness, being renewed up into the image of God by Christ Jesus, so that I say I was come up to the state of Adam which he was in before he fell. The creation was opened to me, and it was showed me how all things had their names given them according to their nature and virtue. And I was at a stand in my mind whether I should practise physic for the good

of mankind, seeing the nature and virtues of the creatures were so opened to me by the Lord. But I was immediately taken up in spirit, to see into another or more steadfast state than Adam's in innocency, even into a state in Christ Jesus, that should never fall. And the Lord showed me that such as were faithful to him in the power and light of Christ, would come up into that state in which Adam was before he fell, in which the admirable works of the creation, and the virtues thereof, may be known, through the openings of that divine Word of wisdom and power by which they were made. Great things did the Lord lead me into, and wonderful depths were opened unto me, beyond what can by words be declared; but as people come into subjection to the spirit of God, and grow up in the image and power of the Almighty, they may receive the Word of wisdom, that opens all things, and come to know the hidden unity in the Eternal Being.[4]

Having opened to the Light Within, Fox is carried back into Paradise where he experiences the newness and freshness of the original creation. In Genesis when God expelled Adam and Eve, he posted an angel with drawn sword at the gates of Eden to prevent their return. Fox has now passed back through this prohibitive and purgative sword to be transformed into pureness and to recover the image of God distorted in the fall. He is given a knowledge into the heart of the world, understanding the nature and virtues, the power and excellence, of all creatures, and the human condition and state of Christ.

This knowing of the order of creation comes through involvement with rather than detachment from the world, and is interpretive and sensuous, making sense of created beings through the senses. Principal among the senses in this account is smell, expressing an intimate knowing of the New Creation. Depths are opened through smell, seeing, and hearing which reach beyond what words can convey. To be renewed into the original Adamic state is to have such intimate knowing of "the admirable works of creation" and is to experience a "hidden unity" and fullness of being in God.

Fundamental to Fox's spirituality then is this intimate indwelling of the New Creation. Not only is he centered in the Light, he is situated in the world in its original vitality. Even though he presents a visionary experience unique to himself, he intends it as a spiritual pattern for all, whether or not we are given to such visions. The New Creation is our present ordinary world but as experienced in depth illumined by the divine Light. On the surface we center ourselves in a context narrower than the community of all being, splitting self from world, spirit from nature, mind from body; in the depths, the Light draws us down to dwell beyond these fragmenting dichotomies.

Spirituality of the New Creation

The method of life seeking such unity is waiting in silence. To reach down to where the Light lives requires a waiting that draws us down from surface preoccupations into our inchoate depths where we do not control nor understand. Silence is the means of this descent. Waiting in silence is a receptive state in which "ripeness is all." Our spirituality does not come from our initiating but rather from our letting go, as Penington was wont to say, in our getting low every day. This silent descent into ripeness is an opening to the Light-centered New Creation, and a readiness for responsiveness within this environment.

In letting go we trust in an unseen power; we trust that power to be there in our region of unknowing and that it will take form in the given moment as word, image, or action to be performed — as the speaking of the Spirit. The manner of our spirituality of Light and New Creation is therefore neither proclamation of the Word (in Bible or preaching) nor celebration of Action (in the Eucharist), but is waiting — a silent descent to the source and anticipation of emergence of a divinely shaped pattern. Beneath the spoken or written word, or the past action of Christ, we wait upon the presence of Christ, the source of word and action.

Philosophically, the nature of Quaker spirituality diverges from traditional western spirituality based upon the Greek distinction between spirit and matter. Aristotle conceives of self and world as constructed by the formative agency of spirit imposing form upon formless matter. Incorporated into Christianity this became, in medieval thought, reason shaping emotions towards the goals of rationality and the vision of God, and in Protestant thought, God conforming a passive self by obedience to divine will.

Neither ascending beyond the world to a vision of God nor leaping a chasm between the world and divine will, Quaker spirituality descends in silent waiting into the depths of the world. There we discover the divine mystery, and from That Which Has No Form, because it is not a form but the source of all forms, arise the Spirit's leading and our own spirit with a felt sense of divine presence. Matter is pregnant with divinity. The forms of our speech and actions, of our lives, need not be imposed on us from without. They emerge from formlessness, a formlessness we know in our silent waiting to be worthy of trust. To open to this divine potential for human form is to grow as a seed, to achieve structure in matter. Spirit (human and divine) is not an abstraction from space and time, but is always experienced in the here and now, in this circumstance by this embodied self that I am.

For this reason Quakerism is a world-affirming spirituality. Spirit and world, as our existential context, are not a dualism, leading to a world-negating spirituality. Rather the matter of our lives is a spiritual incipience potent with Spirit.

Trusting such formlessness, such mystery, beyond the apparent protection of dualism—which excludes the ambiguity of interrelatedness and certifies the superior value of one disentangled part—can be terrifying. Wallowing in it can be destructive, either by refusing ever to come to form or by continually dissolving all forms back into their mysterious source. While returning ever again to the source, we are always being drawn forth by the Spirit to create the forms of our personal, communal, technological, and cultural lives. The ongoing movement between formlessness and form is to keep us close to the mystery and to live in forms filled with Life that do not destroy but enhance our being in the world.

We can watch young Fox coming to awareness of the presence of God in the world early in his *Journal,* in the movement between his convincement of the Light within and experience of the New Creation. He moves from dichotomizing spirit and world, to reducing spirit to world, to affirming the spirituality of the world as divine creation. In his discovery of the Light within in his convincement, he seemingly rejects the outward world, for "I had nothing outwardly to help me."[5] As he turns within, however, to the presence of the Inward Teacher, he finds "two thirsts in me," one "after the creatures" and the other "after the Lord."[6] The world is not only without, it is within, opposing the thirst for God. Later he realizes more clearly that the world is within as symbol: "The natures of dogs, swine, vipers, of Sodom and Egypt, Pharaoh, Cain, Ishmael, Esau, etc. The natures of these I saw within, though people had been looking without."[7] While outwardly the world is objects in space and time, inwardly it is evil, the corrupting and destructive forces in the self. At this point the "world" is negative for Fox, both as outward things and inward symbols.

Discovery that the world is within as inward meaning means that self and world are inseparable. While initially negative in import, it opens Fox to an affirmation. Once he realizes that the world is within, he is overcome by the thought that perhaps there is no spirit (human or divine), that all there is the natural world: "a temptation beset me ... 'All things come by nature'; and the elements and stars came over me so that I was in a manner quite clouded with it."[8] If the world is within as well as without, perhaps all runs according to natural law and causes, and there is no spiritual dimension nor Spirit? But under the weight of this temptation, he waits. In waiting he finds an affirmation emerging that the world is in truth the creation of God: "And as I sat still under it and let it alone, a living hope arose in me, and a true voice, which said, 'There is a living God who made all things.' And immediately the cloud and temptation vanished away, and life rose over it all."[9] While Fox does speak elsewhere of "world" in the Johannine sense as sinful opposition to spirit, he also affirms it as the context of spirituality. The world is God's creation, the place in which our spirit may grow in relation to the divine Spirit within.

Theology of the New Creation

The spirituality of Light and the New Creation provides the foundation for early Friends' theological expressions of creation, sin, and redemption. Mainstream Protestantism separated creation from conversion, the beginning of the world from the individual's turning to God, but Quakers held them together: creation is the context of conversion. Conversion is opening to the Light, which in early Friends' experience brings an initial exuberance of discovery followed by struggle with self-will. They spoke of the Light searching out the dark places in their life. The conclusion of this process, which might take weeks or several years,[10] was a sense of release and willingness to follow the daily leadings of the Light. Such freedom from bondage brings us into unity with the creation. Reconciliation with God by opening to the Light in the depths brings us into unity with the depths of the totality of being, with the New Creation.

Early Friends speak of "convincement" rather than "conversion" because they are not turned around (con-verted) to go in an opposite direction toward a different but absent goal, but rather are brought to stillness where they can be awakened to what is already present. Rather than a passive recipient of grace, as in parts of Protestantism, the self actively participates in its transformation, giving consent and yielding to deeper levels.

The New Creation is neither a past act, the beginnings of the world, nor a future event, the heavenly world at the end of time. It is the present context of our being. As such it is in fact one with the primordial and eschatological creation, but the stress falls on divine and human presence in the present. The Quaker doctrine of creation is not speculative but experiential, based neither on scriptural texts nor on physical nature as the effect of divine causation but on a lived sensitivity to and unity with the world in depth pervaded by divine agency. From its origins this sensitive unity, while not founded on, was nevertheless informed by biblical texts.

Sin is the barrier that veils our eyes from the depths of Light and New Creation. It is living on the surface, preoccupied with outward things. Fox calls this surface existence living in the "flesh": it is "the flesh ... which had veiled me," he says. Living in the flesh is "not [to] give up to the will of God." It is to be living on the surface where we have the illusion of control and full comprehension. To "give up self to die by the Cross"[11] is to open to those uncontrollable divine depths within self and world.

Adam's sin, for early Friends, was not that he ate of the Tree of Knowledge of Good and Evil but that he did not eat of the Tree of Life. Isaac Penington writes that the forbidden fruit was "knowledge without life" which "makes them wise in the wrong part, exalts them against the life, dulls the true appetite, and increases the wrong appetite." Knowledge without life is knowing without depth, knowing only the outward. We are enjoined to feed on the Tree of Life which is the inward Christ. But such tasting will shatter our outward knowing: to "feed on the Tree of Life, they must lose their Knowledge, they must be made blind, and be led to it by a way that they know not."[12] The knowing of life in Eden is not head knowledge but a tasting, feeling, indwelling knowing of the divine presence in the original creation.

Early Friends are reviving the classic Christian doctrine that beneath original sin there is "original righteousness." Augustine and others thought it lost in the fall,[13] but Fox believes it is not obliterated, only obscured. Original righteousness can be recovered when grace opens us to what has all along been there, by pulling us off the surface into the inwardness or depths of things. Redemption is, therefore, the recovery of awareness of the divine life and the restoration of creation. Beneath our sinful experience of a distorted world is the illumined experience of the world in its original freshness and power permeated by divine presence. The redeemed life is to dwell in unity with God and world knowing the true nature of creatures through a felt unity with them in God, and to act in accord with that unity.

There is a danger for us in affirming original righteousness. On the surface it can be taken in a facile way as a justification for feeling good about ourselves or feeling superior to those who stress original sin. For early Quakers, who constantly engaged in self-examination, however, it carried them into the depths and thus touches upon the fear and wonder of awe and the irrepressible passion for connectedness and enhancement of love.

The dominant Augustinian tradition speaks of a completed creation which is then distorted in the fall; a minor Christian tradition, exemplified by Irenaeus and Schleiermacher,[14] speaks of the world being made unfinished. Our responsibility is to complete it. The redeemed life, therefore, shares in divine creativity. Early Friends participate, although unwittingly, in this Irenaean tradition in emphasizing growth from a seed and growing up into the image of God. Penington makes the original unfinishedness explicit in his first Quaker book: "When the Creation of God is finished; when the child is formed in the light, and the life breathed into him; then God brings him forth into his holy Land...."[15]

Perfection is affirmed by Fox as he is brought up into the image of God in which Adam was originally created. In reflecting later on his New Creation vision he says: "I found that none could bear to be told that any should come to Adam's perfection, into the image of God and righteousness and holiness that Adam was in before he fell, to be so clear and pure without sin, as he was." But this is a dynamic perfection involving growth; using Pauline language, he says we "should grow up to the measure of the stature of the fulness of Christ."[16] It is thus possible to affirm perfection within an unfinished world since perfection means being open to the depths in self and world and being responsive to the measure of Light we are given, rather than conformity to a static and abstract idea. The measure of Light we have may vary from time to time; perfection lies not in completeness but in the fittingness of our response to it.

Ethics in the New Creation

Ethical action, decisions, and understanding for early Quakers emerge from this deep level of existence in which we discover the movings of the divine Light and our connectedness with all created being. Spirit and matter are one. From this spirituality we are disposed to be present where we are, in this body and world, in this here and now. William Penn manifests this unity, born of his commitment to center and circumference, in his definition of true religion: "True Godliness don't turn Men out of the World, but enables them to live better in it, and excites their Endeavors to mend it."[17]

Fox, with Paul, affirms the possibility of living now in the Spirit beyond the confusions and surface complexities of the flesh but in the real material world. The Spirit/flesh distinction is not the Greek dualism of spirit/matter. Flesh is not matter but the distorted spiritual condition in which the inward depths are obscured. Body and creation are being redeemed now in the inwardness of Light and New Creation, since in this spirit "is the true waiting upon God for the redemption of the body and of the whole creation." This is evident in the transformation of our senses. Our senses are corrupted in the fall: "And by this invisible spirit I discerned all the false hearing and the false seeing, and the false smelling which was atop, above the Spirit, quenching and grieving it."[18] But in the New Creation they are restored to their original capacity. In his return to Eden as our foundation, Fox's sense of smell, sight, and hearing are regenerated. Through these physical senses he has access to the New Creation and is able to perceive the spiritual aspect of the material world and to live fittingly in matter.

At such depth in self and world the particular and the universal are also one. Opening to the Light within enables us to be led in each particular moment by the Spirit. A leading is always particular, emerging in a specific situation and guiding us toward unity within that given moment, never abstracted from it. The full circumference of each situation is the totality of being. In our depths we discover this universal connectedness. To respond appropriately to a divine leading emerging from our depths is therefore to act in a way befitting the whole of creation, since Light illumines and engenders unity with creation in each of its leadings. The universal is always encountered through the particular, but known as experiential relatedness rather than conceptual abstraction.

Quaker ethics is not based, therefore, on pursuit of ideals nor conformity to external principles, whether scriptural or rational (however much it is shaped by biblical moments or by ideals and principles). It is an ethics of realism, not of idealism or legalism, because it starts with the actual situation and God's specific leading within it. The imperative is not imposed from without but emerges from the indicative, from what is going on—as interpreted, not on the surface, but from the depths.

The foundation of Quaker ethics is, therefore, neither goals nor laws, but being—our being in the world as the New Creation and our being opening to emergent luminous depths within. The measure of Quaker ethics is the felt sense both of depth in which the divine mystery is leading and of unity with creation. From living in such depths come our social testimonies for community, peace, simplicity, equality, and education.

Social Testimonies in the Matrix of the New Creation

While opening to the Inward Light explains Friends' radical individualism, dwelling in the New Creation explains our radical communalism. The Light is God present within, leading each of us in our ownmost way, thus engendering individual strength and identity. But the Light is also the Creator Spirit connecting us one to another in deeply knit worship or group decision and bringing us into "unity with the creation,"[19] thus opening us to our underlying inherent relatedness to being. To be led by the Light is to be situated in the Light-ordered New Creation. While there is no doubt that Friends ethics is shaped by our relation to God, by our belief that there is "that of God in every one,"[20] it is shaped with equal importance by our relations to the matrix of being, the New Creation. To have a center is to have a circumference.

When Fox first articulates his opposition to all war-making, he exhibits this horizon of the New Creation:

> But I told them I lived in the virtue of that life and power that took away the occasion of all wars, and I knew from whence all wars did rise, from the lust according to James's doctrine. Still they courted me to accept of their offer and thought that I did but compliment with them. But I told them I was come into the covenant of peace which was before wars and strifes were.[21]

The life and power which takes away the occasion for war comes from living in the power of the covenant of peace of the original creation which existed before strife in the Fall. Friends' pursuit of peace and reconciliation from Fox down into our own time is not only out of response to the Light's leading but from a felt sense of the possibility of those in conflict coming to dwell in unity with creation in the depths of the world which the Light opens us to and situates us within.

Simplicity as a Quaker testimony also springs from these depths. Speech, dress, and comportment should manifest inwardness of the life of the Spirit rather than outwardness of pride in human artifice. Rhetorical flourishes and many words, preoccupation with excesses in attire, vain and hypocritical behavior are all "destroying the simplicity and betraying the Truth."[22] Puffed up by pride, they are "the spoilers of the creation" who "have the fat and the best of it, and waste and destroy it." They have "lost the hidden man of the heart" and "the adorning of Sarah" but instead "cumber God's earth."[23]

So also with equality; the inequalities and injustices of society are "invented by men in the Fall and in the alienation from God" whereas equality is established in the original creation. Honoring social rank rather than the person is a manifestation of sinful flesh; therefore, Fox refuses to bow or doff his hat, honoring one's presumed social betters, and addresses all people "rich or poor, great or small" with the plain speech of thee and thou. He thus enjoins all "to deal justly, to speak the truth, to let their 'yea' be 'yea', and their 'nay' be 'nay'; and to do unto others as they would have others do unto them."[24] To deal justly and live simply is to dwell in and to exhibit the fitting relations of the New Creation.

When Fox sets up the first Quaker schools, he explicitly connects education with the creation. He advises the women's school at Shacklewell to engage in instruction for women, as serious as that for men, in "whatsoever things were civil and useful in the creation."[25] Within his creation-broad educational concern Fox, contrary to the oppressiveness of his time, makes education available for all regardless of class or sex.

Women Speaking in the New Creation

While our discussion so far has only heard male voices—Fox, Nayler, Penington, Penn—the Founding Mother, Margaret Fell, exemplifies not only sexual equality and these other social testimonies but the unity of theological and ethical thinking from within the spirituality of Inward Light and New Creation. In 1666 she published *Womens Speaking Justified, Proved and Allowed of by the Scriptures, All Such as Speak by the Spirit and Power of the Lord Jesus*, an argument for women's equality with men to preach, prophesy, pray, and engage in leadership and priestly offices in the church.

For her, thinking within a relational approach (connected to Light and the matrix of being) is rigorous, specific, complex, and comprehensive. She offers an argument showing that the Bible supports sexual equality in church leadership. While she is arguing from the Bible to persuade others for whom the Bible is primary authority, she begins from her own experience of sexual equality living with the Light and in the New Creation. Even though she does not mention events in her own life that have formed her perspective, she draws from the Bible that which supports it.

Her argument is that there was sexual equality in the original creation and that when open to the Light within, we are restored to living in the New Creation in which there is sexual equality now. Her argument is based on the creation as the context for equality—the creation as God originally made it, Jesus confirms and exhibits it, the Spirit opens us to it, and the New Jerusalem in its fullness manifests it. She constructs her argument through the elaborate metaphor of salvation-history, tracing sexual equality from creation, through the Fall, Hebraic history, the life and resurrection of Jesus, history of the early church, to the eschaton.

She begins her argument quoting Genesis 1:27–29, "God created Man in his own Image; in the Image of God created he them, Male and Female," and comments: "Here God joyns them together in his own Image, and makes no such distinctions and differences as men do."[26] Not only did God not subordinate woman to man in the creation, but has never done so: "God the Father made no such difference in the first Creation, nor never since between the Male and the Female."[27] Rather God has poured out the divine Spirit upon women as well as men throughout biblical history: "More might be added to this purpose, both out of the Old Testament and New, where it is evident that God made no difference, but gave his good Spirit, as it pleased him, both to Man and Woman, as Deborah, Huldah, & Sarah."[28]

Jesus confirms sexual equality in the original creation by quoting approvingly the Genesis passage; he "owned the Love and Grace that appeared in Women"; and word of his resurrection was carried first by women: "what would have become of the Redemption of the whole Body of Man-kind, if they had not believed the Messsage that the Lord Jesus sent by these Women, of and concerning his Resurrection?"[29] Moreover, the church is spoken of in the Bible as woman; restraint of women's leadership is therefore rejection of Christ and his church: "the Church of Christ is a Woman.... Those that speak against the Power of the Lord, and the Spirit of the Lord speaking in a Woman, simply by reason of her Sex, or because she is a Woman, not regarding the Seed, and Spirit, and Power that speaks in her; such speak against Christ, and his Church."[30] And in the end time the Woman Church in its fullness, the "New Jerusalem," "the mother of us all" and the "Image of the Eternal God," is preparing to come "down from Heaven, and her Light will shine throughout the whole earth."[31]

With the full sweep of the history of the human world from a biblical perspective supporting her claim for sexual equality, she takes on directly St. Paul's injunction for women not to speak in the church. She says we have misunderstood his intentions.[32] While he subordinates women to men, he does so where they are evidently living in the fallen condition as in the unruly church in Corinth. To them he preaches the law which constrains them under inequality. But where people have opened to the Light, they no longer live under law in the fall but live now in the Spirit. She says: "And whereas it is said, 'I permit not a Woman to speak, as saith the Law:' but where Women are led by the Spirit of God, they are not under the Law." Women filled and led by the Spirit now or in anytime are no longer subject to sexual inequality of the fall and the law's constraint, for they dwell in the oneness of Christ—"Christ in the Male and in the Female is one"[33]—which recovers sexual equality (even though she does not use the actual phrase) of the New Creation.

As metaphoric, her thinking is inclusive. God's presence is likened to historical action. God is present in each historical period performing a distinct divine action, yet the periods are connected with each other through the presence of God. She does not separate the periods so as to locate salvation only in one of them, since the time of Jesus. No moment of time is excluded from having a mysterious depth of reconciling power because every moment offers the possibility of opening to the Light and being situated in the divine matrix of the world. And so there have been women (and men) filled with the Spirit in touch with God and creation in all periods of history.

Temporally this means that the beginning of the world and my beginning are present in the end, as the end is present in the beginning, and both present in the middle of our way. Spatially, this means that the universal is present in every particular. Any concrete reality exists within the web of being; when approached in depth we can feel the universal connectedness. Cognitively, this means that intellect and passion are inseparable. As evident in Fell's writing, she engages her subject with clarity and coherence, yet also with energy that connects, that connects particulars together in a pattern, that connects her own woman reality with the world and biblical history. Theology and ethics are inseparable: to think about God is to think about the self and world; to think about the self is to think about society, the world, and God.

The Protestantism that Fell and other early Friends attacked used exclusive thinking, excluding people before Jesus from salvation, excluding Christians from present righteousness. When an event in the past becomes an object by which conformity is measured and from which righteousness is imputed, that event is excluded from the present. Fell tries to avoid the dogmatic and ethical control a church can wield when it insists that all its followers adhere to its interpretation of such an objective event. In her metaphoric inclusiveness, she, rather, embraces the adventure of the uncertain moment with the Light interwoven with creation.

Quaker Spirituality: A Life Deepening

Quaker spirituality, manifest in Margaret Fell's theological-ethical argument for sexual equality in church leadership, is shaped by her and early Friends' discovery of living from the Light and living in the New Creation. It is a life deepening into the depths of divine mystery in self and world. It is thus a life of ongoing transformation, seeking ever new forms to express depth in each new situation, forms of community, peace, simplicity, equality, education, embodied presence, and the fitting word. Spiritual maturing in the New Creation is learning a new language, a new form of life. It is learning to be at home in the silence of being and to speak its language of Light—of the depth and the love and the fullness of being in the world.

Two Lads in Front of a Fire: A Seventeenth-Century Tale

One wintry day in Germany early in the seventeenth century a young lad sat in front of a fire "communing," as he later wrote, "with my own thoughts."[1] He mused on the formation of ancient villages into great cities and how "ill-designed" they were, with buildings "large and small haphazardly, and the streets crooked and irregular."[2] How much better they would be if they were all constructed by one master engineer according to a single, clear plan. So it has been as well with nations, he reflected, and the sciences. Laws have been determined by the mere happenstance of crimes and quarrels; the sciences have been "built up ... little by little, from the opinions of many different contributors,"[3] which in their differences do not get very near the truth. Indeed, our individual lives from infancy have been "governed by our sensuous impulses and by our teachers ... who were often at variance with one another."[4] It would have been better, he says, "had we from the moment of our birth been in entire possession of our reason and been all along guided by it alone."[5]

Recognizing that it is not wise or possible "to pull down all the houses of a town,"[6] to reform a state by "changing everything in it,"[7] or to remodel the "whole body of the sciences,"[8] he decided there and then, safe in his stove-heated room from the wintry blasts without, that what he could do was simply reform his own mind. He "resolve[d] to strip oneself of all opinions hither-to believed."[9] Once having emptied his mind, he would only re-admit those beliefs which could be "shown to be in conformity with reason."[10] Thus he sought a total reform of his thoughts and a "basing of them," he remarks, "on a foundation entirely my own."[11]

To engage successfully in this deracinate act of rooting out all belief, he realized he needed a "true method" which, he says, "I could rely upon as guiding me to a knowledge of all things my mind is capable of knowing."[12] He felt confident that he could find such a method "[s]ince God has given each of us a light for the distinguishing of the true from the false."[13] Inasmuch as only mathematical reason could discover truth that was certain, he devised that day of wintry musing four rules: to accept only that which was clear and distinct, and therefore indubitable; to divide each problem into as many parts as necessary for its solution; to begin with the simplest things moving towards the more complex; and to be comprehensive omitting nothing.[14] In a word his method was to doubt everything and only to accept what withstood such doubt, for only that could be certain; nothing else should be retained.[15]

Three decades later, on a cold morning in Nottinghamshire, another young lad sat in front of a fire. As he was sitting, he suddenly felt overwhelmed by doubt. He says "a great cloud came over me, and a temptation beset me."[16] And he heard a voice say within him: "All things come by nature." The temptation was to doubt the existence of God, and divine creativity, in the face of modern science that reduces the world to a process of natural causation. As he heard this voice, he says, "the elements and stars came over me so that I was in a manner quite clouded with it." Darkened and downcast by this eruption from beneath, he did a very strange thing. He writes: "I sat, still and silent." He neither succumbed to nor sought to dispel the gloom, but allowed it to be. He continues, "I sat still under it and let it alone." As he gave it space to be in his consciousness, he found "a living hope arose in me," and then he heard a voice speaking within himself, "a true voice, which said, 'There is a living God who made all things.'" He concludes his account by noting: "And immediately the cloud and temptation vanished away, and life rose over it all, and my heart was glad, and I praised the living God."[17]

The first lad is, of course, the well-known René Descartes, father of modern philosophy. The second, unknown by most, is George Fox, founder of Quakerism. The first fire was kindled in 1619; the second in 1648. From his stove-heated speculations, Descartes departed to wander around Europe for the next nine years applying his method of rational doubt to all beliefs, coming finally upon what he believed to be the cornerstone of absolute certainty, and therefore of his philosophy: "I think, therefore I am" (*Cogito ergo sum*).[18] From his Nottingham hearth Fox would wander Britain, Europe, and America for the next forty-three years calling on people to wait in the pre-rational depths of silence in order to discover the real and to follow its leadings.

Within several decades of each other, Descartes is founding knowledge and life upon reason (whose own foundation is reason alone), as Fox is founding them upon personal waiting on the pre-rational depths of silence. Comparison of these fire-warmed reflections of Descartes and Fox from whom have flowed the divergent ways of modernity and Quakerism—dualistic and non-dualistic—may shed light on the evident problems of modernity with its dualistic approach to and understanding of reality, of self and world, and efforts to achieve justice, and open up consideration of a non-dualistic approach.

As he sat in front of the stove, Descartes was thinking, engaging in a reflective act. He made a decision and established a goal: to perform an act on his own self—to reform his own mind. He chose to do this through a particular type of methodical thinking: doubt. Fox, on the other hand, was merely sitting in front of the fire. What was transpiring in his consciousness prior to the occurrence he does not say, but he was not performing an act of thought which would bring about what followed, but was simply waiting in silence.

As Descartes mused on the formation of cities, he moved in his thinking to oppose rational planning to traditional development (whether of cities, law, science, or an individual life), and an individual's creativity to a group's. Through a long process of thought Descartes discovered what he could not doubt. He found he could doubt his senses and the world they conveyed to him, because they sometimes deceive us; demonstrative reasoning, because sometimes we err; and all thoughts, because, since they can come to us in dreams, and therefore are not true, they are not reliable in waking. Nevertheless, while thinking all was false, he found he could not doubt that he was thinking, and that therefore he existed as a thinker, or as he says, a thinking "substance" or "thing."[19]

Reflecting on why he finds the "I think" persuasive, he says that he was assured of its truth because "I see very clearly that in order to think it is necessary to be."[20] Unencumbered by the body's sensuous uncertainties and ambiguities, because the self as mind (he is thinking of his own mathematical mind) is "entirely distinct from the body," needing neither place nor matter,[21] rational clarity provides certitude. Hence, he says, "I could take as being a general rule, that the things we apprehend very clearly and distinctly are true" — although he does acknowledge "some difficulty in rightly determining which are those we apprehend distinctly."[22]

For Fox, the stillness of his sitting was shattered by an eruption from "beyond." It was an event unexpected coming from "outside" Fox's initiation, planning, or control. In Descartes' language it was "haphazard," an event in the history of a life, the kind of thing in building a city that results in crooked streets and big and little houses, While a non-rational happening in an individual, it is obviously different from the two aspects by which Descartes depicts the non-rational side of self: its sensuous impulses and learning from teachers. It comes from a depth deeper than these.

Hearing a voice of doubt within, Fox made no conscious resolves but went on sitting in silence. We could say he "chose" to sit silently, rather than to do something else, and that he engaged in an "act," that of waiting. But the "choice" came effortlessly, with no rational deliberation, and the "act" is peculiarly one of inaction. He did not seek to exercise reason or will to cope with the problem, nor to ignore or reject it, but "let it alone" as he "sat still under it," allowing it to be in its full potency. To wait for the large silence to become articulate in the face of a doubt that threatened the vocational and personal identity just forming in this young man took an extraordinary degree of trust and hope, trust in the constructive potency of the inchoate depths and hope for what one does not yet know, for what one cannot yet name nor work towards.

What Fox discovered in waiting was a dimension of depth within himself, and rising from this inwardness beneath all thought and action, a creative expression which he understood to be God speaking. The second voice was not a parental imperative, "You ought to believe in God," but was an indicative, an expression of a committed relationship out of which he unwittingly already lived. Its expression evaporated the doubt. Where Descartes starts with a rational act of doubt and seeks methodically for that which is indubitable, Fox begins with waiting in silence, trusting this dimension of unknowing, for what response will emerge to an event that is happening within his inner life. Descartes acts, Fox waits; Descartes initiates what follows, Fox responds in waiting to what is happening.

The criterion of truth for Descartes is rational clarity; to have an idea that is clear and distinct is to have certain assurance. For Fox, the criterion of truth is a feel of the divine life within, arising out of the unknowable depths in the midst of an ambiguous situation. Against distinctness, there is amorphous depth; against a clear idea, there is a lived feeling; against the dualism of an agent mind separated from an objective body, there is a non-dualistic starting point of divine depth emerging to shape the human surface.[23]

From the Cartesian dualistic starting point has flowed forth modernity with its "critical" philosophy of the last three hundred and fifty years. Whether as rationalism or empiricism, Cartesian critical thought has shaped and expressed modern culture. In the belief that the acids of doubt would uncover certain and irreducible truth, it has sought objective truth divorced from the personal, as if feelings and faith, intuition and insight, arising in our bodies, are not intrinsic to the work of the sciences and philosophy.

Wielding critical reason, modernity has conceived the self as an "autonomous individual." In Kant's words, the rationally autonomous self is "released from the self-incurred tutelage" to the dogmatic control of church and tradition, belief and feeling, and the realm of the personal. It insists on looking closely at nature and self for verifiable evidence of any assertions. No doubt modernity has been a time of creative brilliance that has opened immense vistas into the nature of the world and ourselves, and through technological development has transformed our ways of coping with the basic necessities for survival.

But the solutions of yesterday are the problems of today. For all our success using critical reason, we are brought to our present difficulties of possible annihilation, felt meaninglessness, and anxiety of how to be fully and religiously in the world (I wrote this in 1984). While the Enlightenment's use of critical reason has liberated us in many ways, we have rather found us in a world cast adrift from its religious and moral moorings, shattered in its sense of meaning, experiencing the world no longer as real and shared but as a fragmented, dubious, solipsistic space. Heroically we name the denizen of such an existence an "autonomous individual," yet ironically and menacingly, meaninglessness and alienation have grown as the individual has autonomously increased its technological power. Just when we have acquired the technological capacity to destroy humanity, we have abrogated the human capacity for personal commitments, which alone is the basis upon which we might take responsibility for the continuance of life, and have rather given over leadership to impersonal objectivism (the expert—scientist or technocrat) and the selfinterested manipulator of private desires (the politician).

Dualism, although happily freeing the self from dogmatic control by external authority, has, in the way in which it has done it, severed mind from body: explicit rational thinking from the body's richly complex personal commitments that underlie and lead to knowledge and action. Religiously, Cartesian doubt has dissolved much of our traditional structures of belief and action. Religious language, imagery, and ritual have lost much of their power. Many of us doubt the existence of God as mastermind of creation or Supreme Person who protects us from the world, the horrors of history, and cares exclusively for his chosen people. Either God is rationally demonstrable and ethically supportive of our own values, or escaping critical reason's demand for verifiable evidence, we depict God as an objective reality independent of our ordinary living, with its lived commitments and embodied experience of being in the world, whom we know to exist by faith, i.e. belief.

While it is strange to bring together for comparison an exquisitely rational philosopher, dedicated to mathematics and modern science, who has had a tremendous influence shaping modernity, with a little-known religious leader and social reformer, lacking intellectual sophistication and opposed to philosophical speculation, why have I called it one tale from the seventeenth century? The seventeenth century has proved fateful for our destiny. As we return to this source and watch the crystallization of the foundation of modernity, we can glimpse other possibilities in solution that did not become precipitates in the Cartesian amalgam but coalesced in other ways.

While there are others, such as Blaise Pascal, contemporary in the seventeenth century with Descartes and Fox, who, while participating in the rise of modern science, refused to separate the personal dimension of experience and underlying commitment from intellectual life and action,[24] Fox's avoidance of the dualistic separations of mind and body, thinking and feeling, coalesced in the Quaker movement he initiated, through affirming that knowing and acting arise from the pre-rational depths in our personal experience and beneath-consciousness commitments.

In our time [1984] some thinkers are recognizing these problems of modernity and seeking transformation of the modern way. One theologian, Stanley Romaine Hopper, calls for nothing less than a "radical revisioning" of our western way of perceiving, thinking, speaking, and acting—our manner of doing theology and of being in the world:

> The traditional symbol systems have been sprung: the classical metaphysical model for talking about "God" and the manifold of our experience is no longer our "house of being." We are shorn and bereft of these plain and comfortable perquisites. It is not even a question as to whether we can come up with a theology "in a new key"; it is a question rather as to whether theology, in so far as it retains methodological fealty to traditional modes, is any longer viable at all.[25]

Confronted by such a crisis we would do well to find where we have gone astray in our own Dark Wood, and return to our source. To speak and to dwell in our house of being, and to do theology, we must let go of our rational mode of thought to descend into the theopoetic depths in which "Presence fills our being before the mind can think ... [and] prior to our speech,"[26] and "presences" in the poetic play of metaphors.[27]

The difference between Descartes founding knowing upon reason itself and Fox founding knowing and acting upon the experiential depths is a central distinction Michael Polanyi, another philosophic thinker, makes in our time. For him Descartes is the founder of our "critical era" who "declared that universal doubt should purge his mind of all opinions held merely on trust and open it to knowledge firmly grounded in reason."[28] The methodical application of doubt over the last three hundred years has not resulted in the expected "residue of knowledge," certain and unassailable, but rather in alienation of self from its body, community, and world, severance of reason and passion, subject and object, science and humanities—in an irrepressible deluge of skepticism and solipsism.

Polanyi seeks, therefore, a "postcritical" philosophy that will transcend the shortcomings of our critical starting point:

> We must now recognize belief once more as the source of all knowledge. Tacit assent and intellectual passions, the sharing of an idiom and of a cultural heritage, affiliation to a like-minded community: such are the impulses which shape our vision of the nature of things on which we rely for our mastery of things. No intelligence, however critical or original, can operate outside such a fiduciary framework.[29]

"Belief," "tacit assent," "fiduciary framework" underlie, for Polanyi, not only all knowing, but our use of language, acquisition of culture, and participation in community. All human acts emerge from and are dependent upon a tacit dimension of commitment. While Polanyi will move from this to elaborate a theory of knowledge and of being, and Fox will initiate a religious movement seeking divine presence to be guided by the Inner Light (Inward Teacher, Light of Christ), they are both starting from a postcritical foundation affirming personal unconscious commitment to emergent reality.

There are other contemporary philosophers who start from the same postcritical foundation. Maurice Merleau-Ponty develops his phenomenology on the basis of tacit commitment to our bodies and through them to backgrounds from which emerge, through our creative gestalt-making activity, the various figures or explicit forms, of things we perceive and words we speak. Ludwig Wittgenstein works with our tacit commitments to language as forms of life we live.

There is, of course, no conscious connection between these philosophers and Quakerism, nevertheless, it is curious that Wittgenstein knew about and admired Fox. Norman Malcolm in his memoir of Wittgenstein says of him: "The Journal of George Fox, the English Quaker, he read with admiration — and presented me with a copy of it." Even though Wittgenstein was not in any way overtly religious, Malcolm says, "he looked on religion as a 'form of life.'" He recognized in two kinds of experience he had the possibility of such a life form. In one Wittgenstein says: "I wonder at the existence of the world," thinking "How extraordinary that anything should exist!" In the other, he had "the experience of feeling *absolutely*, safe. I mean," he goes on, "the state of mind in which one is inclined to say 'I am safe, nothing can injure me *whatever* happens.'"[30] While Fox did not engage in intellectual wonder at the being of the world, nor reflect philosophically on the nature of language, he lived a form of life and of language redolent of such wonder and confidence, which may explain Wittgenstein's admiration.

Not only is there difference between Descartes and Fox on how we know reality, but as well in how we act, and our relation to justice and social oppression. Modernity using Cartesian critical reason has defined the self as autonomous with natural rights and with freedom to bond together in a social contract. It has sought to control life by law, asserted human equality, established democracy to solve conflicts nonviolently through rational argument.[31] While all to the great benefit of humanity, modernity has nevertheless also used critical reason to assert its superiority toward the body, seeking domination of our own bodies and the bodies of others—whether those of women, persons of color, the third world, the body politic, the animal world, or the presumably inert earth itself. Reason is indispensable to achieve a just existence for all, but when it is separated from our bodies' tacit commitments and interrelating with reality, it can be used to affirm systems of oppression as a natural part of the human condition.

When the inward pre-reflective dimension is taken as the source of thinking and acting, as in our example of Quakerism, a non-dualistic approach can result in transformed social patterns. While in no way perfect, Quakers made great progress in sexual equality because of their affirmation of a commonality in our depths in which each person, man or woman (or child) can be led by the Inward Light if they will enter and wait in the silence.

Women in the beginnings of Quakerism shared equally with men in the formation and administration of the Quaker movement (Margaret Fell, later wife of Fox, helped create and then administered the movement from its "headquarters" at her estate, Swarthmore Hall), the rigors of itinerant missionary life (the most extraordinary story being Mary Fisher's journey alone to and safely from the Sultan of Turkey), the terrors of British persecution and imprisonment (Margaret Fell Fox was herself imprisoned for four years in the dungeon of Lancaster castle, many other women were incarcerated throughout England, and in New England, Mary Dyer was hanged on Boston Common), and leadership in worship (women preached as well as men; the earliest document justifying women's right to speak in church is Margaret Fell's *Womens Speaking Justified* of 1666). While continuing historical research is showing pockets of sexist practice, this tradition affirming and living sexual equality continues down to our time. It is not insignificant that a disproportionate number of women in the nineteenth- and twentieth-century women's movements have been Quaker.

Feminists have begun to be aware of this tradition and would benefit by knowing more about it and its underlying principles to articulate more fully their own visions. Rosemary Radford Ruether cites this tradition in *Sexism and God-Talk: Toward a Feminist Theology*, but misunderstands it by importing into it traditional dualisms of church and world, redemption and creation. She writes:

> Quaker theology affirmed as the true Christian message
> the original equality of men and women in creation and its
> restoration in Christ. Quakers saw this only as mandating
> women's equality in the Church, including women's right
> to preach and to govern. But in the world, including in
> the marriages of believers, the male was still to rule. Thus
> Quakerism also implicitly accepted the duality of orders
> of creation and redemption. Patriarchy was regarded as
> appropriate for the order of society. Equality could be
> affirmed only for the eschatological order anticipated in the
> Church.[32]

For Fell and other Friends, the "original equality of men and
women in creation" can be lived in now because the original
creation is not separated from the present but rather is in our
inward depths and can be reentered by descent and dwelling
in the silence. Sexual equality is not eschatological, something
to be achieved in the future, for the order of the world beneath
consciousness in our depths is the original creation which when
we sink into inward silence can become for us the new creation
to live in now. So, also redemption is not a future event: the
redeemed are those who are awakened and knowingly dwell
within the Light-filled new creation.

Church and world are not separated. The true church are
those dwelling in silence and being led by the Light. When so led,
they are living in the depths of the world as originally created.
The institutional church and human world when absent of the
Light's leading are neither the true church nor the true world.
Patriarchy is the order of the fallen world not of the new creation.
Authority among Friends was not hierarchical but emerges from
the group gathered together in the Light, in the Spirit. Marriages
were not conducted by a male priest, but in a nonhierarchical

Quaker meeting for worship under divine guidance in which the couple said their own vows. Coming with traditional Christian dualisms, Ruether was unable to see the non-dualistic starting point of Friends that led them to establish what she herself was advocating, a nonhierarchical community in which men and women share authority. Equality was present in practice and aspiration, although never without sexist intrusions.

Other social patterns flow from beginning in silence. Quakers began a Christian-Jewish dialogue during their first decade of the 1650s which, while certainly Christian in perspective, attempted "to answer to that of God in every person," so as to encourage them to be faithful to God as they experienced the divine mystery.

Friends reached out to Native Americans, evident in William Penn's attempt to deal fairly with them, and later in John Woolman's journey to the Delaware (Lenni-Lenape) Indians on the banks of the Susquehanna River during the French and Indian War, not only to share his religious insights but to learn from them what the Light Within had taught them.

Slavery in America was seen by many as the natural human condition, endorsed by God in scripture or the unfortunate result of our unchangeable sinful nature. Because redemption was not a future event, but a possibility of transformation now, society, and not only individuals, could be transformed; slavery could be eliminated.

Friends maintain a testimony for peace and refusal to fight throughout its history which originated with Fox and a group of Friends declaring to King Charles II at the Restoration that they would never take up arms against him because the Spirit would not lead them into violence.

Because nature and spirit are not dualistically split, since Spirit is in the depths of the world, nature was seen as a proper object of study, so that a disproportionate number of Quakers became involved in the development of modern science. Quakers have also made contributions to the business community which they understood to be a spiritual undertaking: establishing a fixed price for commodities and a reputation for trustworthiness, contributing to the beginnings of the Industrial Revolution by inventing a new way of making steel, setting up major banking firms and chocolate manufacturing.

In all of these efforts towards social justice and engaging the world from a spiritual perspective, Friends have sought guidance and energy from beneath the power of reason. While using reason in the service of depth leadings, they have been led often to do what seemed unreasonable, such as trekking through the wilderness during war to visit Indians, or rationally impossible, such as eliminating slavery.

Descartes and modernity, he helped initiate, have benefited humanity significantly by liberating the mind to use critical reason on world and selves. Its self-incurred difficulties, because its way of liberation depended upon dualistic splits, need now, however, to be confronted for our survival as well as our flourishing.

In this seventeenth-century tale of two lads before a fire we can glimpse some virtues and self-handicapping aspects of dualistic modernity, and the possibility, arising at the same historic moment, of a non-dualist alternative. Affirming the dynamic unity of mind and body, self and world, inward and outward, spirit and nature, by recognizing our dimension of inward silence that sustains and guides emerging into thought and action, we can mend our torn world and unraveled souls by nurturing a deeper understanding of reality and how to live in it fittingly.

II. What Is Quaker Philosophical Theology?

Theological thinking was extensive in the beginnings of Quakerism but has become suspect for various Friends in our time. While in its beginnings it nurtured social action, many today see it as an abstraction or dogmatism that distracts from our justice work. Seeing the Life in it that holds faith and practice together, then and now, is one challenge. Another challenge is to see the philosophical innovations in early Friends obscured by both their divergence from the development of modern philosophy in the same period, and by being embedded in a religious movement, expressed in Christian language, intent on transforming self, society, worship, and church business.

The philosophical innovations and the more visible theological ones of early Quakerism are perceptible in the writings of Isaac Penington and Robert Barclay. In tracing Isaac Penington's shared journey with his wife, Mary Penington, from their Puritan despair to Quaker vitality, we can see the nature of Quaker spirituality as it leads for him into innovative thought and for her into practical living, symbolizing in their marriage the interaction of thought and action arising from Silence in Quakerism.

The innovations are in philosophical issues of being, knowing, language, how to think, and the nature of the self. *Being* is both inward and outward reality, not dualistically separated but interactive: the Silence of Being is the inward depths of the outward. *Knowing*, rather than observing reality with reason alone detached from life and emotions, is participative in reality arising from inchoate Silence through feeling and sensing into conscious awareness. *Words* are forms of life expressive of, or closed off to, inward depths, conveying and creating meaning through multiple uses. *Religious words* reach beyond to reality that cannot be said, but can be evoked, especially through the transformative power of symbolic metaphors. *Thinking* is emergent, arising from Silence through the relatedness and embodiedness of our lives and action into thought: dialogical not dualistic, experiential not abstract, more poetic than logical, blending philosophical and theological. *Self* has levels of awareness in mysterious depths, sensuous relatedness, explicit consciousness.

Theological innovations approach traditional ideas of God, Christ, sin, justification, sanctification, salvation, scripture, through the lens of inwardness, as forms that arise out of formless Silence. With Silence as the basis, the theological is inseparable from the philosophical, since the meaning of theological ideas are inextricably tied up with the meaning of the nature of self, world, reality, how we know, and how words work. Quaker thinking does not split religious life from intellectual thought in the modern dualisms of self/world, subject/object, spirit/matter, reason/feeling, mind/body.

Barclay's thought has been a point of contention from the beginning. While there seems to be a scholarly consensus that Barclay is dualistic, claiming that he separates the inward and outward Christ, embraces Descartes's dualism, and differs from Fox on these matters, I argue that like Fox he affirms an emergent, rather than dualistic, relation of inward to outward that does not separate the inward and outward Christ. His use of Descartes is apologetics not dogmatics, that is, he seeks common ground with his opponents in order to engage them in their own language about his different view. While it is easy to treat his big theological book as systematic theology, it is in fact apologetics, as he calls it, *An Apology*.

As I have sought to understand Quaker thinkers and how we think, I have been helped considerably by looking at them, not only from within my own Quaker perspective, but from the viewpoints of particular non-Quaker philosophical, theological, and religious thinkers who through their questions, angles of vision, and unfamiliar forms of expression open new insight into what is going on in our writings and its importance in the larger intellectual dialogue of our western culture. In my essays you will therefore encounter aspects of the thought of René Descartes, Michael Polanyi, Maurice Merleau-Ponty, Paul Ricoeur, Ludwig Wittgenstein, H. Richard Niebuhr, Paul Tillich, Stanley Romaine Hopper, Martin Buber, Mircea Eliade, T.S. Eliot, Rumi.

Writing these essays in Quaker thought—theological, philosophic, historical—has been a journey through the years carrying the conceptual into the personal, the individual into the communal: the germinating of some Seeds of Silence. Behind the last essay in this section, *Reflecting Theologically from the Gathered Meeting*, are four previous versions in which this movement can be traced in their changing titles.

The first essay focused on the individual thinker as *Dwelling in the Life: The Quaker Roots of Quaker Spirituality*, begun during a study-leave year 1990–1991 while I was a Procter Fellow at Episcopal Divinity School in Cambridge, Massachusetts, and a Friend in Residence at Pendle Hill, Wallingford, Pennsylvania. My second writing was a journal entry right after the first Quaker Theology Seminar (QTS) at Woodbrooke, Birmingham, England in April 1993 as I took pleasure and time to ruminate theologically as I explored the English environs. I called it *Quaker Reflections in a Wichcombe Tea Garden*, in which I reflected on Quaker systematic theology, Cartesian dualism, and Barclay's theology. I expanded and re-envisioned my 1990 essay for the QTS in April 1994 as *Beginnings of Quaker Systematic Theology*, moving thought about life and spirituality into dealing with my fascination with systematic theology. With second thoughts (actually third thoughts), chastened in dialogue with Beth, my wife—who asked, Am I really interested in the dogma of the church?—I again refocused the essay beyond systematic doctrines to *Dwelling in the Life: Quaker Spirituality as Theology*, for the November 1994 QTS.

Finally, I break out of my individualistic approach to embrace the communal experience of Silence. Silence is the source of Quaker theological creativity. While I experience this intensely in my individual solitude, the corporate meeting for worship ("corporate" as being bodily together with one another), especially its deepest form we call "a gathered meeting," is the communal space in which I experience the engendering creative Silence. It symbolizes and embodies the relatedness of person to person in the world, embedded in a tradition and practice, environed by Silence.

What then is Quaker philosophical theology? How does the Quaker vision become embodied in theological thinking; how does theological thought relate to Quaker ethics of acting under guidance of the Light? Quaker thought is something more than Quakers doing theology or philosophy, or arguing for Quaker principles. It is emergent thinking: thinking emerging from Silence through metaphor and concept; situated in the linguistic world of Friends' life and thought, stories and writings, and the larger cultural worlds we inhabit; carrying the mysterious depths of our being in the world into articulate forms; intending an "answering that of God in everyone" by evoking awareness in each reader's personal depths of Silent Mystery in living and reflecting on their lives.

A. Becoming Quaker: Doing, Speaking, Thinking

Felt Reality in Practical Living and Innovative Thinking: Mary and Isaac Penington's Journey from Puritan Anguish to Quaker Truth

Writing in different genres, with different audiences in mind, Isaac (1616–1679) and Mary (1625–1682) Penington both depicted dramatic contrasts between the fullness of life they found together as Quakers and their previously unfulfilled, though earnest, religious searches. Raised as English Puritans in a "world turned upside down"[1] by the revolutionary discrediting of religious and royal authority, they passionately hungered to know God's reality and divine acceptance, but found themselves eventually mired in radical doubts that such knowledge was available.

Isaac, by the time of writing the final of his eleven books (ten theological, one political) as a Puritan (1648–1656), sensed an absolute distance between the transcendent God and earth: the "Kingdom is not to be found in this world, but in heaven."[2]

Mary wrote of her fervent and anguished pursuit of truth and "true prayer"[3] in childhood and early adulthood. Marrying Sir William Springett in 1642, she found partnership of equality and simplicity in search of true religion, rejecting most church ceremony. After the tragically premature death in 1644 of William and their firstborn, she "went from … simplicity into notions,"[4] believing God to be "inaccessible," having "no religion I could call true." Yet, even in this doubting state, she "waited upon the Lord" to embrace "what the day would bring." In moments she would "be melted into tears and feel inexpressible tenderness," yet dared not (as she and Isaac would later as Friends) consider such feelings to be the inner workings of Spirit. Her remarkable dreams show in her depths a "thirst after that which I did not believe was near me."[6] In 1654, she married again, joining to

Isaac Penington's overt spiritual disquiet her own turmoil.

Despite their shared weariness of seeking and not finding, they were both struck in their first encounter with a Quaker by his witness to the "light and grace which had appeared to all men."[7] The process of convincement took two years (1656–1658), given their aristocratic and academic prejudices. Isaac was put off at first by what he saw as sub-standard theological discourse; Mary was dismayed by the leveling effect of plain speech and attire. Yet the power and authority they felt from these people were finally unmistakable; convinced at last of the Truth as divine presence and transformative power in their own lives (in 1658), they each wrote ecstatically of what, after so long a search, they had found in the company of Friends.

Drawing from the silent depths that opened in him through Quaker worship, Isaac continued to write religiously. His books and letters constitute one of the most voluminous legacies of Quaker thought, containing gems valued through the centuries luminous with life of the spirit. His leadership exemplifies the innovative theological and philosophical thinking of first-generation Friends. He shows Friends' array of ground-breaking ideas about how to know and talk about reality, how to think and write about "self" and "God," and how to pursue wisdom on a Quaker path.

Mary Penington

Mary exercised public leadership, writing to authorities on behalf of imprisoned Quakers, including Isaac, urging religious tolerance. To Quakers she advocated women's leadership through Women's Business Meetings where female control over marriage challenged patriarchy.[8] More importantly, her leadership was in modeling the Quaker way in domestic life as daily attentiveness to divine guidance. She writes of her spirituality of the everyday in *Experiences in the Life of Mary Penington*, her compilation of writings from the years pre-1668,

1672, 1680, and 1681, not published, however, until 1821.

The pre-1668 account of her Puritan childhood and Quaker convincement, with a 1672 Postscript, was addressed to "my children and some few particular friends who know and feel me in that which hungereth and thirsteth after righteousness, and many times being livingly satisfied in God my life."[9] Her 1680 account of her life with, and death of, her first husband was addressed "To Her [and William Springett's] Grandson, Springet[t] Penn," son of her daughter Gulielma and William Penn. Also, at the close of her life, she wrote (April 1680–November 1681) "an addition to the foregoing narrative," telling in detail her experiences managing finances and estates, Isaac's death, and anticipations of her own.

Mary gave a vivid account of daily divine leadings in her gifted and fearless managing of her family's financial and physical arrangements complicated by loss of Isaac's property during seven imprisonments. She told how, taking the initiative, she moved from place to place, drawing creatively upon resources from her own properties. In these and other practical matters, she supported Isaac and five children in the confidence and humility of the Quaker way of wisdom, waiting upon the Lord's presence moment by moment: "Sweet is this state, though low, for in it I receive my daily bread, and enjoy that which He handeth forth continually."[10]

Although Mary's initial reactions to Quakerism were less intellectually inflected than Isaac's, a transformative epistemological insight was inspired by a scripture quoted by Friends invited into the Penington home. In their coming she felt dread: "Their solid and weighty carriage struck a dread over me." This was not on the level of belief or thought, rather she *felt* the sacred in their comportment: "I now knew that they came in the power and authority of the Lord." Hearing "He that will know my doctrine, must do my commands,"[11] she realized that religious truth is existential, not conceptual, requiring one's whole being.

Her opening to doing the will of God precipitated a tremendous inward struggle with "evil inclinations in me," "my beloved lusts," my "deceit," "my honor and reputation in the world," what today we call ego. To obey God's will was to relinquish control of one's own self-image, opening instead to divine presence and guidance. She "felt under judgment," what she called the "wrath of God." After many months, "by the stroke of judgment," she was "brought off from all those things, which I found the light made manifest to be deceit, bondage, and vanity, the spirit of the world."[12]

In seeing herself in the Light, accepting and letting go, she "take[s] up the cross to my honor and reputation in the world." Taking up the cross, a letting go of ego-driven life, "divested of reasoning," was to live in Spirit. No longer self-directed, she found direction in the depths. Joy overwhelmed her:

> But oh! The joy that filled my soul in the first meeting ever held in our house at Chalfont. [T]he Lord enabled me to worship Him in ... his own, and ... to swim in the life which overcame me that day.... [L]ong had I desired to worship Him with acceptation ... without doubting,... for I could say, "This is it which I have longed and waited for, and feared I never should have experienced."[13]

Owned and accepted by God, when she had felt unacceptable, giving up her ego-dominated life and the deceit that obscured her true being, she now felt immersed in "life." The long sought sense of God's presence she discovered within.

Living as a Friend in the felt truth of God's indwelling presence supplied her with "a large portion of his light, and ... love and acceptance of his beloved ones." The Light dissipated her class prejudice and revealed the truth of her own condition: "In his light do I see those temptations and infirmities." She acknowledged fallibility: "I feel and know when I have slipped in word, deed, or thought." Personifying these temptations to live again under ego's domination, she had "a lively hope of seeing Satan trodden down under foot by his [God's] all-sufficient grace," and kept "low in the sense of my own weakness."[14]

Mary recorded three archetypal dreams. Friends published dreams as expressions of Spirit to support their spirituality, community life, and to address the world.[15] Unintended for publication, Mary's reveal contrasts of divine workings in her unconscious before and after becoming a Friend. Unprecedented (as far as I know) in the history of Christianity is her dreaming non-allegorical feminine and marital imagery of Jesus and wife as sexually equal divine humans.

After losing her first husband and son, deciding no longer to think about religion or God, she recorded (1658–1668) this first dream (which she dreamt 1644–1647). She saw "a book of hieroglyphics" that spoke of the future of church and religion. Feeling oppressed, she left the group she was among and went alone at night into a field and prayed: "Lord ... show me the truth." Immediately her hand was struck by a "bright light, like fire" from the sky. Dreaming assurance of religious truth, she was terrified upon waking, "believing there was nothing manifest since the apostles' days, that was true religion; for I knew nothing to be ... certainly of God."[16]

In "thirst after that which I did not believe was near me," she dreamt (1647–1654) a dream of even greater import. Sitting alone and sad, she heard a great noise of "shrieking" and "hallooing" because "Christ was come." Waiting in "dread," she sat "still in the same place, cool and low in my mind." Someone entered her room and said: "Christ is come indeed, and is in the next room; and with Him is the bride, the Lamb's wife." Eagerly she arose to express her love to him, but "stood still at a great distance."[17]

What she saw at the hall's end was Christ as "a fresh, lovely youth, clad in gray cloth, very plain and neat ... of a sweet, affable, and courteous carriage." She watched as he embraced poor people she found contemptible, and concluded he has a "wisdom" for seeing in them a "hidden worth" she does not see. Having considered the options of how Christ would relate to her—to own her as one of his own or to treat her as she treats herself as unacceptable—she said, "At last He beckoned to me to come near him," which she did "tremblingly and lowly" with "great weightiness and dread."[18]

Soon she saw the "Lamb's wife," "a beautiful young woman, slender, modest, and grave, in plain garments, becoming and graceful. Her image was fully answering his, as a brother and sister." Mary then turned to a fellow "seeker" and said:

> Seeing Christ is come indeed, and few know it; and those that in the confusion mourned or rejoiced, know it not, but Christ is hid from them; let us take the king's house at Greenwich, and let us dwell with and enjoy Him there, from those that look for Him and cannot find Him.[19]

Receiving no reply, she awoke.

Who is this "wife" as "sister" whose image fully resembles Christ's? Instead of orthodoxy's bride of Christ as the Church, is she, with beauty and grace like Christ, the feminine embodiment of the *imago dei*? This dream shows a Puritan's unconscious commitment to simplicity and models gender equality, values that will be lived out as a Friend.

Whereas in her first dream, the divine presence merely struck her hand as a beam of light in Nature, here God in the form of Christ and wife have come into Mary's social world. Where in the first dream she left the company of people and went outside into solitude, here she shares with a fellow seeker her desire to occupy the king's palace—a politically revolutionary idea—and to enjoy Christ there. Christ accepted her as she is in her religiously confused condition, showing compassion towards lower class people Mary finds contemptible, revealing her class vanity.

While Mary obviously considered dreams potent with spiritual meaning, she provided no interpretation. In her third dream, in 1676 as a Friend, however, within the dream itself she contrasted memory of this second dream, between twenty and thirty years earlier, with her current dream, again encountering Jesus and his wife. In this subconscious inquiry into the difference between a young and mature couple, a creative theological mind expressed imaginatively the contrast between her Puritan and Quaker experiences of the sacred.

Unlike her solitude in her two previous dreams, this dream began with her and two others in an "upper room." Looking out the window, they were struck with dread at a black and dismal sky, and waited "keeping cool and low in our spirits, to see what would follow." As the sky was cleared by "one great vent of water," there appeared "a very bright head, breast, and arms, the complete upper part of a man." Beautiful, he was "holding in his hand a long, green bough," imaging "a signification of good"; "being overcome with the greatness of our sense," they felt "astonishment and joy." "[R]unning swiftly about the room, with constant acclamations of admiration and joy," they "could not set forth in words" because their "voices [were] unable to deliver us of what we were so big with."[20]

Mary saw a man and woman in an "oval, transparent glass" below the bust of the first man, "nearer the earth," reminding her of her earlier dream:

[T]he man wore a greater majesty and sweetness than I ever saw with mortal: his hair was brown, his eyes black and sparkling, his complexion ruddy; piercing dominion in his countenance, splendid with affability, great gentleness, and kindness. The woman resembled him in features and complexion; but appeared tender and bashful, yet quick-sighted.

Falling on their faces, Mary and her companions reverenced these "heavenly forms" crying "glory!" As the man ascends, "the woman came down to us," and said, "with great gravity and sweetness. ... that we should not be formal, nor fall out,"[21] and then disappeared.

Within her dream Mary reflected on the differences between this and her earlier dream:

"This is a vision, to signify to us some great matter and glorious appearance; more glorious than the Quakers at their first coming forth." I added, that I had a distinct vision and sight of such a state in a dream, before ever I heard of a Quaker; but it was in a more simple, plain manner than this. For I then saw Christ like a fresh, sweet, innocent youth, clad in light gray, neat, but plain; and so, likewise, was the bride, the Lamb's wife, in the same manner; but under this plain appearance, there was deep wisdom and discernment; for I saw Him own and embrace, such as I could not see any acceptable thing in; such as I thought Christ would not own, being old, poor, and contemptible women. "But now," said I, "his countenance and garb are altered: in the former was united to sweetness, majesty; in the latter, to plainness and neatness is joined resplendence."[22]

The images are archetypal, occurring in "an upper room," suggestive of Christ's last supper. She witnessed there the image of the upper half of a beautiful man, and below him, Christ and his wife. Emerging beauty out of a context of dread, signifying good, beyond words, this sacred image resembled the *imago dei* Ezekiel saw: "the Lord in a likeness as it were of a human form."[23]

While early Friends did not speak much of the image of God *per se*, but rather of "the seed within," "the inward light," and "that of God in everyone," Isaac spoke of "the true image of God raised in persons, and they knowing and loving one another in that image."[24] If this male upper body is God in human form, then the divine male and female below resonate with the Genesis account of God creating in their ("God" is plural here) own image humans as male and female. If Christ is the actualization of the image of God, it made sense for Mary to witness the *imago dei* outside the upper room in which Christ shared his last supper. The upper room is empty now, since Christ as *imago dei* is, as Mary knew, within people.

The differences between Puritan and Quaker dreams expressed the fullness she had discovered as a Friend. In her first dream she was terrified at the truth that God is and has touched her; as a Friend she took joy in God's Presence. The light that struck her was external; as a Friend she will come to know the felt depths of the inward light. Truth and light she will use interchangeably to signify reality both of God within and our condition. The light struck her hand "like fire," her capacity for doing things. When convinced, her vain doings will, with much struggle, be inwardly burned away.

Young in the Puritan dream, the couple has matured in the third dream, as has Quakerism. The couple's countenances now have "majesty" added to "sweetness," and in clothing "resplendence" added to "plainness and neatness."[25] For a Quaker or Puritan to affirm majesty and resplendence is shocking. While offering no explanation, she found in her felt depths what her culture looked for outwardly. Not in the ritual splendor of the Anglican Church, royal splendor of monarchy, nor scriptural beauty of the King James translation, but in experience within of Christ and consort, the male and female *imago dei*, she found spiritual magnificence.

Isaac Penington

Isaac's anguished search for the truth of God in life as a Puritan, while similarly emotionally intense, is more intellectually fraught than Mary's as he experienced God, his friend, becoming his enemy, shattering his Christian thought and life. Sometime before 1648, Isaac experienced a dark night of the soul:

> [T]hen was I shaken, smitten, and thrown down into the depth of so great misery, darkness, and anguish.... The thing which I could not fear, overtook me: He, whom I looked upon as my indissoluble friend, became my greatest. enemy.... These breakings ... came upon me in one hour.... [T]hey entered deep, seizing upon the very life of my spirit.... [I]t was the purity, the integrity, the ingenuity of my Spirit..., my new life in ... the Gospel, which was rent from me: and this was death indeed.... [T]here was nothing spared, no knowledge..., no Holy inclination that was not born down, and made visibly sin and darkness to me.[26]

After this collapse he struggled to make theological sense of self, world, and God. Ramifying through his pre-Quaker writings as despair, bitterness, and self-loathing, he wrote: the self is "polluted, unclean, filthy, noisom, offensive."[27] God is absolutely transcendent, who does what he pleases: "I will feed on thee, and devour thee, and ... by the warmth of my stomack, convert thee into within my self,"[28] for "There is Nothing but offence and war ... between God and the Creature."[29]

Correlative with God's absolute transcendence was absolute relativization of knowing and ethics. "There is no true knowing of God by the understanding of the creature." "While he hides from us the true and original colour of things,... he may cosen us as often as he pleases." "Man hugely likes the God that he frames in his own imagination ... as lovely ... [but is] a dreadful God, and in no wise desireable."[30]

Good and evil are but appearances of original undifferentiated unity: "Perfect and wicked are both of the same lump, only differently clothed to act their several parts, which when they have done, their clothes must be taken off, and they turned back into the lump again."[31] God and Satan: "from one spring come these two Fountains ... called God ... [and] Satan."[32] Ranters, "Your life I love,"[33] but "it were ... good for them in this present state, to chuse the good, and refuse the evil."[34]

Growing weary of his search for true fullness, he moved in his last book before convincement toward an other-worldliness: "God's earth [is] fitted by himself for his Seed, filled with his own fullness,... this is not ... this earth as it now is ... but in heaven."[35]

A seed nevertheless remains from childhood. As a Quaker he realized that little stirrings within when young were Spirit's movements: "For though I had a true taste of life and power from God; yet not knowing the foundation, there could be no true building with it; and so the spirit was quenched";[36] "the great deceit of man; he looks for a great, manifest power in or upon him to begin with, and doth not see how the power is in the little weak stirrings of life in the heart."[37]

Letting go of ego's unrequited search for divine power manifest in this life prepared him for encounter with truth of this seed in depth through Quakers. When first encountering Friends, Isaac, like Mary, disdained them intellectually but is touched in inwardness: "at the very first they reached to the life of God in me ... [but] the more I conversed with them, the more I seemed in my understanding ... to get over them.... [Yet] I felt them in the secrets of my soul; which caused the love in me ... to increase towards them."

After attending several Quaker gatherings with Mary, he went to Meeting on May 31, 1658 determined to embrace the truth: "that I might not receive anything for truth which was not of him, nor withstand any thing which was of him." Experiencing truth in inwardness of divine reality and his own condition, "I felt the presence and power of the Most High among them, and words of truth from the Spirit of truth reaching to my heart and conscience, opening my state as in the presence of the Lord." Not merely "words and demonstrations from without,... I felt the dead quickened, the seed raised."[38]

He then spoke ecstatically of finding truth of the Seed within:

> [M]y heart (in the certainty of light, and clearness of true sense) said "This is he, there is no other: this is he whom I have waited for and sought after from my childhood; who was always near me, and had often begotten life in my heart; but I knew him not distinctly, nor how to receive him, or dwell with him ... But some may desire to know what I have at last met with?... I have met with the Seed..., my God..., my Saviour..., true knowledge ... of life..., virtue..., the Seed's Father, and in the Seed I have felt him my Father..., true holiness, the true rest of the soul...."[39]

In convincement he let go of his controlling "veiled self"[40] "sinking low out of wisdom,... reason, imaginations."[41] He experienced "the melting and breakings of my spirit"[42] as he opened to the truth of God and self in the divine depths in life.

Isaac and Mary's convincement added an upper-class couple to a movement made up in the 1650s mostly of ordinary people: Mary as daughter and wife of knights, and Isaac as Cambridge educated, much published Puritan theologian, and son of a Lord Mayor of London. For these reasons, when Isaac supported John Perrot against Fox's condemnation of him in the early 1660s, advocating Friends stay open to discern whether the Spirit is at work in him, Quaker leaders handled him gingerly but firmly, persuading him to submit to Fox's leadership.[43]

While Mary's writings showed the felt depths of divine presence and guidance in illumination of her practical life as a Friend, Isaac probed these depths with an extraordinary richness. Unrecognized by philosophers then and now, his contributions to philosophy are obscured by his participating in a religious group of peculiar worship and justice activism. Exemplifying Friends' innovative thinking, Isaac showed: philosophically how to know and talk about reality; theologically how to think and write about "self" and "God"; and spiritually how to walk the Quaker way of wisdom.

Beginning his philosophical reflecting waiting in the silent depths of mystery in self and world, he conceived *being* as inward and outward; *knowing* as participating in being beneath words rising through feeling and sensing into conscious awareness; *language* as forms of life expressive of, or closed off to, inward depths, which convey meaning through multiple uses, especially the evocative transformative power of symbolic metaphors.

Reflecting on his and Friends' being in the world, Isaac distinguished surface and depth in life by utilizing correlative terms from scripture: inward and outward, spirit and letter, and power and form.[44] "Outward" for Isaac meant visible structures that are political, social, economic, ecclesiastical, and thus the words we speak, the clothes we wear, the way we worship and live in society. "Inward" meant our personal, experiential, existential, lived being.

All outward forms we create have an inwardness. They are created and maintained by an inward spirit, orientation, impulse: either from the inward light "in the Life" or from the deceitful ego of the veiled self of "any form, out of the Life"[45]: "The outward which is right in God's sight, must come from the inward, but not from the inward will or wisdom of the flesh, but from the inward light and Spirit of God; but it is a great matter to receive singly and go along with the inward light, and avoid the inward deceitful appearance of things."[46] Church services, for example, Friends rejected, not because they were forms but because they were spiritually empty and imposed on people by ego's defensive conformity of belief and practice.

Forms are not merely outward. Inwardness too has its forms: words, ideas, decisions, beliefs. If these come from the ego, they are expressions of the spirit of domination; if from the inward light, they are expressions of the holy spirit. Beneath outward forms, we have inward forms, and beneath both kinds of forms we discover in inwardness a formless reality of spirit—spiritual energy not structures, form-making agency that is not itself a form, what Isaac called Mystery, Spirit, Life, and Inward Light. Being is relational, never detached: reality, as we relate to it in the world, always has a depth of mystery.

Arising as expression of mystery, a form—a work, practice, social structure—does not retain depth automatically. The "life" or "spirit" in forms is evanescent. We experience mystery; then it is gone: "it is hard retaining it, nay, impossible rightly so to do, but in the spirit which gave it."[47] A form is not itself the reality it is expressing. A form can be retained after spirit is lost; we deceive ourselves into thinking we are holding the reality when we are left clutching an empty form, maintaining it for its own sake—such is idolatry. The deeper mystery in the reality is evanescent. Connection with it must be refreshed.

While memory of the past and anticipation of the future is important, Isaac stressed the present, for it is in the present that we experience mystery in inwardness, that new or old forms refreshed are activated. So Friends experienced Protestantism's worship and belief focused on the past as empty, and experienced silence in worship as a crucible in which mystery could be felt and refresh or generate life-filled relatedness, new insights, leadings, and words to speak in one's present situation.

Awareness of such mysterious depths does not come through ideas, although once aware, we can think about it, as Isaac did. We are aware of Mystery or the Life through what Isaac called sensing and feeling by abiding in it from which awareness arises into consciousness: "wait to feel the thing itself which the words speak of, and to be united by the living Spirit to that, and then thou hast a knowledge from the nature of the thing itself; and this is more deep and inward than all the knowledge that can be had from words concerning the thing."[48]

By knowing "the thing itself" he did not mean objects observed but mystery felt that issues in particular beings. Beyond modernity's conceiving reality as of two kinds—subject and object—Isaac attended to a third underlying reality— mystery: "That which God hath given us the experience of ... is the mystery, the hidden life.... So that in minding this, and being faithful..., we mind our peculiar work ... which God hath peculiarly called us to."[49]

While principally talking about knowing God, all knowing for Isaac involved connecting beneath consciousness. By participating in the mystery, we know "ere we were aware."[50] At the same time that Descartes is originating modern philosophy, grounding true knowing in reason without pre-thinking awareness, and denigrating feeling as merely subjective, Isaac and other Friends are grounding knowing in feeling and sensing. Knowing is affectional. To know something in its mysterious depths is to be affected, moved emotionally, to be changed. Detached, unemotional knowing is an illusion. Knowing is emergent. Waiting in silence, knowing arises through sense and feeling into patterns of thought, not, as in modernity, through imposing frameworks on phenomena—putting Nature on the rack (Francis Bacon).

If not in our thinking minds, from where then does feeling-ful awareness arise? While Descartes conceived bodies as objects moved by external causes, Isaac and Friends located such pre-thinking awareness in our bodies. Arising "ere we were aware," that is from our unconscious bodies, our first conscious awareness appears in our non-conceptualizing senses of tasting, touching, smelling, which provide more intimate contact with reality than sight and hearing. If opened to these pre-conceptual depths, all physical senses are intensified: "Life gives it a feeling, a sight, a tasting, a hearing, a smelling, of the heavenly things, by which senses it is able to discern and distinguish them from the earthly things.... [F]rom this Measure of Life the capacity increaseth, the senses grow stronger; it sees more, feels more, tastes more, hears more, smells more."[51] If open to mystery, the physical senses become spiritually discerning: grasping deeper meaning in reading, talking, and inhabiting a situation.

For Isaac, body was not passive, separated from agentic mind, but was involved in all knowing and experiencing. Rooted in our bodily contact with reality, ideas always present only an aspect of truth. The whole of a mysterious reality exceeds our partial grasp through ideas emerging from our spiritually sensitized senses working from our angle of experience. Isaac's pre-Quaker relativism became Quaker perspectivalism. Isaac's grasp of aspects of reality through his angle of experience of mystery did not achieve the absolute certainty that modernity since Descartes has sought, and never found, but did, nevertheless, result in confidence and power to live in the world.

Words, therefore, express aspects of a fuller reality, depending on how they are used: to express something of realities "known" bodily, to give greater form and clarity to feeling and sensing, to interpret scriptural meaning, to argue theologically, to offer pastoral counsel, and to evoke feeling-ful awareness of mystery in our depths. Words are forms of life issuing from these silent depths. They are then maintained as filled or emptied of their original meaning or spirit, as "in" or "out of the life."

The Quaker way is distinguished from Puritan, Anglican, and burgeoning modern thought by this affirmation of ineffable mystery. Where forms of word and idea—as scripture, belief, doctrine, and reason—dominated and represented reality, Friends experienced reality deeper than all forms. Words grasp aspects, but never the whole, of reality. Rather than dogmatisms of the word in Puritan and Anglican thought (right belief), and of reason in modern thought (Cartesian dominating body with mind, object with subject), Isaac showed the Quaker way as a dynamic process of interaction in which the outward emerges from the inward. We can see and say what emerges as aspects of reality, but the whole we "know" through indwelling it and becoming aware of it through sense and feeling—which is the beginning of philosophy. Depth emergent word, thought, and forms of life as aspects of mystery are deeper than words can say and than we can know. Yet we can say something—which is the beginning of theology. Religious words grasp aspects of an unsayable whole of reality, and carry us back into feeling originating mystery. Their primary function is not to present notions of God and salvation, for "the end of words is to bring men to the knowledge of things, beyond what words can utter."[52]

The language of early Friends is rife with metaphors because they can bear people into unsayable depths. Metaphors interrelate aspects of felt reality beyond concepts' boundaries, integrating places in ourselves, awakening passions for new ways of being, and shaking our world-view. When they reach into ineffable depths, metaphors function symbolically: expressing a hidden dimension through an everyday level. Speaking of the metaphor "Christ is a rock," Isaac said believers use this as an idea who are "without knowledge of the mystery.... My meaning is, they have a notion of Christ to be the rock,... but never come livingly to feel him the rock ... inwardly laid in their hearts.... Where is this to be felt but within?"[53] Neither experiencing metaphor's tension of relating Christ and rock, nor feeling Christ symbolically as a rock inwardly, believers know this idea but not the mystery in it.

Hence Isaac's approach to scripture was not through logic to get ideas conceptually "right," but to carry us beyond words: to evoke, express, and grow in experience of divine mystery: "my spirit hasteneth from words ... [to] sink in spirit into the feeling of the life itself,... and cease striving to ... comprehend."[54] Ideas can be held with passion, but if we do not have an inward feel of the life of reality of which they speak, we are dealing with an empty shell of meaning, not the kernel of reality. Scriptural ideas approached as notions are read as "letter" not in the "spirit." If the forms of scriptural words are read in the "spirit" that engendered them, we feel the divine life and transformative power of the Spirit which "causeth life ... and love to spring up in him."[55]

For Isaac, as for Quakers then and now, theology emerges from the mystery we feel waiting in silence. Indwelling a whole of reality beyond words, theology says "somewhat": "Indeed there is so much wrapped up in it, as the heart of man cannot conceive, much less the tongue utter; yet somewhat have I felt, and somewhat is upon my heart, to say."[56] Starting with an idea, rather than experience, of God, words do not express reality, but only refer to our constructed image: "without the knowledge of the mystery, [knowledge] is not sufficient to bring them unto God."[57] Thinking about God for Isaac was thus done as we indwell God.

Over against Protestants beginning with the Word, controlling divine and human spirits by biblical texts, Friends trusted the unsayable depths of Spirit within. Discerning what emerges as from Spirit, rather than from the veiled self, was by sensing the Spirit's presence rather than by conformity of words to the Word. Word does not control Spirit; Word expresses Spirit. Friends discern the Spirit-filled Word "in the life" of the Spirit.

While Isaac spoke of Father, Son, and Spirit, these are metaphorical, expressions of inward experience of divinity. Used interchangeably rather than having conceptual boundaries, metaphors radiate and interconnect. These three are also "light" and "breath," manifesting his experience of being drawn out of darkness into unity with the godhead through the Breath of Spirit: "hearkening to this breath, the mind and soul is led out of darkness, into the image of light...; being transformed by this breath,... there is a unity with ... Father and ... Son, who themselves dwell in this breath,... in whom all are, who are one with this breath."[58]

Christ was central for Isaac: "every spiritual thing, refers to

Christ, and centres in him."[59] Christ is God, "the infinite eternal Being," who was fully manifest in Jesus "but cannot be confined to be nowhere else but there."[60] To the accusation that Quakers spoke of "two Christs, one manifested without, and another revealed within," Isaac answered: the "mystery of life, and hope of glory," manifest in the earthly Jesus, is "revealed and made known within unto us, by the same eternal Spirit."[61]

Jesus was the paradigmatic embodiment of a Spirit-led life. Stressing servanthood, he did not "lord it over" his disciples, "requiring them to believe,"[62] but nurtured Life in them. To drive the listener off the intellectual level into Spirit's depths, he spoke parabolically—"sometimes he was silent, and gave no answer at all; at other times, he answered not directly, but in parables. And how offensive is this to man's wisdom, who requires a positive and direct answer!"—and paradoxically—"with many contradictions to the fleshly understanding," saying, "'I judge no man'" ... yet was he not continually judging?"[63]

Salvation for Isaac was dwelling in and living from the Spirit or eternal Christ within. Salvation was not a transaction between Father and Son through sacrificial atonement on the cross but revelation within of a divine Seed and its growth. We have within us "two seeds": "profane" and "true."[64] Sin was not a past event, but our present choice to nurture the profane seed, living in "any form, out of the life," in our own natural will and understanding. Adam's fault, repeated by us, was not disobedience but choosing Knowledge rather than Life.[65] As we open to the true seed, grace grows us now as children of the Light, to live "perfection,"[66] not a fixed ideal but humble daily dwelling—in one's measure—in the Life. A true Christian was not someone who professed the name of Christ[67] but someone who is a "new creation" by the creativity of the divine Spirit, "feeling the thing ... though they had never heard the outward ... name Christ."[68]

Daily breathed through by divine Mystery—"He breatheth

the breath of life upon me every moment"[69]—Mary modeled practical domestic life illumined and led by Spirit. Dwelling in the fullness of life, Isaac engaged in innovative thought probing Truth in inwardness, urging all to "wait for, and daily follow, the sensible leadings of that measure of life which God hath placed in you, which is one with the fulness, and into which the fulness runs daily and fills it, that it may run into you and fill you."[70] Through dramatic searching and finding the felt reality of God in inwardness, and faithful living in turbulent times with its consequences of enduring persecution, they exhibited centeredness and passionate caring borne of silent daily dwelling in the depths of existence.

In their transformed lives and theological discoveries, Mary and Isaac modeled the Quaker way to their contemporaries. Mary had no impact after her generation until the publication of her *Experiences* in 1821. She has gained recognition with feminist inquiry into Quaker women writers. Isaac's writings remained in print throughout Quakerism's centuries because of the theologically insightful mystical gems in his pastoral letters. Deserving further attention are Mary's theological acuity expressed in dreamwork and her spirituality manifest in domestic creativity, and Isaac's passionate and poetic articulation of early Friends' alternative depth theology of inwardness, philosophical innovations of emergent knowing, and spiritual way of living into fullness in the Light.

"Gathered Inward to the Word": The Way of Word and Silence in Quaker Experience

Hidden in the middle of his *An Apology for the True Christian Divinity*, Robert Barclay describes his own convincement as being touched by the silence in a meeting for worship:

> For not a few have come to be convinced of the truth after this manner, of which I myself, in part, am a true witness, who not by strength of arguments, or by a particular disquisition of each doctrine, and convincement of my understanding thereby, came to receive and bear witness of the truth, but by being secretly reached by this life; for when I came into the silent assemblies of God's people, I felt a secret power among them, which touched my heart, and as I gave way unto it, I found the evil weakening in me, and the good raised up, and so I became thus knit and united unto them, hungering more and more after the increase of this power and life, whereby I might feel myself perfectly redeemed.[1]

It is perhaps ironic that this five hundred and forty-two-page book should have its origins in experience of silence. Yet any Quaker discussion of "language and experience" must explore silence as their underlying dimension. To approach the nature of language from within the context of silence, however, results in a distinctive view.

Words related to silence have multidimensional meanings. Words not only carry meaning as explicit content; they have tacit meaning intertwined with our living, that shapes and expresses life. Friends call this dimension "silence." In the twentieth-century philosophical paradigm shift from knowing to language, philosophers, such as Maurice Merleau-Ponty, Michael Polanyi, and Ludwig Wittgenstein, call it "background,"[2] "the tacit dimension,"[3] and "the mystical,"[4] that which "can't be said, but shows itself."[5] Friends at variance with religious and philosophical thought of mid-seventeenth-century Europe, anticipate many insights of such twentieth-century philosophers. In order to describe the Quaker understanding of language and silence, I will focus on one philosophically and theologically sophisticated leader in the seventeenth century, Robert Barclay, and draw him into dialogue both with such twentieth-century philosophers of language as Wittgenstein, Merleau-Ponty, and Paul Ricoeur, and with our own contemporary Quaker experience.

Meaning in Silence

While his *Apology* is extensively argumentative, it is the meaning and power of silence in a meeting for worship that reaches Barclay and touches his heart. Silence is a vast realm of meaning that lies before and after and beneath language. We know from our experience in meeting for worship that silence can affect, sustain, integrate, free, and transform our lives without a word being spoken, either audibly or in one's mind.

As we enter the silent assemblies of Friends, we center ourselves, descending from the surface of our everyday concerns into the depths of our being. We let go of our ideas and plans, our tasks and obligations, our hopes and fears, and enter a stillness in which we expect something to happen that is beyond our imagining and control.

Just prior to his description of his convincement, Barclay explores the meaning of silence in Friends' worship. He, like other Friends early and late, says: "the great work of one and all ought to be to wait upon God."[6] Such waiting is this expectant stillness in which we are simultaneously calmly at rest and yet actively open to what will happen. We are unfocused upon any particular thing and yet are attentive in and to the silence, waiting to receive feelings and sensations; a focus of image, idea, story, or scriptural word; and perhaps a leading to rise to share such with the meeting.

To reach this level of waiting we have already undergone a change. The obstacle to reaching this level is our own ego which must be overcome—or slipped loose from. Our individual inclination, supported in major ways by modern culture, is always to control what is going on within and without. Yet our descent to the level of waiting detaches us from our structuring activities—both intellectually making things cohere and morally making things conform. We detach from our active thinking, willing, and imagining and from our conscious commitments and obligations. This then requires a trust to be in a structureless state that we will not ourselves disintegrate or be overwhelmed by destructive psychic forces. To reach for this level can be disorienting if not downright terrifying. To be waiting in silence is, therefore, an act (which is simultaneously a gift) of faith as a reliance upon the unknown, being patient amidst mystery.

Barclay says it this way: in entering the silence, participants are "to cease from their own forward words and actings,… from all their own thoughts, imaginations and desires."[7] Each "layeth down his own wisdom and will;"[8] each "man's part and wisdom … [is to be] denied and chained down in every individual."[9] No one is to "[bring] forth his own conned and gathered stuff."[10] Even scriptural words, along with ritual, are to be set aside. Silent waiting upon God "was not preached, nor can be so practised, but by such as find no outward ceremony, no observations, no words, yea, not the best and purest words, even the words of scripture, able to satisfy their weary and afflicted souls."[11] There "can be nothing more opposite," he says, than this is "to the natural will and wisdom of man" so that it cannot be "rightly comprehended by man, but as he layeth down his own wisdom and will."[12]

In letting go of our own will and wisdom—what we call today the "ego"—we are to become "subject to God,"[13] "to be silent before the Lord." Participants "being directed to that inward principle of life and light in themselves, as the most excellent teacher,... came thereby to be taught to wait upon God in the measure of life and grace received from him."[14]

The meaning of "God" to whom we become subject, upon which we become dependent, as we slip away from our ego confines, and wait, is, in experiential terms, a moment of revelation, the manifesting of divine reality in our present experience. Beyond stillness, the experience is one of presence: "to feel the Lord's presence, and know a gathering into his name indeed, where he is in the midst."[15] And it is one of power: as the divine life is felt within, selves "may move with it, and be actuated by its power" which makes "effectual" the "life, power, and virtue" in one's life, ceremony, and language—in words that "pray, preach or sing" or quote scripture.[16]

The power of this presence actuates us, according to Barclay, in many ways. Selves are "inwardly taught to stay their minds upon the Lord, and wait for his appearance in their hearts."[17] "[T]he pure motions and breathings of God's Spirit are felt to arise" and "to refresh the soul."[18] Within the whole meeting this power can be experienced as a "glory [that] breaks forth, and covers all" with "a holy awe and reverence upon every soul."[19] In its teaching "the soul cometh to see its own condition" as one inclining to live within the ego confines of its own volitional and intellectual control and the grace-full potentiality to live more deeply and fully. We are thus illuminated but also changed, for if in the awe-filled presence of the divine glory, "the natural part should arise in any, or the wise part, or what is not one with the life, it would presently be chained down, and judged out."[20]

As Barclay recounts in the anecdote of his own convincement through the "secret power" of silence, "I found the evil weakening in me, and the good raised up"[21]—the "evil" of an ego-controlled life excluding divine presence and the "good" of a life open to the movements within it of the divine Life.

And the "good" of a life open to the Life in others: as selves are "actuated" by the divine Life and their life arising within them, they are "gathered thus together."[22] "[G]athered into the life," he "became thus knit and united unto them," and—as evidence of an erotic dimension in silence—he felt himself "hungering more and more after the increase of this power and life."[23] From this experience of the motions of life in the silence, "words ... arise"[24] and are understood by becoming "sensible of" the "same life" in the hearers that "answers"[25] to the life in the speaker.

Nevertheless, there is a problem here for us in our effort to understand the Quaker use of language. While Barclay speaks of words and understanding arising from the silence, he says emphatically that all the effects of silence we have noted do not require language. He speaks, for instance, of "an inward travail and wrestling" in which we are "renewed in the spirits of our minds without a word."[26] So also for silent worshippers who are "straying in their minds," one "in whom the life is raised" can become "a midwife through the secret travail of his soul to bring forth the life in them" "so that the rest will find themselves smitten without words."[27] And when "rude and wicked" men seek to disrupt worship, "if the whole meeting be gathered into the life, and it be raised in a good measure, it will strike terror into such a one ... reach to the measure of grace in him, and raise it up to the redeeming of his soul."[28] But even when there are no disruptions or wandering minds:

> [I]t may, and hath often fallen out among us, that divers meetings have past without one word; and yet our souls have been greatly edified and refreshed, and our hearts wonderfully overcome with the secret sense of God's power and Spirit, which without words hath been ministered from one vessel to another.[29]

Can this be true, that language is not involved in the silence? One of the great insights of the paradigm shift in twentieth-century philosophical thought is that all our conscious life is pervaded by language, that language is the medium within which the fish of human consciousness swims. Yet I have suggested at the outset that Quaker understanding of language anticipates this present revolution. There seems to be a contradiction here. In any case, what use are words if all that is spiritually needful can occur in the nonverbal silence? We turn then to the meaning and importance of words used in the Quaker context of silence.

The Way of Words

Let us look in Barclay's discussion of silence at how religious words are spoken in order to deal with our dilemma. Religious language issues from the "heart," from the deep well of our feelings, of our passions and compassion, of our opening up, reaching out, and taking in others. What is "uttered forth" is that "which the Lord puts into their hearts."[30] But what is this; are these dictated words? Then we are given words by God, as the gospel writers are often portrayed in the Christian tradition, and we simply repeat them?

What Barclay says, however, is that what God puts in the heart is God's own self: "the pure motions and breathings of God's Spirit are felt to arise."[31] What God "puts in the heart" is the divine Spirit, once hidden, now becoming active within the self, stirring and inspiring it to come to expression in such a way that bears the Spirit in and through the words. God gives, not specific things to say, but a particular *way* of speaking, out of which we are inspired to create the particular words of the moment. Speaking, religiously, is a creative endeavor, like writing poetry. Not an act of conforming to a set form, such as scriptural words or church doctrine, words are created by us as we are moved by "the free motion of life itself."[32] From this divine life arising, breathing, within our life in the silence, "words of declaration, prayers or praises rise."[33]

He speaks of such words as bearing truth. But this is not the truth of words conforming to objects. Rather the truth is something in the silence that we "grow up in," which takes over our soul and enables us to come to utterance:

> Now as many thus gathered together grow up in the strength, power, and virtue of truth, and as truth comes thus to have victory and dominion in their souls, then they receive an utterance, and speak steadily to the edification of their brethren, and the pure life hath a free passage through them, and what is thus spoken edifieth the body indeed.[34]

To speak religious truth is not to match the content of our words with a divine object, such as with redemption or God, but is to be in the *way* of truth, which is the way of the Spirit—to have our life so moved by the divine Life that we speak. What we speak certainly has a content but the meaning of what we say is more fundamentally our way of being in the life in this moment. What we communicate in religious speaking, beyond what we say, is the way we are relating to the Spirit as it has motivated us to speak. The Spirit, in its particular motion of the moment, is carried by the words. This is why we must be in the same spirit as the speaker in order to understand what is being said, whether in sermon or scripture. So Barclay says: "when any are, through the breaking forth of this power, constrained to utter a sentence of exhortation or praise, or to breathe to the Lord in prayer, then all are sensible of it; for the same life in them answers to it."[35] To become "sensible of it" is to feel the way the Spirit is moving in the words and to discover the same way resonating, "answering," within oneself. It is to dance, in our hearing, the same life the speaker dances in speaking.

Words as Forms of Life

Barclay presents religious words as ways to live, as forms of life.

Now this is one of the central insights of the great philosopher of ordinary language, Ludwig Wittgenstein. He says: "to imagine a language means to imagine a form of life"[36] and "the *speaking* of language is part of an activity, or of a form of life."[37] To mean by speaking words is an activity of the self. Words are actions of the self and thus ways of behaving—even if "[f]ine shades of behavior."[38] As actions, words have their meaning in their use: "the meaning of a word is its use in the language."[39] The meaning is in "how" words are employed, not simply "what" words are uttered. For instance, the same word "chair" can be uttered in an assertion, a question, and a command; but it will have a different meaning in each because of the way it is used.

Barclay understands this distinction between "how" and "what." Early in the *Apology* he distinguishes between two different ways in which the same words can be used:

> Here the apostle doth so much require the Holy Spirit in the things that relate to a Christian, that he positively avers, we cannot so much as affirm Jesus to be the Lord without it; which insinuates no less, than that the spiritual truths of the gospel are as lies in the mouths of carnal and unspiritual men; for though in themselves they be true, yet are they not truth as to them, because not known, nor uttered forth in and by that principle and spirit that ought to direct the mind and actuate it in such things: they are no better than the counterfeit representations of things in a comedy.[40]

To take one of Paul's favorite phrases, "Jesus is Lord," Barclay is saying that when the "how" of saying this is not in the Spirit, this declaration is false because it is not "actuated" by the Spirit and therefore not "uttered forth in and by that ... spirit." This sentence does not carry the Spirit, just as a theatrical performance of Julius Caesar does not give us Caesar's real "doings."[41] So when we say the "what" of "Jesus is Lord" in the "how" of the Spirit, we have the Spirit's real "doings" — motivating the words, carried in the words, and present as actuating Spirit in the hearers.

In Wittgenstein's words, then, for us to imagine Quaker religious language is to imagine a form of life — the way of life lived forth from the experience of silence. He says: "It is easy to imagine a language consisting only of orders," or "reports in battle," "questions" and "answering yes and no."[42] Just as playing "the language-game"[43] of commands is a way of living — of relating to others, the world around, and to oneself — so playing the language-game of the life of the Spirit is a form of life. It is the life form of the language of the heart.

The Event of Sensible Meaning

What we have said so far is that for Friends there is a vast realm of silence, rather than a vacuous nothing, which is profoundly meaningful and that religious words arise from and bear across to hearers. But to speak and to be understood requires a shift in living, a letting go of ego and descending into the heart in which the life can come to play. As the life stirs in us in the silence, our words that issue forth are forms of life. They are true not because their content represents an external object but because they are bearers of reality, of the divine Life, that touches us, indwells us. They are bearers of truth as actions, as they are used, in the way in which they are used, in the "how" of their use, not simply in the "what" of their content.

But we still have not answered our question of why words are needed at all, since the silence is laden with meaning. Let us look, then, at the non-explicit level of meaning in words, at the "sensible meaning" in words that is beneath their idea content.

In the language of the heart there is a "sensible meaning" communicated beneath the level of explicit content. Beneath the conceptual meaning of "Jesus" as an historical person and founder of a religion, and "Lord" as an authority to submit to, and beneath the functions of the parts of speech of subject and predicate, resulting in a confession of faith, what other meanings are there? How can we make more sense of the life of the Spirit being conveyed along with these concepts and functions?

A simple but paradigmatic example in Quaker history of this sensible meaning of words we feel beneath their cognitive content is that moment when John Woolman, meeting in silence with non-English speaking Delaware Indians and beginning to pray, asks the interpreter to cease translating, in the belief that his spirit of love will communicate. As you will recall, Chief Papunehang's later gloss on this "sensible" communication was: "I love to feel where words come from."[44] Where they come from is the Spirit or the Life. When the content of Woolman's words were no longer comprehensible, because translation had ceased, there was still something being communicated—the way of the Life and the way in Woolman's life that he was being stirred by the divine Life. While the content was, presumably, about divine love, presence, and activity of the Spirit, the reality of love and Spirit was being borne by the spirit in which Woolman spoke—that is, the way in which he used those words.

What more, however, was Chief Papunehang hearing? Consider: all our speech is sound that we utter with tongue, teeth, lips, larynx as we force breath through them in their particular configurations. The sounds we utter all have a rhythm and tone. Woolman's words were like music, whose words were incomprehensible, to the Chief's ears. Yet there was meaning in the rhythm and tonality, and there was a palpable, although not conceptualizable, intentionality. The Chief could feel that Woolman was intending something, that the intention was to share the act and attitude of love, and that he spoke from depth—from the place that is the source of words, from the Great Spirit.

No doubt the Chief was aware as well of the situation—of how Woolman held himself, standing or sitting, the physical surroundings, and the practice of the Native Americans to gather in silence, and their recent assembling to listen to the Moravian preacher—which were all a part of, what Paul Ricoeur calls, the "event" of a speech-act:

> The event is not only the experience as expressed and communicated, but also the intersubjective exchange itself, the happening of dialogue. The instance of discourse is the instance of dialogue. Dialogue is an event which connects two events, that of speaking and that of hearing.[45]

The setting of "the intersubjective exchange" between speaker and hearer, even when untranslated words are being spoken, is dialogical. Speech always happens in a context. The context always plays a part in the meaning. When explicit content is being shared, the words are always to some degree ambiguous. The context helps clarify meaning. As Ricoeur says:

> Most of our words are polysemic; they have more than one meaning. But it is the contextual function of discourse to screen, so to speak, the polysemy of our words.... And it is the function of dialogue to initiate this screening function of the context. The contextual is the dialogical. It is in this precise sense that the contextual role of dialogue reduces the field of misunderstanding concerning the propositional content and partially succeeds in overcoming the non-communicability of experience.[46]

When the "propositional content," as Ricoeur calls it, is uncomprehended, the context is still clarifying meaning—as the Chief knew that Woolman was praying in a religious gathering and felt his caring for the Native Americans and openness to the Spirit.

A simple example of how context shapes meaning is in asking "What's that bark?" You will understand me differently if we are walking amidst a wood, or out searching for our lost dog, or standing with Dante on the banks of the Acheron watching

Charon steer his craft towards us.

Sensible Meaning as Gesture

Another great philosopher of the twentieth century, Merleau-Ponty, calls this sensible meaning beneath content "a *gestural meaning*, which is immanent in speech." If we can disengage ourselves from inhabiting the dialogue of speech and look at it from outside, hearing sounds and seeing one creature surrounded by other creatures (we call humans), we can see that this physical event before us is a gesture, is an effort to signify something. Go back to Barclay's description of coming to utterance in silent worship. The words are a gesture of the Spirit. The Life of the Spirit is "immanent in speech" and is, as it were, signaling those gathered, addressing us and evoking an answering signal back from the same Life that is in us.

Merleau-Ponty says that this gestural significance in language is a "sense [that] was everywhere present, and nowhere posited for its own sake."[48] He explains that when we speak, we do "not think before speaking, nor even while speaking." Rather an orator's "speech is his thought."[49] The speaker "does not think of the sense of what he is saying, nor does he visualize the words which he is using." Speaking is a flow of words. As we speak, we do not stand outside of our saying, objectifying the idea of it, but inhabit it. The meaning is incarnate in the words as we use them. The speaker in improvising is caught up in his or her words. A word is an "emotional essence," an "existential meaning,"[50] it has a "style." "I possess its articulatory and acoustic style as one of the modulations, one of the possible uses of my body." "I do not need to visualize the word in order to know and pronounce it." Rather it is like "reach[ing] back for the word as my hand reaches towards the part of my body which is being pricked."[51] The sensible meaning in speech, then, is the expression of a complex emotional essence and existential meaning, the exhibiting of a style—the display of a form of life.

So also for the listener: he or she is caught up in that emotional essence and that style in the flow of words: "we have no thought marginal" to what is being said,

> for the words fully occupy our mind and exactly fulfil our expectations, and we feel the necessity of the speech. Although we are unable to predict its course, we are possessed by it. The end of the speech or text will be the lifting of a spell. It is at this stage that thoughts on the speech or text will be able to arise.[52]

So it is in a Quaker meeting; the speaker and listeners are wrapt up in the Spirit of what is being said as life answers to life. In the particular words spoken, the general style of the Spirit is present in a very particular way in those words of that moment and place. Only later do we conceptualize what it was about as we try to report what was said to someone not there.

The Embodiedness of Meaning

The sensible meaning that we feel in silent meeting, in which life answers to life in the silence and the speaking, is what Barclay calls "spirit." Often he does not capitalize it so the reader cannot be sure whether it is the spirit of God or of the self. Such ambiguity is, I believe, intentional because "spirit" is both the divine Spirit and the human spirit within which the divine is stirring.

While Barclay's philosophic insight into the nature of language is developed in terms of religious language, he, nevertheless, is seeing in this realm of discourse much of what Wittgenstein, Ricoeur, and Merleau-Ponty see in ordinary language. They are, like Barclay, understanding language, not as pointing to external objects, but as action and energy, and therefore as spiritual—as affecting our way of being. While there are differences, the way Barclay speaks of life and spirit in words is similar to the way

Merleau-Ponty speaks of a pervasive sense, style, existential meaning, and emotional essence in words. Both insist there is a meaning that is alive central to words beneath their explicit content. Both understand similarly the relation between word and sensible meaning.

Sensible meaning is embodied in words. Just as for Merleau-Ponty, thinking is not separate from the gestural significance of words, so, for Barclay, doctrinal thinking and scriptural talk—to be true—is not separate from utterance of life in the Spirit. Meaning—as thinking for Merleau-Ponty—then, is not "self-conscious thought" occurring independently from words but "*is*," he says, "the subject's taking up of a position in the world of his meanings," giving a certain shape to that world, "a certain modulation of existence."[53] Similarly, meaning—as theological thinking for Barclay—is not talking separate from our living but is the self's taking up a position in the world of silence, giving a certain shape to the breathings of the life of the Spirit.

Meaning is embodied; it does not float free from our words. As sensible or gestural meaning, it is incarnate in our living. But, as Merleau-Ponty says, it "is not contained in the word as a sound"; it "is not contained in it like some physical or physiological phenomenon."[54] Rather the meaning is our living enacted in a certain form, a form of life. As Merleau-Ponty says: word and sense "are intervolved, the sense being held within the word, and the word being the external existence of the sense."[55] And as Barclay says, the inward life is within the outward word, and the outward word is—or should be—the actuation of the inward life.

Merleau-Ponty's affirmation of sense embodied in words is part of a much larger affirmation of the body's centrality to all thought and action. His entire philosophy is based on the sense- and meaning-making capacities of the "lived body"—that is, the body as we live it, rather than study it. But Barclay's affirmation of inward meaning embodied in outward word is also part of his larger affirmation of the embodiedness of the spiritual life.

He says: "God hath seen meet ... to make use of the outward senses ... to convey spiritual life, as by speaking, praying, praising, &c., which cannot be done to mutual edification, but when we hear and see one another."[56] Friends gather together "outwardly in their persons," and "in one place,"[57] as well as "inwardly in their spirits."[58] When they are "inwardly gathered unto the life," while "seeing of the faces one of another,"[59] there is "occasion for the life secretly to rise, and pass from vessel to vessel"[60] so that each individual "partakes of the particular refreshment and strength which comes from the good in himself" and at the same time becomes "a sharer in the whole body."[61]

This affirmation of embodiment results in concern for the particularities of our existence. The inward sense or spirit is not some abstract generality of life—as some mysticisms would have it—but in its outward embodiment is concrete, manifest in the particularities of our bodily lives—not only in our speaking, but in our eating, plowing, and doing mechanical work.[62] The Spirit is involved in all these things, although differently as "general" or "particular inspiration." The general is "to comfort, refresh, quicken, influence and assist us, without any particular command to any particular action,"[63] while "particular inspiration" leads individuals "to preach, or expound scripture"[64] or to engage in certain actions, such as traveling. One of Barclay's objections to making scripture the primary rule affirms this particularism. From scripture the apostles "could not learn their duty, as to those particulars" such as "to go here or there to preach the gospel." They could only learn this "immediately from the Spirit"[65] as it gives particular directions.

As the inward is embodied in the outward in vary particular ways, it can be discerned there in the outward: "the free motion of the life itself, as it pleaseth God to bring it forth, is to be attended in all outward, spiritual performances."[66] The inward life is attended to in the outward by "a spirit of discerning"[67] which involves "spiritual senses" working through the "bodily senses": "the fruits of the Spirit, which, although they remain in the souls of holy men, yet send forth a savour of that life and Spirit ... through the outward works and conversation,... [which] reach unto the spiritual senses of others, where they are."[68]

The Transformative Power of Words

The power of silence, that so touched Barclay's heart, becomes the power of words, as they arise from within the silence and bear its life in their expression. This is why Wittgenstein's phrase is so apt for understanding the early Quaker understanding of religious language: words spoken in meeting are forms of the divine Life that arises in the corporate silence, moving us to a momentary form of our life in which we will express the divine Life in our life in the form of our words.

Words themselves, for Wittgenstein, Merleau-Ponty, and Ricoeur, as for Barclay, have power—as forms of life. The meaning is in this action, in how the speaker uses words. The prevailing view in modernity, against which all these twentieth-century thinkers are reacting, and the view that was just getting started in the mid-seventeenth century, against which Barclay was reacting, was that words point or refer to objects. The assumptions here are that words do this referring without the action of a speaker using them, and that the meaning of words are the objects to which they point, as if objects were alone real. Such a view, as all these thinkers make clear in their own idioms, empties words of power and separates meaning from the action and living of selves.

The power of words for Barclay is the power of silence and therefore has the same effects we have seen the silence to have. The self is "actuated by God's light and grace in the heart."[69] The self is already changed as it slips away from ego, from its own will and wisdom, and opens its heart to discover the light and life arising within it. Then as it is influenced to speak, the self gives particular expression of the Life or Spirit, which shapes the self as it acts in this particular form. In Merleau-Ponty's words, speaking involves "a certain structural co-ordination of experience, a certain modulation of existence,"[70] "a synchronizing change of my own existence, a transformation of my being."[71] The self's relationship to itself and to the Life is to some degree re-ordered by the form in which the Life and the speaker's life is uttered. Speaking is a way of giving further significance to the meaning already present in the silence by giving it the shape of particular words. Through the power of speaking, "this open and indefinite power of giving significance—that is, both of apprehending and conveying a meaning"[72]—the self thus "transcends himself towards a new form of behavior."[73] It "brings the meaning into existence ... opening a new field or a new dimension to our experience."[74] Thus it is, in speaking in meeting, if deeply moved, we experience our life from before the meeting being drawn into a new dimension and modulated.

But language not only changes the self, it shapes new meaning that reaches beyond the self "towards other people."[75] Language establishes relations. It relates us to others and the world as well as to ourselves. Barclay acknowledges this in saying the Life in the speaker "answers" the Life in the meeting participants, becoming "a flood of refreshment" as it "overspreads the whole meeting" as an "awe"-filled "glory" that "chained down" anything that "is not one with the life."[76] Not that we are unrelated to others until the Life moves within us in the silence or our speaking, we are already existing in relationships to self and others, but the words intensify and give concrete form that coordinate and enhance these relations. They "edifieth the body"[77] of those present. And they change these relations: for instance, as the lives of those one thousand Seekers were changed who heard Fox preach on Firbank Fell in 1652. Words are not, therefore, merely "a means," according to Merleau-Ponty; they are "a manifestation": "As soon as man uses language to establish a living relation with himself or with his fellows, language is no longer an instrument, no longer a means; it is a manifestation, a revelation of intimate being and of the psychic link which unites us to the world and our fellow men."[78] Words are revelatory of the sensible or gestural meaning they carry, of the particular life we are living in this moment of utterance, and of our links to the world and others, as well as to the divine.

Words as Configurations of Silence

Now we are in a position to deal with the apparent contradiction that words are not necessary in the silence for Barclay and yet he anticipates the twentieth-century revolution in philosophy that affirms that words pervade our conscious existence. Words do pervade our lives but as potential forms of life we can enact. The silence, as the great well of all potential forms, contains the possible forms of life we can speak. What Barclay is denying to the silence is the explicit content of words, not their sensible meaning. The way in which he describes the power of life and spirit in the silence shows that it is potent with sensible meaning. When we are not speaking words nor are they running inaudibly in our heads, but we are being affected in the silence, we are feeling the sensible meanings stirring and spreading among those bodily gathered there. This he calls the spirit or the life— both divine and human—at work in our hearts. Merleau-Ponty makes this point in saying "this supposed silence is alive with words, this inner life is an inner language."[79] Because there are these meanings in the silence, words can arise from within the silence and bear the silence across to its hearers, opening that well of the heart within them. But words can also lose their rootage in the silence. These become the outward words of theology and scripture that people speak without having the currents of life swirling through them. The modern view of language that sees words as referential, rather than as forms of life, has defined the nature of language, in Barclay's terms, as essentially outward.

Merleau-Ponty recognizes the need in our day to return to the source of our language—to the primordial silence:

> Our view of man will remain superficial so long as we fail to go back to that origin, so long as we fail to find, beneath the chatter of words, the primordial silence, and as long as we do not describe the action which breaks this silence. The spoken word is a gesture, and its meaning a world.[80]

This is what early Friends have done—returned to the primordial silence—and what Barclay has done. Not only has he made this return, but he has described the breaking of that silence by utterance of the life of the divine in human spirit.

The silence is something we experience again and again, but it is also a metaphor for the whole in which we live and move and have our being. As such our words are parts of that whole; they make aspects of the silent whole explicit by giving them verbal shape.

When we speak, we actualize certain potentialities in the whole; we draw attention to these aspects of the whole; we relate to the whole through them; and we give shape to our own lives as we live momentarily in the whole through these explicit forms. The meaning of words is, therefore, very much connected with the meaning of silence, with our prelinguistic life in the world. Verbal meaning depends upon nonverbal "lived" meaning. Verbal meanings are configurations of nonverbal meanings— lifting them to visibility, giving them new shape, actualizing and revealing what was only inchoate and perhaps dimly felt.

Words are, therefore, emergent. They emerge from silence as particular expressions of it. They carry this silent whole in a momentary, selective, conscious focus. They change the self as they give verbal form to the self, more intimately connecting various elements in the self, the self and others, and the self with the silent whole. And they can bring the self in return, beyond all words, back to the silent whole enriched. As Isaac Penington says: "the end of words is to bring men to the knowledge of things beyond what words can utter."[81]

This understanding of language expressing a larger, deeper whole of meaning that is silent, that is not articulate, contrasts dramatically with the modern view being formulated by such thinkers as Descartes and Galileo in Barclay's own century. For them there was no whole to which words gave expression, rather there were merely separate objects, words, and thinkers. Silence was disregarded as an empty nothingness between subjects and objects or was redefined scientifically as the gravitational field of physical space.

For Barclay, and other early Friends, silence is the pre-articulate whole in which selves and things are connected. Words draw out certain aspects of that whole into explicit figures. When we speak, our words become ways that we live—they become configurations of the silence.

The Inward Way of Words

The way of word and silence in Quaker experience is an inward way. In our silent meetings we are gathered into the divine Life that arises and moves within the silence. Barclay and other early Friends use the word "inward" for wherever the life is present. It is not a term of subjectivism, that separates the individual psyche from real objects. As we have seen, the life spreads through the whole group and unites us with the whole of world and divinity. Gathered in the inward life of a meeting for worship, Friends can be gathered inward to speak or to hear as an expression of divine in human life that modulates the life of all present.

Another great philosopher of the twentieth century shows that the Greek word for "word"—*Logos*—means "to gather."[82] Martin Heidegger says: "*Logos* is the steady gathering, the intrinsic togetherness of ... being."[83] Friends speak in the language of the Spirit rather than in the language of the Word—

which is central to mainstream Protestantism—and so attribute this gathering power to the Spirit. The gathering of our being in relation to the being of the world and God goes on in the silence through the motions of the Spirit. To recognize this etymology of *Logos* is to make more pointed the realization that the gathering by the Spirit in the silence is a situation charged with the possibility of speech. The way of both word and silence is a gathering—a knitting together into certain verbal forms of life and a holding of each in the whole of being. The gathering in silence is indispensable to the gathering in words as they give partial expression to the silent whole. And the gathering in words is crucial to the gathering in silence as potentialities are realized, made manifest, and selves are further configured in their concrete and corporate richness.

If words are forms of life, then every speech-act is a manifestation of self. As Rumi said—to switch worlds from twentieth-century European philosophy to thirteenth-century Turkish poetry—"Every spoken word is a covering for the inner self."[84] But if they carry a sensible meaning others can catch, an emotional essence or existential meaning that others can dance, then they also manifest something more than the individual self. By understanding this "more" as silence, and therefore as the whole in which we dwell here on earth and as divine energy, then our words as forms of life manifest not only self but the whole of being. Our words, and more complexly our lives— complexified largely by our words—are therefore configurations of the whole, choreographings of the silence, in which we live and move and have our being. In every word we speak, then, there is something of the particular self I am and of the universal Life that pervades all things. Words then carry with them, however hidden, reminiscences of their emerging, longings for home, and resonances of our present dwelling. To return to the place from which words come, the silence, the Quaker experience is to be gathered into this whole by the gathering power of the divine—Spirit, Life, Light, *Logos*—and from within this heart of inwardness, again and again, to be "gathered inward to the word."[85]

B. Quaker Thought: Relational and Emergent in Robert Barclay

Touched and Knit in the Life: Barclay's Relational Theology Beyond Cartesian Dualism

Robert Barclay's theology is a laboratory for discovering one's own Quaker way of doing theology. Controversy has swirled around him both in his lifetime and ever since. While alive he argued extensively with Puritans. After his death Friends have either claimed him for their side in fratricidal conflict or rejected him for distorting Quaker ways of thinking. Having wrestled with him since my youth, both to understand him and to figure out my own Quaker approach to theology, I recommend him as a challenge to head and heart. As I am seeking understanding, I am responding to George Fox's challenge to Margaret Fell when they first met in the spring of 1652 at her home Swarthmore Hall and then she heard him preach in her Ulverston Puritan church. She was, as she said, "cut ... to the Heart" by his challenge: You know what the scripture says, but "what canst thou say?"[1]

Amidst his arguments with Puritans, Barclay develops, I want to show, a Quaker way of doing theology—using a relational method which contrasts significantly with Puritans' use of a dualistic method and dogmatic thinking. Two-thirds of the way through his *Apology* Barclay speaks of his convincement as being touched in the heart by the life and power among people gathered in silent worship. This is the beginning of his relational theology—relating to selves open in their depths and to the divine presence moving in their midst. Theological thinking, like messages delivered in meeting, emerges from these non-rational depths of shared silence. Knowledge of scripture and Christian principles does not precede such experience but rather emerges out of such experienced depths: "afterwards the knowledge and understanding of principles will not be wanting, but will grow up so much as is needful, as the natural fruit of this good root."[2]

While this non-dualistic way of thinking can be shown in George Fox, Margaret Fell, and Isaac Penington (see my efforts cited in bibliography), Barclay draws upon Descartes implicitly in his *Apology* and explicitly in an essay entitled *The Possibility and Necessity of the Inward & Immediate Revelation of the Spirit of God*. Scholars have concluded that Barclay is, therefore, irretrievably dualistic. Barclay's explicit engagement with Cartesian dualism has obscured for them his relational way of doing theology and the meaning of this engagement within his apologetic context. To show that Barclay's way of doing theology is relational, we must confront this charge of dualism by exploring his use of Descartes.

Cartesian Dualism and Relational Thinking

Under the impact of the rise of modern science, René Descartes (1619–1650) carefully crafted a mind/body dualism from the Greek spirit/matter hierarchy, in order to free the scientific exploration of the natural world from ecclesiastical and theological domination and to protect the realm of selves and its truth from science's encroachments. While English intellectuals, such as the Cambridge Platonist, Henry More, were excited by Descartes' philosophy, the danger was recognized in his thought of a mechanistic view of body and world absent of and alien to the personal. Less recognized at the time, Descartes initiated for both rationalist and empiricist modern philosophy an insatiable search for absolute rational certainty through the method of doubt. The result, however, as Michael Polanyi so well has shown (see *Personal Knowledge* and *The Tacit Dimension*), has been skepticism and totalitarianism, for the method attempts to uproot all commitments by which we dwell in the world.

Dualism means a separation of realms so there is no interaction between or participation in one another. Descartes' dualism isolates mind and body from each other totally (except for his dubious effort to connect them at the pineal gland). The theological implications are to separate self and God, self and world, and the experienced Christ from the biblical Christ. The mind severed from the body's participation in and interaction with the world, looks out from its enclosure upon a world of objects — natural, human, and divine — to which it is unrelated and about which it is uncertain. The biblical Christ as external to the knowing self similarly becomes problematic: how can we know with certitude anything that happens in history?

Descartes thought he discovered a foundation of absolute certainty in the self, specifically in critical reason. In his realization of *Cogito ergo sum* ("I think therefore I am") he grounded reason in reason: he realized in doubting all things, he could not doubt that he was doubting. He did not apply his methodology of doubt to God's existence. Rather he found ideas of God within his reason that he believed only God could have caused since they were of perfection and we as imperfect creatures could not have made them. On the basis of trust in such a perfect creator he decided he could depend sufficiently on his senses to convey a knowable world, but the point of certainty was in reason itself, not in sensuous relations to the world. Protestantism found certainty in the scriptures; even though external to the self, its objective certainty was assured by God's self-validating revelation. The separation of God and Christ from our minds was thus bridged by this contact point with the divine through scripture as the certain Word of God.

But the Quaker way, which we will see in Barclay, was to look for certainty neither in reason nor in scripture, but in personal experience. Through pairs of terms, Friends spoke of inward and outward, life and form, spirit and letter, silence and words in such a way that the first term was a dimension of depth in the latter term. While some recent Quaker scholars construe these pairs as dualistically separate in Barclay, I want to show that they were in fact used by him as interrelated, with the former participating in the latter and the latter emerging from the former. Inwardness was the level of life and spirit that Barclay and his seventeenth-century Quaker contemporaries descended to over and over again in meeting for worship and daily living. From this spiritual dimension word and action emerged filled with vitality as outward forms. The outward was thus the inward made manifest; the inward was the outward in potentiality. Only when these split apart so the outward form was empty of life, or the inward vitality was prevented from coming to expression, was there a problem.

But the certainty embraced here in inwardness was a "lived" certainty rather than a rational one—the assurance that comes in experience of things that are deep, that feel really real and ultimately significant, that transforms lives and calls forth the giving of one's life in commitment. As a lived certainty, it is better to speak of this as a trust and confidence since it does not eliminate, as rational certitude attempts to, the many ambiguities of living.

By this relational mode of religious knowing, Barclay and other early Friends held together interactively self and God, mind and body, self and world, and the experiential and biblical Christ. They did this by seeing God as a transcendent presence within the self, the mind as an embodied consciousness discerning truth through the spiritually enlivened physical senses, the self as inherently connected with all creatures within the original creation present in our depths, and Christ as the eternal divine presence dwelling in all people and in fullest measure in Jesus.

A Growing Scholarly Consensus on Dualism in Barclay

There is a growing consensus among Quaker scholars, however, that Barclay's involvement with Cartesian thought is a capitulation to it, setting the stage for the development of quietism and its separations of mind from body, divine from human, and the inward Christ from the outward biblical Christ. Maurice Creasey says:

> [A]t the hands of Robert Barclay, and largely in terms of a confused and illegitimate application of the originally clear and valid distinction between "inward" and "outward", Quakerism became wedded to a prevalent and quasi-Cartesian dualism and, as a consequence, set its feet upon paths which, for many a year, led it into the barren places of quietism and formalism.[3]

He argues that in Fox and Penington "outward" and "inward" were used to distinguish "a formal or conventional or notional knowledge of Christianity as a body of 'revealed truths' and religious and ethical practices" from "a transforming and creative personal acquaintance with and relation to Christ in the Spirit."[4] But Barclay, according to Creasey, distinguishes these as

> a contrast between two modes of revelation, and ... between two distinct organs whereby these modes of revelation are respectively received. There is no recognition of any possiblity [sic] of mutual interaction or communication or influence between these two modes, or these two organs.[5]

Barclay has taken, Creasey explains, the earlier definition of inward and outward as two different ways to apprehend the same revelation given in history, and turned it into "two kinds of Revelation," one of which is "without any essential connection with History" and is known by an "organ within man, which yet is no part of man's essential being, dependent in no way upon the constitution of man's mind."[6] The reason for this presumed separation is Barclay's imbibing Cartesian dualism. Thus "Quakerism early took the form of a kind of spiritualized

Cartesianism" leaving it as "a religious movement lacking an adequate intellectual formulation and means of self-criticism."[7] Over and against this "religion of immanence," Creasey proposes "a religion of incarnation" in which "the 'inward' made itself known in and through the 'outward', and is still to be encountered only so"[8]—that is, through the Jesus of scripture, the Johannine incarnate Word.

Mel Endy agrees with Creasey about Cartesian dualism in Barclay but sees this separation of inward and outward going back to Fox and the beginnings of Quakerism[9] stemming from Cartesian and Platonic thought.[10] He sees in Barclay "spiritual-corporeal" and "divine-human" dualisms—the former because Barclay separates the physical and spiritual senses, and the latter because the human is made entirely passive, with no free will, as the old self, its will and personality, is annihilated and replaced by the Spirit and will of God.[11]

John Punshon suggests that "Barclay unintentionally expressed the central ambiguity of Quakerism and posed a problem which the evangelical and liberal traditions were later to solve in characteristically different ways." [12] The evangelical tradition, overlooking Barclay's relegation of scripture to secondary authority, springs from his theological development of redemption through Christ. And the liberal tradition, overlooking Barclay's holding the mystical light and historical Jesus in an "indissoluble link," springs from his development of this inward spiritual reality. With Creasey, and in contrast to Endy, Punshon sees a significant difference between Barclay and Fox:

Then there is a tantalising difference in atmosphere between the two men. Barclay is obviously a scholar, at home with the Fathers as well as the Bible, capable of taking nice points and making fine distinctions. Fox breathes the air of an Amos or Paul, and sees the whole sweep of God's covenant relationship with his Church in a far more dramatic and concrete way. Basically, Barclay has put Quakerism into a quietist kind of straitjacket by his philosophical dualism and distrust of the powers of the human mind. Fox's profoundly scriptural faith contains so many counterweights to enthusiasm in one direction that there is a diversity and comprehensiveness there that Barclay has not quite caught.[13]

In the most recent consideration of Barclay's dualism, Hugh Pyper similarly identifies Barclay as Cartesian in interpreting him as representing the self as an "individual [who] is fundamentally a mental being."[14] But he qualifies this by recognizing the experiential and communal dimension in Barclay's thought evident in his convincement. Yet he argues that Barclay's theological and philosophical commitments to dualism "do not allow him to express them [i.e. 'these communal experiences'] in his systematic writings."[15] Moreover, this "inherent dualism of Barclay's thought ... ultimately pulls apart the divine and the human in the incarnation."[16] He thus has a "deficient doctrine of the Holy Spirit"[17] because he does not distinguish between "the spirit already at work in the world" and "the power of the son at work in the man Jesus."[18]

Starting with Barclay's Starting Point

In the face of this growing scholarly consensus of Barclay's capitulation to Cartesian dualism, I would propose a different angle of approach in order to understand Barclay's use of Descartes' concepts and his way of thinking theologically. Rather than bringing the experiential in at the end of a study of Barclay as a contradiction to his assumed Cartesianism, as Pyper has done, I suggest we start from experience in community since that is the context of his convincement and hence the springboard for all his Quaker reflections. From this perspective we can follow him developing a non-dualistic theology, though admittedly not into its fullness, and eventually return to the question of the meaning of the apologetic form of his thinking, which Pyper has so well discussed,[19] for his engagement with Cartesian dualism. Before we explore the relational nature of his convincement and subsequent reflection, we must assess Barclay's epistemological emphasis as he begins his *Apology*, for here we see the unmistakable influence of Descartes.

Writing for university trained readers in the common scholastic form of rational argumentative defense of propositions, Barclay starts his book by establishing the true foundation of knowledge. Within the latter half of the seventeenth century this suggests two particular influences—John Calvin and Descartes. Calvin in 1559 begins his *Institutes of the Christian Religion*: "Nearly all the wisdom we possess, that is to say, true and sound wisdom, consists of two parts: the knowledge of God and of ourselves."[20] Calvin here shifts the focus from medieval preoccupation with being to the modern question of knowing. One hundred years later Descartes is fixing epistemology as the central question and starting point for modern philosophy. But he intensifies the quality of what is sought, redefining "true and sound wisdom" as certain knowledge: as that "which I knew to be true and certain."[21] The influence of both Calvin and Descartes is evident in the title of Barclay's first proposition: "Concerning the true Foundation of Knowledge."[22] Furthermore, when he speaks of what he wants to find as "quietness and peace in the certain knowledge of God,"[23] he exhibits Descartes' preoccupation with certainty.

When Barclay speaks of his convincement, however, we are in an epistemological approach that shows no trace of Cartesianism:

For not a few have come to be convinced of the truth after this manner, of which I myself, in part, am a true witness, who not by strength of arguments, or by a particular disquisition of each doctrine, and convincement of my understanding thereby, came to receive and bear witness of the truth, but by being secretly reached by this life; for when I came into the silent assemblies of God's people, I felt a secret power among them, which touched my heart, and as I gave way unto it, I found the evil weakening in me, and the good raised up, and so I became thus knit and united unto them, hungering more and more after the increase of this power and life, whereby I might feel myself perfectly redeemed.[24]

He speaks of being convinced by the truth as the divine life reached and touched his heart in the silence of meeting for worship. Not by rational argument and theological inquiry that would convince the understanding, but by the power of the divine life he felt among the assembly gathered in silence he received the truth. The effect of being touched by and giving way to the life was to discover the evil within himself weakened and the good strengthened, himself to be knit and united with the worshippers, and a hunger to feel himself fully redeemed.

Mind and body are not split apart. In entering physically into this space where people are sitting in silent worship, he is touched in his mind, but it is the mind as heart, not as head merely (a distinction he uses from the beginning[25]). In the heart he feels and wants; it is the place of his passions, of affectional understanding. He is affected in his heart through perceiving the situation, through sensing the power in it, not by conceiving it. Just as his understanding is not separated from his body but they are working together as they are touched by the life, so also the self is not separated from God. The life of God is immediately present making its redeeming and uniting power felt in his whole bodily and ensouled being. While the agency is the divine life radiating from the gathering, so that he is acted on by this power, contrary to Endy's claim, Barclay is not entirely passive, for he speaks of giving way to that which has touched his heart. He presumably could have resisted it. While he will speak later of the Spirit's leading from within himself, here is no annihilation of the self. Indeed, there is an enlargement of the self, as he not only feels the good being raised up in him (which presumably was already present, but not pervasive in him), but discovers himself, by the grace of this divine life, being brought into unity with these people.

There is no dualism here of mind/body or divine/human oppositions. Nor are there any Cartesian concepts at work. He is using concepts—convincement, truth, heart, life, good and evil, unity, redemption—but they are emerging directly from his experience as he attempts to give account of what he felt and the effects that followed as he entered this gathered meeting. Nor is there any reference to Christ outward or inward, except the metaphor of "life" which is a Johannine term for both the inward and outward Christ.

In his larger discussion of Proposition XI "Concerning Worship," within which this account of his convincement occurs, Barclay develops further his relational views of self and God, mind and body. God is present "in the midst," whose "presence" is known through "feeling" and being "gathered" by it.[26] Words in worship "are felt to arise" from the "pure motions and breathings of God's Spirit."[27] An intimacy is present in the divine-human relations in which the divine actuates the self from within it empowering it to "words and actings." Friends learn "to wait upon God … and feel after this inward seed of life; that as it moveth, they may move with it, and be actuated by its power, and influenced, whether to pray, preach or sing."[28]

"Waiting" is not passivity; it is an activity in which the ego—what Barclay calls "the natural will and wisdom" and the "imagination"[29]—is to be laid down. Waiting thus involves "denying self, both inwardly and outwardly, in a still and mere dependence upon God." It involves "being emptied as it were of himself," of all "the workings, imaginations, and speculations of his own mind." It is being "thoroughly crucified to the natural products" of the self so as "to receive the Lord," in which "the little seed of righteousness which God hath planted in his soul ... receives a place to arise."[30]

While this place of "holy dependence"[31] and the growth of "the little seed" is in inwardness, it is not separated from the outward but is the depth within it. "God hath seen meet, so long as his children are in this world, to make use of the outward senses." He uses them "to convey spiritual life" by "speaking, praying" which can only contribute to "mutual edification ... when we hear and see one another." The "seeing of the faces one of another, when both are inwardly gathered unto the life" "causeth the inward life ... the more to abound."[32] As "many are gathered together into the same life, there is more of the glory of God."[33] So the meeting together of people "outwardly in their persons,"[34] in their bodies, and "outwardly in one place"[35] is important to the nurture of their inward lives. Hence "the name of Quakers, i.e., Tremblers": when selves engage in worship in "inward travail," the inward struggle may result in an outward "trembling and a motion of body." The body may be shaken resulting in "many groans, and sighs, and tears, even as the pangs of a woman in travail."[36] Literal birthing is used as a metaphor for the inward life struggling to come forth. The body, in its physical shaking, may show forth visibly the inward spiritual condition of giving up one's natural will and wisdom.[37] The outward expresses the inward. Mind and body are not separated.

The Senses Natural and Supernatural

But what of Barclay's distinction between the natural and supernatural senses: "The senses are either outward or inward; and the inward senses are either natural or supernatural.... [S]ome beings are natural, some supernatural; so some ideas are natural, some supernatural...."[38] Many Quaker scholars see this as evidence of the mind/body split. The spiritual senses are, on the contrary, I would say, not only like the physical senses but work through them. What they sense is not light and sound as received by the outward senses but through the physical light and sound they sense the spiritual light and voice of God. Barclay says that, while voices in scripture are usually not outward but inward voices, God has spoken outwardly to people through angels or through dreams and visions. The way in which they knew, however, that this was God speaking was through the spiritual sensing of the "secret testimony of God's Spirit in their hearts, assuring them that the voices, dreams, and visions were of and from God." The outward senses are fallible; even hearing an outward word spoken to you in a mystical audition cannot "credit"[39] this experience as from God. This can only be known inwardly in the heart through the Spirit's assurance.

When Abraham entertained angels, Barclay says, he did not recognize them as angels through his outward senses. Seeing men walk towards him—receiving light from them on the retina of his eyes, as we would say today—does not tell him their spiritual quality; it is the spiritual sense that does. "And seeing the Spirit of God is within us, and not without us only, it speaks to our spiritual, and not to our bodily ear."[40] So also with all the other senses. Like Fox and Penington, Barclay speaks of the spiritual senses in terms of each of the physical senses: "thou shalt feel the new man, or the spiritual birth and babe raised, which hath its spiritual senses, and can see, feel, taste, handle and smell the things of the Spirit."[41]

The issue of the outward and inward senses is not whether there are two ways of knowing, or two modes of revelation, as Creasey has said, but how do we discern the full meaning of things, how do we catch the full meaning of what we receive through our outward senses and of what occurs within us that may not be detectably connected with any perception but only with being ourselves in our bodies? Barclay speaks of a blind man not knowing the full meaning of sunlight, while a mere child, who can see, grasps its meaning. And he speaks of words, obviously seen or heard—whose true meaning can only be grasped by an inward taste:

> neither can the natural man, of the largest capacity, by the best words, even scripture words, so well understand the mysteries of God's kingdom, as the least and weakest child who tasteth them, by having them revealed inwardly and objectively by the Spirit.[42]

What is known inwardly through this spiritual or supernatural sense Barclay says is "immediate" and "objective." "Immediate" means "no mention of any medium." The meaning does not come from "writings or books" but comes first hand in one's own experience. Barclay does not, however, recognize that any words, even those "words put into the mouth"[43] by God, are a medium, as are the feelings one has of God's inward working. Nevertheless, his point is well taken, even if word and feeling are recognized, as they would be today, as media; God works immediately in the feeling and words.

Inward revelation by the Spirit is not merely immediate but "objective." The inward workings of the Spirit are real and are the object of our faith. He says: "That which any one firmly believes, as the ground and foundation of his hope in God, and life eternal, is the formal object of his faith."[44] What this formal object is is inward revelation: "And what was the object of their faith, but inward and immediate revelation."[45] The Protestant alternative, which Barclay is rejecting, is that scripture is the object of faith:

> Such as deny this proposition now-a-days use here a distinction; granting that God is to be known by his Spirit, but again denying that it is immediate or inward, but in and

by the scriptures; in which the mind of the Spirit (as they say) being fully and amply expressed, we are thereby to know God, and be led in all things.[46]

This Protestant view makes the inward revelations of the Spirit merely subjective, which is subordinated to the outward words of scripture, so the function of the Spirit is reduced to merely understanding the objective words. In this view, there is no reality and meaning apart from explicit external forms, which is apart from the words of scripture. This Protestant view believes, says Barclay:

That the Spirit doth now lead and influence the saints, but that he doth it only subjectively, or in a blind manner, by enlightening their understandings, to understand and believe the truth delivered in the scriptures; but not at all by presenting those truths to the mind by way of object,... of whose working a man is not sensible.[47]

But there are "many truths" which "are applicable to particulars and individuals," Barclay argues, which "are in nowise to be found in the scripture" but which we yet learn—by the Spirit, who "objectively present[s] those truths to our minds."[48]

In current philosophical language we can say Barclay is locating all true knowing in the inwardness of what Michael Polanyi calls the "tacit dimension" (see Polanyi). The reason we trust tradition (for Catholics) or scripture (for Protestants) is finally that both have been revealed to the church "doctors and fathers" or to the Bible writers by the Spirit in inwardness: "all ends in the revelation of the Spirit."[49] And we, in our inwardness, discern through the motion of the Spirit in us the presence of the Spirit in them.

What is delivered immediately and objectively to us by the Spirit in our inwardness has a certainty about it: "the divine revelation, and inward illumination, is that which is evident by itself, forcing the well-disposed understanding, and irresistibly moving it to assent by its own evidence and clearness, even as the common principles of natural truths do bend the mind to a natural assent."[50] Like the astronomer who rightly calculates an eclipse, or like the mathematician who knows "that the three angles of a right triangle are equal to two right angles," the "spiritual senses ... can savour the things of the Spirit, as it were in prima instantia, i.e., at the first blush, can discern them without, or before they apply them either to scripture or reason."[51]

What Barclay finds as common in these examples between scientific and religious knowing of the spiritual senses is their instantaneity of discernment. Pyper understands Barclay as finding a different commonality: rational abstraction and geometrical demonstration. He rightly points out that "Descartes' model of truth is geometry"[52] which seeks truth by "get[ting] behind the fallen world of matter and appearance."[53] Pyper then attributes this dualistic thinking to Barclay: "Barclay makes geometrical demonstration his ideal form of truth."[54] He thus "prioritises the mental over the physical. The prevailing model of western anthropology has been centred on the head, on mental activity and on the higher sense; the eye, the ear, and the activity of speech. The rest of the body tends to be relegated...."[55] While Pyper draws a reasonable inference from someone using astronomical and geometrical analogies, Barclay is, I believe, more subtle and more consistent with his Quaker perspective than this. What he in fact likens to the scientific in the religious is instantaneous discernment—"in prima instantia, i.e. at the first blush." Moreover, the nature of this discerning is not grasping an idea through rational abstraction nor axiomatic argument separate from the sensuous world; it is rather a "savor[ing]." As we have seen, Barclay does not privilege, as the Catholic and Protestant traditions do, the physical senses of sight and hearing, but rather speaks of the inward spiritual sense working through all of the five senses. The spiritual light, as well, works through, not separate from, reason: to "be rightly and comfortably ordered in natural things [is] to have their reason enlightened by this divine and pure light" —and the same for conscience.[56]

Barclay's Christology

Similarly, I would argue that there is no dualism either in Barclay's Christology when he is speaking from experience. The divine indwells both Jesus and us; the difference is in degree. Within a trinitarian context—without working out a trinitarian doctrine (that is, without working out the nature of the three persons and how they relate to one another)—Barclay says there is no knowing the Father except through the Son, and no knowing the Son except through the Spirit.[57] Father, Son, and Spirit dwell within the outward man Jesus and within all humans. The difference is that "the fulness of the Godhead dwelt bodily" in Jesus. Each person has a measure of the divine within: "God hath communicated and given unto every man a measure of the light of his own Son, a measure of grace, or a measure of the Spirit."[58] But only Jesus has the fullest *measure*.

Son "or" Spirit: Barclay, like Fox and other early Friends, does not separate Son and Spirit as metaphysically distinct as the classical Greek influenced tradition does. The divine present in Jesus is the Son, in us and in the world is the Spirit, but the divine presence is Spirit so Barclay also speaks of the divine in Jesus as Spirit. Since the Spirit as divine presence is central to his theology, his doctrine of the Spirit only appears deficient, as Pyper insists, if measured by the abstract metaphysical categories of Greek Christian rationalism. But Barclay and early Friends are offering an alternative to that with their experiential approach.

Barclay introduces a notion into his Christology that I do not know of Fox or other Quakers using. He says that all people have the divine dwelling within through a *"vehiculum dei, or the* spiritual body of Christ, the flesh and blood of Christ, which came down from heaven, of which all the saints do feed, and are thereby nourished unto eternal life."[59] This is a vehicle or a medium, or what he calls in "Revelation" "the organ or instrument of God."[60] It is "a spiritual, heavenly, and invisible principle, in which God, as Father, Son and Spirit, dwells; a measure of which divine and glorious life is in all men as a seed, which of its own nature, draws, invites, and inclines to God." God and Christ are present in this agency: "God and Christ are wrapped up therein" and "it is never separated from God nor Christ."[61] He calls this vehicle, as well, the "light," "seed," and "Christ."[62] The difference this makes between Jesus and other humans is that God dwells immediately in Jesus, but mediately (that is, through this instrumental medium) in all others: "Christ dwells in us, yet not immediately, but mediately, as he is in that seed, which is in us; whereas he, to wit, the Eternal Word, which was with God, and was God, dwelt immediately in that holy man."[63] Christ dwells "mediately" in us as a seed but Christ dwells "immediately" in Jesus, not as a seed, but in its maturest measure.

The work of the divine in us through this instrument is to redeem us. Redemption is the transformation of the self by raising it to new life. This seed of God in us begins to grow so that "Christ comes to be formed and brought forth."[64] This means that people are brought "to a sense of their own misery" and become "sharers in the sufferings of Christ inwardly" and "partakers of his resurrection, in becoming holy, pure, and righteous, and recovered out of their sins."[65] Redemption is, therefore, a present event within the inwardness of a self. Whatever the connection between the past event of God working in the historic Jesus and someone's present redemption, redemption is the transformation of the self, the forming of Christ within the individual self — growing into a spiritual maturity of a God pervaded life.

What then is this connection? The atonement language Barclay uses shows the influence of the classic theory of atonement put forward by Abelard. Barclay says that Christ "gave himself a ransom for all" as "a reason of God's love to the world."[66] Like Abelard's God who woos us to turn to him, for Barclay "God, in and by this Light and Seed, invites, calls, exhorts, and strives with every man in order to save him."[67] While he does sometimes use language of the Anselmian transaction model of atonement—"sacrifice," "transacted," "satisfactory sacrifice,"[68] "purchased"[69]—he does not talk about a historical event in which God "satisfies" his justice while managing to be merciful to humans. The death of Christ for Barclay is not a transaction but a revelation, a divine manifestation focused in love upon persons, not upon God's maintenance of his own rectitude. The biblical portrait of Christ reveals what is revealed within each person but it is only the inward revelation, the inward taste, within each person that saves, not the knowledge of Jesus as the historical revelation of God.

Salvation does only come, for Barclay, through "the name JESUS indeed."[70] But this does not mean an outward knowing of the biblical Christ but an inward knowing of the divine presence within—even if one is ignorant of the biblical tradition:

> I confess there is no other name to be saved by: but salvation lieth not in the literal, but in the experimental knowledge; albeit, those that have the literal knowledge are not saved by it, without this real experimental knowledge: yet those that have the real knowledge may be saved without the external.[71]

The light which saves "could not be understood of Christ's person" but "must be that inward spiritual light that shines in their [all people's] hearts."[72]

Just as people are inclined to evil after Adam's fall, though they may be ignorant of Adam, so also Christ can transform the self within even though the person never has heard of the historical Jesus: "many may come to feel the influence of this holy and divine seed and light, and be turned from evil to good by it, though they knew nothing of Christ's coming in the flesh." Barclay ends this sentence: "through whose obedience and sufferings it is purchased unto them."[73] Yet the "purchase" is not a transaction but revelation, since the seed and light have been at work throughout the history of the world transforming people, before as well as after the historical event of Jesus. Barclay explicitly redefines "purchase" in terms of revelation: "we witness this capacity brought into act, whereby receiving and not resisting the purchase of his death, to wit, the light, spirit, and grace of Christ revealed in us."[74]

Knowing the outward biblical Christ does make a difference. It "humble[s]," "strengthen[s]," "encourage[s]," provides an "excellent pattern" and "example that we should follow his steps," "edifie[s] and refreshe[s]." "The history then is profitable and comfortable with the mystery, and never without it; but the mystery is and may be profitable without the explicit and outward knowledge of the history." In fact, if you are aware of the biblical tradition, Barclay says, "it is absolutely needful that those do believe the history of Christ's outward appearance, whom it pleased God to bring to the knowledge of it."[75]

Christ dwells in all. Any and all can respond to this light and seed, and have them fructify within to the raising up of new life in God, saved out of sin into purity of life. Yet Barclay qualifies "Christ" here. He distinguishes between Christ as seed within the self and Christ as growing and formed up into new life. In the latter sense Christ is not present in everyone. Christ is only present in everyone as the divine seed that has the potential to grow into maturity and to illuminate the darkness of control over life by one's own will and wisdom. Only if the *vehiculum dei* or seed or light "is received and closed with in the heart, Christ comes to be formed and brought forth: but we are far from ever having said, that Christ is thus formed in all men, or in the wicked." "Neither is Christ in all men by way of union, or … inhabitation" but "is in all men as in a seed." In this sense, as a seed, Christ is within everyone.[76]

The self is entirely passive to saving grace—in its initial workings. The self's nature is "wholly corrupted"[77] so it cannot save itself. This corruption is not imputed from Adam, yet each person repeats Adam's sin when "they actually join with it."[78] For this reason Barclay says Quakers speak of "the old Adam, in which all sin is;… and not that of original sin."[79] Righteousness through justification is not imputed but actual: "by this justification by Christ … we understand the formation of Christ in us,… this inward birth in us, bringing forth righteousness and holiness in us."[80] In justification we are "being made really righteous, and not merely a being reputed such."[81] While the self cannot "move one step out of the natural condition, until the grace lay hold upon him," it does have the nature to be "capable to be wrought upon by the grace of God" and the capacity to resist or receive it: "he that resists its striving, is the cause of his own condemnation; he that resists it not, it becomes his salvation." So "the first step is not by man's working, but by his not contrary working." And after the initial step by grace, the self cooperates with grace: "afterwards, as man is wrought upon, there is a will raised in him, by which he comes to be a co-worker with the grace."[82] Endy is right that grace is indispensable but the self is not annihilated. Rather it is reordered, as it was originally meant to be, so the divine, rather than the natural will and wisdom, pervades and guides the self.

So here there is no dualism separating the biblical, historical Christ and the inward Christ. For those who assume redemption is a transaction, as Creasey does, such an emphasis on inward transformation would split the inward Christ from the objective Christ of the Bible. But Barclay's view of redemption is not transactional but revelatory: what was fully present in the historical Jesus and recorded in the Bible is what can be revealed in varying measures within every person from the beginning of time, as God, as seed or light, strives from within each person to get them to receive and not resist the growth of this seed.

If Barclay's view of redemption is not dualistic, is there, nevertheless, an influence of Descartes' subject/object split on his notion of the *vehiculum dei* as it separates the historical Christ from other humans? Barclay does separate the divine and human here, but not because of Descartes. Rather he proposes this out of a commitment to the Christological tradition, that maintains the impassibility of God: God the Father does not suffer because he is not divisible into parts. He conceives a *vehiculum dei* because "the seed, grace, and word of God, and light" strive with the self and are "crucified" by human response, but this is: "not the proper essence, and nature of God precisely taken." God "is not divisible into parts and measures," because God is "a most pure, simple being, void of all composition or division," who "therefore can neither be resisted, hurt, wounded, [nor] crucified."[83] While this insistence that God in essence is simple and undivided whereas we are finite and partial is a curious mortgage to his past theological education at the Catholic Scots College of Paris, he qualifies this disjunction between God and self by conceiving of the entire trinity, and not merely the Son, as indwelling the seed or light, and thus indwelling everyone. While God and self are distinguishable ontologically, they interact intimately as the undivided God dwells mediately within us and engenders our growing up in Christ—just as whole and part are different yet interact.

Barclay's Apologetic Use of Cartesianism

What we have been seeing is that there is no dualism in Barclay when he is reflecting on his own religious experience. The supernatural sense works through the natural senses to discern the moving of the Spirit within the spirits of those gathered together bodily in silence. Evoked by grace, the self is actuated into being more fully itself, being united with others, and becoming an active co-worker with the divine. The divine he discovers within as the inward Christ is the same Spirit manifest in fullness in the outward Christ of scripture. Nevertheless, a year after the *Apology* he employs Cartesian dualism in response to Adrian Paets, a Dutch diplomat and philosopher. Here Barclay separates mind and body, denies synaesthesia, denigrates the body as brutish, and affirms innate ideas. What can explain this seeming capitulation to Descartes' dualism?

Most of Barclay's published theology, as evident in the title of his *Apology*, is "apologetic." What this technical theological term means, as he says at the outset of his magnum opus, is "to declare and defend the truth."[84] Apologetic theology addresses people of a different point of view and seeks to defend one's own views against their criticism and to persuade them at least of the reasonableness of one's own views if not their truth. The way in which this is done is by finding common ground with one's critics. The Bible and the Protestant theological tradition obviously provide common ground between Quakers, Puritans, and Anglicans. Hence his frequent references to scripture, Protestant doctrines, and general reasonableness; yet when he presents common texts he invariably gives a Quaker interpretation. This often leaves his audience dissatisfied, yet they must admit that there is some basis in scripture, tradition, and/or reason for his view—as Adrian Paets recognized, according to Barclay's report, that Quakers "could make a reasonable plea for the foundation of their religion."[85]

Why then does he use Descartes in responding to Paets? To write apologetics is to let your opponent set the agenda to which you respond. Descartes had become all the rage among erudite thinkers both on the continent and in England. Not that people necessarily agreed with him, but serious thinkers knew they had to deal with him. When the Dutch thinker writes to Barclay making the Cartesian separation of outward senses from the mind, Barclay writes back in kind, using the coin of the realm.

Paets works from the empiricist side of the outward senses of the Cartesian split, arguing, according to Barclay, that the Christian religion, based on Christ Jesus, is merely "contingent truth" because it deals with the "matter of fact" of history. Since matters of fact can only be known by the outward senses and since "God cannot make a contingent truth to become a necessary truth," then faith only comes through the outward sense of hearing, as he understands Paul to have meant when he said: "Faith cometh by hearing."[86]

Barclay is wrestling with what will later be known as "Lessing's ugly ditch." In 1777 Gotthold Lessing wrote: "accidental truths of history can never become the proof of necessary truths of reason." He calls this distinction between historical and rational truth "the ugly, broad ditch which I cannot get across, however often and however earnestly I have tried to make the leap."[87] Where Lessing desired a certainty on the other side of the ugly ditch, Paets has an answer which satisfies him on this side of the ditch: that the truth comes by hearing the gospel preached.

Barclay, however, requires more certitude and intimacy than contingent history provides. Taking the rationalist side of Descartes' split, he looks for truth, as Descartes does, within rather than outside the self. And like Descartes, he insists on certainty—indeed, "infallibility," since he approves of Catholics' desire for certainty, though not their locating it in the church tradition.[88] He locates it, rather, in inward immediate divine revelation, by God speaking directly within the soul. He likens the certainty of such supernatural revelation to the certainty of a necessary truth of definition: "that this proposition, every divine revelation is necessarily true, is as clear and evident, as that proposition, that every whole is greater than its part."[89] Using Descartes' criterion for truth,[90] such truth is "clear and evident" or "clearly and distinctly known."[91]

Pyper takes such talk as evidence of Barclay's capitulation to

Descartes. He argues, further, that the belief that "God can and does implant contingent truths in our minds, and by that act they become eternal truth"[92] fits with Barclay's use of geometrical analogies that seemingly denigrate historical knowledge. As we have seen, however, the point of such geometrical analogies is not their disembodied rational conceptualizing but their instantaneity of understanding that is sensing and trusting. While Barclay does speak of God making contingent truths of history into eternal truths, this is not an assertion of reason's capacity to work separately from historical existence. Rather Barclay makes this claim through an appeal to experience. Those few occasions of God implanting historical truths in people's minds were when prophets were enabled to foretell various characteristics of the historical event of Jesus. But the truth of Jesus is not that of outward facts, whether known in anticipation or looking back, but the inward truth of the eternal Christ. Since Christ dwells within all of us, we can know this inward truth without knowing the historical facts of Jesus. When attending to Jesus, we only know the spiritual truth about him by grasping the inward truth in him that is already within us. This is not denigrating history but affirming that its important meaning is not outward but inward, which we only know by engaging our inwardness with it.

In answering Paets, Barclay does separate mind and body: "the mind can move itself; and operate in itself; which a body cannot do: but as body can be moved by another."[93] He isolates the function of each sense from the others (denying what today is called "synaesthesia"): "it is no less absurd ... to require us to see sounds, and hear light and colours." He denigrates the body: restricting knowing God to the outward senses, as Paets does, "turn[s] men into brutes" since the outward senses "the beasts have common with us."[94] Yet we have seen Barclay affirming the embodiedness of spiritual sensing through the outward senses and of participating inwardly in silent corporate worship.

Because he believes in inwardness and denies that the outward senses alone can provide spiritual knowledge, he feels he can use Paets' Cartesian language.

With Descartes, Barclay also affirms innate ideas: "the ideas of all things are divinely planted in our souls."[95] Rejecting Empiricism's belief that ideas are caused by things imprinting themselves through the physical senses on the mind, he says that external things "stir up" ideas but cannot form them. These "divinely planted" ideas:

> are not begotten in us by outward objects, or outward causes,... but only are by these outward things excited or stirred up..., for the outward object does nothing, but imprint in our sensible organs a corporal motion. Now there is nothing in a corporal motion, that can form in us the ideas of those things; for all ideas are of a spiritual nature?[sic] Now, nothing that is corporal, can produce that which is spiritual, because the less excellent cannot produce the more excellent, else the effect would exceed its cause....[96]

Barclay explicitly accepts that there is a "natural idea of God, which Cartesius and his followers so much talk of," that all persons have "some sort of idea of God, as of a most perfect being."[97] Our supernatural ideas are also "stirred up" but by divine causality, which he calls "the organ or instrument of God,"[98] the same as the *"vehiculum dei."*[99] Here again he is finding common ground with Descartes' interiority because he knows in his own experience of meeting for worship the stirring up of words by the divine presence innate within the self, but this is a far cry from Descartes' rationalistic understanding of inwardness.

The Usefulness of Barclay's Relational Approach
A commonality exists between Descartes and Quakerism, even

though they are fundamentally opposed, and Barclay mined this similarity in his apologetic writing to Adrian Paets. Barclay, like Descartes, starts with the individual in its interiority and what it can know within with certainty. Authority for both is in nothing external but is found within inwardness. The nature of that inwardness is, however, very different. For Descartes it is explicit reason searching out its own rational foundation which becomes the basis for all further philosophical reflection. For Barclay, it is a dimension of spiritual sensing, not reasoning, of being touched in the heart and the life. While Descartes' knower is isolated from its own body and community of knowers, Barclay speaks of being knit into the life of others and of the Spirit as they sit together in silence or go about their daily lives. Certainty is similarly important, but comes for Descartes through doubt that eats away at all relations in search of an absolute idea that can be held beyond trust. For Barclay it comes through the sensing and trusting of experience felt within the inwardness of the individual self in the world and in community.

Barclay has lifted the phrase "clear and distinct" from Descartes and uses it to describe our grasp of truth. For Descartes, it means rational clarity; for Barclay, however, since the true is discerned through a sense not reason, it means spontaneity and immediacy of discernment—it tastes true at first blush. Certainty comes in relatedness for Barclay; for Descartes it comes in detachment. Only in "Revelation" does Barclay speak of "stirring ideas." This is an inadequate description of the process by which he knows, in his experience of the silence, the moving and actuating, the stirring, power of the Spirit, which can bring us to speech. While the emergence of words from the tacit depths is not Cartesian, nevertheless, there is a commonality in that we are moved to words by an agency at work in us beneath notice.

When he is arguing apologetically with Paets, Barclay depends on Cartesian categories. But when he reflects on his own experience, he does not. When he is philosophically alert in his apologetic theology, he is confronted with two options: empiricism or rationalism—either truth comes by the outward senses or by the inward seeing of reason. While his non-dualistic reflections on religious experience had implications for a third philosophical method, he was unaware of this option. Today in the wake of twentieth-century existential, phenomenological, postcritical, and feminist thought, we can grasp a way of thinking that is neither objective nor subjective, but reflective on our being in the world. Barclay did not realize the philosophical potential of his religious reflections and so, faced with these two alternatives, chose the Cartesian inward side but redefined it, not as lucid consciousness, but as the place of spiritual experience and sensing that works through reason and the natural senses.

When he engaged apologetically with the empiricist Paets, he argued for inwardness using Cartesian categories. Whether we interpret Barclay as having generally capitulated to Cartesianism depends on whether we view him through his apologetic or his experiential approaches. Because he says explicitly that it was his experience of the life in a silent meeting that brought him into Quakerism and because he develops theological reflection, as we have seen, from such experience, I see the experiential approach as fundamental to Barclay's theology. From this perspective, I have argued, there is no dualism in his articulation of the nature of self, God, and Christ. I think, therefore, that his evident engagement with Cartesian dualism did not distort his theology, although it was seriously employed in answering a philosophically astute non-Quaker. While we might regret his preoccupation with apologetics and wish he had become more aware of the relational method implicit in his theological reflections, he did, in fact, use it as he reflected at length on his own experience and its background of silence, within the context of the Christian theological heritage.

If he had shifted from apologetics with dualists to theology as reflection upon experience, he could have restructured his

Apology by beginning with his experience on first entering "the silent assemblies of God's people."[100] It could still be apologetics, seeking common ground, however, not with dualistic reason but with wholistic experience of being human—as we feel, know, and speak, as we relate to divinity and other selves in the world, informed by the biblical heritage. Within the laboratory that is Barclay's thought, one can discover a way of doing Quaker theology that responds to George Fox's challenge, "what canst thou say?"

The Growing Up of Principles: Otherness in Robert Barclay's Emergent Thinking

Friendship is at the heart of the transformed life for early Friends—friendship with fellow Quakers, other people, earth creatures, and especially with God. Robert Barclay, speaking of justification by faith in a Quaker perspective, says emphatically that it means that the self is "really redeemed" and "made righteous" so as to "come ... to a sensible union and friendship with God."[1] In a tradition devoted to being friends with God, self, and world, you do not find an emphasis on God as "wholly other." In 1917 Rudolf Otto in *Das Heilige* provides an influential definition of the religious which focuses on God as "the wholly other." In 1923 Martin Buber responds to his definition in *Ich und Du* in a manner that resonates with early Friends:

> Of course, God is "the wholly other"; but he is also the wholly same: the wholly present. Of course, he is the *mysterium tremendum* that appears and overwhelms; but his is also the mystery of the obvious that is closer to me than my own I.[2]

A Relational Approach

Early Friends, embracing "the mystery of the obvious that is closer to me than my own I," develop a way of theological thinking that is relational. Thinking begins beneath notice in our relatedness within the silence experienced in worship and at the roots of daily living. As we have seen in the previous essay, "Touched and Knit in the Life," two-thirds of the way through his *Apology*[3] Barclay speaks of his convincement as being touched in the heart by the power of silence felt among Friends gathered together in a meeting for worship. Not by rational understanding—prior knowledge of scripture and Christian principles, or theological argument—he discovered truth of the divine life in the silence he felt radiating from the assembled worshipers, which he realized "is the surest way to become a Christian."

He discovered, as well, truth of his own condition. He felt the evil within himself weakening and the good strengthened. He is connected with his passions, knowing God as immediately present through the affectional understanding of the heart, longing to feel himself fully redeemed, and feeling himself drawn into a deep relationship with the worshippers. In this communal experience of intimacy with God, he feels power that can divinely *actuate* himself into word and act. As Friends learn "to wait upon God ... and feel after this inward seed of life; that as it moveth, they may move with it, and be actuated by its power, and influenced, whether to pray, preach or sing,"[4] When actuated in *waiting*, the self lets go of its connections with "the workings, imaginations, and speculations of his own mind"; is "emptied as it were of himself."[5] When waiting bodily together in one physical place with others in the silence, the outward relatedness is filled with spiritual fullness of unity with each other and with God as we become active "co-worker[s] with the grace."[6]

This relational way is opposed to the dualism that was becoming established as central to seventeenth-century thought. In the middle of the seventeenth century in England, in response to the social and religious "world turned upside down," modern philosophy was building its own foundations in critical reason. Through a method of doubt that presupposed a dualistic separation of the knowing mind from the known of world and body, it was believed possible to attain absolute certainty. In the light of such rational clarity all non-rational sources of our living and speaking—such as silence, feeling, intuition, faith—were dissolved in order to found all knowing on the basis of "reason alone."

The otherness of God, selves, and the biblical Christ conceived within such a dualistic framework detaches and alienates the knowing self from these realities making them wholly other. Conceived within a relational framework, however, the otherness of these realities is as "the wholly present" from which the knowing self is not separated but within which it participates. Otherness is thus conceived very differently within a dualistic or relational way of thinking.

This relational thought of early Friends is emergent. Rather than dualistically separating inward and outward, as in the modern view, the outward for Friends is emergent from the inward. In what follows we shall consider the early Quaker manner of emergent thought and then reflect on the nature of otherness as expressed through it. We shall explore this emergent relational way of thinking in one of the most astute thinkers of early Quakerism—Robert Barclay. To do so is not uncontroversial, since many recent scholars have seen Barclay as immersed in Cartesian dualism. Having discussed at length in "Touched and Knit in the Life" above what I consider a mistaken attribution of Cartesianism to Barclay, I focus here only on his use of an emergent method in his *Apology*.

Emergent Thinking

Quaker thinking is emergent from within the experiential relatedness of the non-rational depths of silence. Knowledge and principles do not precede such experience, which would be to separate knowledge and experience, but rather emerge out of such experienced depths he discovered in the silence of Friends gathered together in worship: "afterwards the knowledge and understanding of principles will not be wanting, but will grow up so much as is needful, as the natural fruit of this good root."[7]

While he is not explicitly aware that he has developed a philosophical alternative to the dualistic method being propounded in his time by Descartes and others, he has, nevertheless, developed a new way of thinking—that today we would call "phenomenological." While theoretically unaware, he uses this method of reflection on experience to explore corporate silent worship and the meaning discerned in it of the nature of God, Christ, and self. Within these reflections, he exhibits a relational approach that involves an emergent way of thinking that is an alternative to dualistic thought.

Beginning from experience of silence, Barclay's thinking in general and conceiving principles in particular emerges from our pre-cognitive experience in the silence. Beneath explicit knowing and noticing—and therefore beneath "arguments," "a particular disquisition of each doctrine," and "convincement of my understanding"—Barclay is "secretly reached by this life."[8] His heart is touched by feeling a "secret power." In Michael Polanyi's language Barclay is speaking of action upon the self on the "tacit" level which the self unconsciously embraces and integrates, from which a pattern may emerge of conscious recognition through a word, image, or thought. Barclay speaks initially of the moral impact this secret power has of weakening evil and raising up the good within, and then he speaks of the social impact: "so I became thus knit and united unto them." The tacit power of the Spirit, working beneath our notice, elicits a growing goodness and connectedness of self. The result is to hunger for "the increase of this power and life" that is stirring in our depths so as to be transformed into spiritual maturity (to have Christ formed in us through the germination of the divine seed within). As "natural fruit" emerges from a "good root," so "knowledge and understanding of principles" will emerge from the movement of this secret power in our tacit dimension.

Conceiving explicitly relies, therefore, upon this tacit motion and our becoming sensible of it, and thus a change in ourselves. While he is speaking specifically of a religious experience, this is true of knowing anything. We can understand something as an outward form, recognize it and repeat it, but to understand it truly we must "stand under" those forms by feeling and being sensible of them in our inward lives, which changes the self.

Barclay says it this way: "though thousands should be convinced in their understandings of all the truths we maintain, yet if they were not sensible of this inward life, and their souls not changed from unrighteousness to righteousness, they could add nothing to us."[9] Polanyi would say that even this recognition of an external form is dependent upon the tacit dimension. Barclay does not, however, see this as he is working within the dialectic of outward and inward knowing. What he affirms in the religious dimension, Polanyi affirms in all knowing.

If the movement of the Spirit emerges into the forms of ideas and deeds, then concepts are, as Wittgenstein says, "forms of life."[10] Our life and the Spirit's life fills our words and ideas. They only have meaning as we use them, or more precisely they only have true meaning in how we use them. Hence Barclay says:

> [T]he spiritual truths of the gospel are as lies in the mouths of carnal and unspiritual men; for though in themselves they be true, yet are they not true as to them, because not known, nor uttered forth in and by that principle and spirit that ought to direct the mind and actuate it in such things: they are no better than the counterfeit representations of things in a comedy.[11]

Concepts have their meaning in how they are used, in the spirit in which they are used. In using words and ideas so as to give form to the Spirit and my spirit, within which it is at work, our ideas draw up a skein of connections from the depths. The silent assembly Barclay enters is already a mesh of relatedness. As he is moved by the secret power, he is knit together into this mesh. So when words and ideas emerge from this inchoate mesh as its sensible meaning becomes articulate, the word, and even more so the concept, becomes a center of resonance and radiance. Thus when we encounter a concept emergent from the tacit depths we feel in it, whether we notice it or not, a potential fullness. This idea can make sense of many things because it carries this skein of relations beneath its surface. We feel a sense of reality: these relations connect to what is real outside of me but also inside of me and inside the group. And we may discover novelty: as we explore these relations within a concept, we may find surprising connections between things we did not think belonged together. Even though people may interpret a concept in only one way, the fact it carries relatedness means that it is possible to use an idea in a way that is different from its conventional meaning. This is what Barclay is doing throughout his apologetic theology, building bridges through common ideas but picking up elements in those ideas which others did not notice or did not intend.

Emergent thinking is different from dualistic thinking. Where a concept has a sense of fullness that wants to be explored in various directions, a concept used dualistically draws sharp boundaries. It is either/or rather than both/and. Things get cut away, get excluded from the realm of the idea. The self as well gets separated from what is known through the concept. It speaks of objective reality and does not illumine aspects of the knowing self as it is involved with the known. The meaning for dualism is in the external form to which it points. The Cartesian method of doubt seeks to dissolve all relations that cannot withstand the acid of its doubt. Thus are eliminated both the knower's relatedness to the known, as the knower is represented as detached, and the web of tacit relations in the concept that beckon for exploration. What is left is the isolated idea referring to an isolated object by an isolated subject.

Summarizing Barclay's emergent way of thinking in comparison to dualistic thinking, as epitomized by Descartes, we can say the following. Barclay's thinking is *experiential*, as he takes up as subject matter for his reflection his experience of first entering a silent meeting for worship. Descartes' starts, as well, within the interiority of the self, not, however, with experience, but with reason. Secondly, it is *relational*, as he is drawn in by his experience of relating to the power in the meeting and to the people sitting together. Descartes' is separative. Thirdly, it is *committed*, as he opens himself to what is happening in the meeting, participates in it uncritically (or rather beneath the level of criticism), and does not resist but welcomes it making its impact on him. Descartes' is detached and doubting. Fourthly, it is *affectional*, as it begins in consciousness as feeling, being touched in the heart. Descartes' distrusts and denigrates the emotions. Fifthly, it is *tacit*, as feeling is the first level of conscious response to the deeper non-explicit secret power, the moving of the Spirit, in the silence. Descartes' is incandescently explicit. Sixthly, thinking is itself a *form of life* that uses forms of life so as to express a fullness of meaning which is evocative of what is really real and of still richer meaning yet to be discovered. Barclay's way of thinking is *emergent*, therefore, as his words, concepts, and principles arise from the pre-cognitive tacit depths of experience becoming feelings that elicit heart understanding. Upon reflecting on what emerges "principles will ... grow up so much as is needful."[12]

Friends' Thinking about Otherness

How then do we Friends experience otherness—the otherness of self, Christ, and God —when we approach it through relational and emergent, rather than dualistic, thinking? For Karl Barth, thinking within a dualistic framework, God is wholly other— totally separated in his being from us and totally unknowable by any act of ours. But for Friends, who like Barclay are touched in the heart by the moving of the Spirit in the silence of meeting and of the depths of our lives, God is, as for Buber, both "the wholly same" and "the wholly present." We experience God in our lives not over against us. We experience God guiding us, sustaining us, and transforming us.

Mircea Eliade defines the religious as experience of the sacred. The sacred he defines, using Otto's definition, as the *"mysterium tremendum"* and *"mysterium fascinans."*[13] In his work as a historian and phenomenologist of religion he says religious experience always has the characteristics of that which is terrifying and that which is alluring—simultaneously. While Friends do experience the divine as terrifying, the ordinary experience we have is of the divine as mystery, a mystery, in Buber's words, that is "obvious" and "closer to me than my own I."

The times when God is experienced as terrifyingly other is when we are undergoing major transformation. Early Friends spoke of the Light revealing and burning away the places of control by the natural will and wisdom. For them this seems to have happened at the beginning of their opening to the Light. For many of us today that is a recurring experience as we resist divine guidance we had earlier found easy. Sometimes the resistance has to do with places of our internal control of which we do not want to let go. Other times it is an action, perhaps a prophetic protest, we seek to avoid. These are moments of terror where we experience God as standing over against us demanding we let go and become open and responsive to the Spirit. Perhaps one of the most frequent times this occurs is when we are moved to speak in Meeting, which is usually a terrifying experience, a moment in which we experience the *mysterium tremendum*. More painfully, we experience the terror of God in suffering due both to natural causes and human evil. Since we look for the divine presence in every moment and in every place, we look for God in the midst of the terrors of our lives. Sometimes God appears as reassurance and sometimes takes on the terror of the situation demanding of us to learn what the Spirit wants to teach us even in the face of death.

God as the wholly same is, nevertheless, different from us. God is mystery that reaches beyond our knowing and control. When that beyondness lures me towards fulfillment of unrealized possibilities, I experience it as *mysterium fascinans*. When that beyondness curbs my ego rampages and shatters my ego structured identity, I experience it as *mysterium tremendum*. But in either case this mystery is the whole in which I live and move and have my being, and thus always stretches beyond me even though it moves within me. Each of us is a particular part. The whole is always other to any part. Yet the part participates in what transcends it and the whole participates in every part making it part of the whole.

Since we experience Christ dwelling within us, we experience a sameness between what we find within our own experience and what we find in the Bible. But of course the biblical Christ and the biblical response to God's indwelling presence in the world stands complexly over against us. Every religious group's take on the Bible and Christ is selective. We are comfortable with certain aspects but we experience the otherness of Christ as the Spirit confronts us with aspects that are foreign and threatening to us. The experience of this otherness of Christ can expand and deepen us, can elicit humility towards other people who take up Christ in very different ways. We modern Friends may find it easier to hear the Spirit speak to us through sacred texts from non-Christian traditions than through parts of the Bible we prefer to overlook. We rightly do not want to perpetuate the sexism, militarism, Christian imperialism, and endorsements of slavery and homophobia in the Bible by simply conforming to whatever is said in scripture. We try to read it in the Spirit in which it was written, but that Spirit is larger than what I am comfortable with and so Christ in the biblical context confronts me as other from which I may learn.

Grace and Human Otherness

Conceiving the otherness of God from within a relational emergent way of thinking, we have described in Barclay, is a theological endeavor that bears significance for our wrestling with one of the greatest problems facing us in the next century: the otherness of selves. W.E.B. DuBois said in 1903: "The problem of the twentieth century is the problem of the color-line."[14] Complexifying his notion of race, I would say the problem of the twenty-first century is the otherness-line—to learn how to live with, and become enriched by, human otherness. How we relate to the otherness of God and Christ can model how to

135

relate to the diversity of humanity we are brought up close to, face to face, in our countries and in the global setting. Just as we are not separated from the divine, so are we not separated from this multifarious humanity. Just as we seek to accept, learn from, be transformed by that secret power that works within our silent depths, so we can open beyond tolerance and respect to an enrichment by others. Our individuality is enhanced as we are made more complex by encountering such otherness, even as we become more acutely and humbly aware of our own uniqueness.

A word for living and living fully with the divine in our lives as both the wholly same and the wholly other is "grace." As we depend upon grace to touch us in the heart to open us to the workings of the Spirit, so do we rely upon grace to open our hearts to the otherness of our fellow human denizens of our world. In such opening we experience, and reflect in a relational and emergent way, on the otherness of God—within "the friendship of God"[15]—from which we may find understanding and principles growing up from our experience of silence—as needed.

C. The What, How, and Why of Quaker Theology

The Quaker Vision and the Doing of Theology

The Quaker Vision

The Quaker vision of the inaugural period of Quakerism was understood through and articulated in theological language. Yet many Friends today believe theology to be antithetic to that vision. They see theology as preoccupied with the *letter* while the Quaker vision is about the *life*—the life of spirituality lived in the presence of God and the life of social action seeking, in Penn's phrase, "to mend ... the world."[1] While the life of the mind can be actively engaged with rigor and precision in any other field—scientific, political, economic, social, historical, literary, even artistic (as witnessed to by this conference)—when it comes to what is most important to us, to what are the roots of all our intellectual and ethical undertakings, we become strangely silent. We avoid making sense of them to ourselves, to our children, and to non-Quakers, in the belief that our lives will speak and that this will suffice.

I agree that lives must and do bespeak what is of central importance to us, that fine words disengaged from our ethical behavior are empty, and that the ultimate realities of our existence are ineffable mysteries which can never be adequately caught in words. Nevertheless, I find in my own experience the need to make sense through words of the ultimate meaning of our lives: in order to achieve an integrated wholeness of being, doing, and thinking; to raise up the next generation; to make our most effective contributions to contemporary efforts to overcome social oppression; to engage non-Quakers in dialogue both to help them and to learn from them; and finally to deepen our spiritual lives of love.

This attitude that opposes "letter" and "life" roots in the

origins of Quakerism, for this is precisely the distinction early Friends used to criticize their non-Quaker contemporaries' writings and to evaluate their own Quaker writings. The "life" as experienced in worship and daily existence became the measure of truth and the principle of coherence. Yet the "letter" for them did not mean all words but only those words empty of the life. Many words were spoken and written by early Friends that they believed were engendered by and filled with the life. These words were indefatigably theological.

The Quaker Vision of early Friends was incarnate in theological language. That vision was rooted in the discovery of the divine within the self, experienced as: presence, sacred mystery, what is really real, transforming power, guiding illumination, and integrating agency (making us aware of and bringing us into a felt sense of unity with all other selves and with the entire creation). The foundation of this vision is beneath words in experience of the depths of self and world. The primary authority is not, therefore, in words but in what early Friends called "the Spirit," which is known first through experience of being "in the Spirit."

For this reason Quakerism was from its beginnings a non-creedal and non-dogmatic tradition within Christianity. From life in the Spirit actions issue, both non-verbal and verbal. The efforts to transform the political socioeconomic system of mid-seventeenth-century England emerged from these non-verbal depths but so also did words, theological words. Words and non-verbal actions were all parts of a whole that encompassed every aspect of life that were experienced as a unity in the divine depths within.

For this reason Quakerism offers a model today, as it has throughout its history, of two things sought for passionately by many today in our larger society—an approach to justice and relief work grounded in spirituality, and a tradition of spirituality centering the whole of life in meditation, which as the focus of Quakerism from the start makes it unique among Christian denominations. The warp and woof of our distinctive pattern of life is language. And I believe that we can provide another model, that will help our larger society and ourselves, of a way of doing theology based in this meditative spirituality. We already speak of a Meeting for Worship, a Meeting for Business, and a Meeting for Education. In our Quaker heritage, as we explore it from our present dwelling in "the life," we possess today a remarkable as-yet-unrealized potential for a Meeting for Theology.

Theological Fatness and Quaker Muscle

But this is hidden both from ourselves and from the rest of the world. A mainstream Protestant biblical scholar and head of his church is reported to have once said to a Quaker colleague: "Quakerism lives off the theological fat of other traditions."[2] While he is right that Quakerism's theological output is modest compared with Lutheran and Calvinist writings, there is, nevertheless, a considerable amount of it. But among its bulk— he is again right—one does not find the kind of systematic treatises that mainstream Protestantism is known for. Yet it is a mistake to take either quantity or a certain kind of theological form as the measure of theological seriousness.

Quakers have not lived off of the "fat" of mainstream Protestant thought. Such "fat" is the result of rational elaboration of objectified biblical ideas. Starting formally with some external principle lifted from the scripture—such as the Word of God, justification by faith, or election—mainstream Protestantism has developed its logical implications. The measure of its truth is, therefore, rational—whether the logical elaboration has been consistent, coherent, and comprehensive—and scriptural—whether the starting point conforms to what is central to their understanding of scripture and whether its development takes up the salient biblical texts in comprehensive and insightful ways.

Such an objective starting point located in scripture, in fact, has an experiential foundation. Martin Luther's doctrinal principle of justification by faith is quite obviously based in his acute personal struggle with a sense of ineradicable sinfulness and discovery of God's forgiving grace. John Calvin's doctrinal structure of divine glory, original sin, justification, and sanctification is founded upon a personal experience of divine acceptance and transformation, which—while intentionally obscured—is discernible in his *Institutes*. While these experiences of God are there, the focus theologically is not, however, on them but on their objective doctrinal truth.

Early Quakers, on the other hand, begin beneath words with experience of divinity in their depths which, to be sure, comes to be named in the words of Spirit, Light, eternal Christ, Inward Teacher. The focus is not on the clarity and certainty of the doctrinal concept focused in scripture but upon the reality experienced over and over again in worship and daily living. From such an experiential beginning the theological fat of logically elaborated long treatises does not accumulate. Rather Friends have grown their own lean muscle feeding on the direct experience of the life, which has led them to put it to work to mend the world, to develop their own peculiar form of spirituality, and to give expression to meaning of this experience of the life—which has been through theological language.

The Variety of Early Quaker Theology

While the amount of Quaker seventeenth-century theological writing does not approach the output of mainstream Protestant writings, it amounts, nevertheless, to a sizable bulk. The published writings of Fox were collected in eight volumes, Isaac Penington's in four (although there is a considerable amount that has not yet seen the light of print), Barclay's in three, Margaret Fell's and James Nayler's each in one long volume, Mary

Penington's in one short volume, and much more by numerous men and women in single volumes or multifarious short pieces. Contemporary Quakers are largely unaware of this since we have during much of this century only kept in print George Fox's *Journal*, two pamphlet selections of Isaac Penington, an abridgment and translation of Robert Barclay's *Apology*, and a few of the political and religious writings of William Penn. More recently Margaret Fell's *Womans Speaking Justified* has been published in several places and efforts are being made to publish or reissue other texts.[3]

Not only is the amount somewhat staggering but the variety of kinds of writing is astonishing: journals, letters, polemical writings (broadsides, debate tracts, trial records), essays, treatises, queries, frames of government, economic models, catechisms, maxims, minutes (of business meetings and memorials for the deceased), dreams, prophecies, apocalyptic visions, anecdotes, history. While some of this is written to and for Quakers, much is written for non-Quakers. They address a wide range of concerns: spirituality, doctrine, religious organization, evangelizing, politics, economics, social oppression, the problems of daily living, relief to the suffering, and visionary experience. All of it is expressed in theological language, because that was the coin of the realm in which people in mid-seventeenth-century England discussed politics, economics, social issues, and ethics as well as religion.

What is the meaning of such variety of written forms? Such an array is dramatic evidence that early Friends were not focused on formal boundaries; the truth did not lie in certain forms. Nor were they focused only on certain subject matters, such as God, belief, and religious practice. Amidst such multifariousness, in what did early Friends find a principle of coherence and what was the measure of its truth?

Coherence and the Measure of Truth

The principle of coherence is not an explicit boundary by which things are objectively demarcated as either included or excluded, but is the experience of life at the center of one's being and world. From this center such variety springs as multiple expressions of the life. The unity in their writing, as in their living, was found, not at the periphery, but at the center. The primary authority, experienced at the center, is the divine Spirit. The measure of truth—which not only permitted but engendered such variety—is the presence of *life* in what is said or done. The life is known experientially by being, as Fox says, "in the life" or being "in the spirit."[4] As William Penn puts it, the question is whether the various forms "are such Means as are used in the Life and Power of God, and not in and from Mans meer Wit...."[5] As Sarah Jones says, the forms which are "manifestations, that proceed from the word" have the purpose "to lead it [the creature] to the substance": "so let not your eyes nor minds be gathered into the manifestations, but sink down into that measure of life that ye have received, and go not out...."[6] The measure is whether the life is manifest in the form and whether it is a means to lead us into that life.

But how do you know that either you or a set of words are "in the life?" You know it by its *feeling, fullness, fruits,* and *fittingness.* Fox says over and over again: "Live in the Life of God, and feel it."[7] For Fox, everyone is given their own "measure of the spirit of God"[8] with which to be responsible and by which to understand. Isaac Penington speaks of entering into that measure in order to feel its fullness of divine presence:

[W]ait for, and daily follow, the sensible leadings of that measure of life which God hath placed in you, which is one with the fulness, and into which the fulness runs daily and fills it, that it may run into you and fill you.[9]

Penn speaks of distinguishing the "Spirit of God" from the "Spirit of this World" in terms of their fruit:

> [T]he Tree is known and denominated from the Fruit, so Spirits (are) by their Motions and Inclinations. And the Spirit of God never did incline (any one) to evil;... [but] the Spirit of God condemns all Ungodliness, and moves and inclines to purity, mercy, righteousness, which are of God....[10]

And the life, as Fox says, brings one into unity—with oneself, with one's fellows, and with creation itself. It is thus fitting as it "speak[s] to thy condition"[11] as "you all have unity in the same feeling, life, and power"[12] and as it brings you into "unity with the creation."[13]

What this means is that the measure of truth for Friends in writing, as in other actions, is not a concept, such as the doctrine of justification by faith, but is an intuitive sense, not an idea but a felt reality. This reality in our experience gets verbalized as "the life" or "Spirit" and it can be articulated within a doctrinal framework as the creative and connecting agency of the trinity, but the truth of it is not in its conceptual manifestation but in its experiential substance.

The Purity of Systematic Theology

We can see more clearly now how the Protestant scholar's accusation misses the mark. His norm is the purity of systematic theology. But as we have seen, the starting point is not some idea as an objective systematic principle but an experience of divinity. The form is not singular as a rational development of belief, but is multifarious in reflecting, in appropriate ways, on diverse aspects of our living. And the truth is not the clarity and distinctness of idea but the experiential sense—the feeling, fullness, fruitfulness, and fittingness—of a reality. Because Quaker theology springs from the life and is measured in the life, it is intuitive and integrative. Yet exactly because it is working from a sense and integrating the different parts of our lives, it seems less serious than the pure logical elaboration of ideas about God, sin, and salvation. The richness of systematic theology is its purity of rational clarity and comprehensiveness—that is its systematicness—whereas the richness of Quaker theology is its abundance of life.

Yet some Friends do speak of certain kinds of Quaker theology as systematic.[14] It is right to call Barclay's *Apology* a systematic theology in the sense that it attempts a comprehensive expression of Quaker belief and does so in an orderly manner. It is, of course, technically "apologetic" theology because it is written to present Quaker views to non-Quakers and to try to find common ground that will enable genuine understanding. As a comprehensive apologetics it is a systematic theology. But it is not systematic theology in its other definitive meanings—of starting from an objective systematic principle and elaborating it logically.

Barclay, in fact, witnesses in his *Apology* to his own intimate experience of the divine life within corporate worship. He says he was convinced "not by strength of arguments.... but by being reached by this life," and then goes on:

for when I came into the silent assemblies of God's people, I felt a secret power among them, which touched my heart, and as I gave way unto it, I found the evil weakening in me, and the good raised up, and so I became thus knit and united unto them, hungering more and more after the increase of this power and life, whereby I might feel myself perfectly redeemed.[15]

On the basis of this experience of the divine life, he begins his book with the epistemological issue of the "true Foundation of Knowledge"[16] and the nature "Of Immediate Revelation"[17]—no doubt shaped by his audience, with whom he found common ground in their attention to this issue under the influence of Calvin and Descartes. While Barclay is erudite in the use of reason in the development of his apologetical theology, he does not use it to elaborate an objective systematic principle but to explain Friends' experiential knowing of the life of God in ways that non-Friends can understand.

Measured by an objective systematic norm Quaker theology is, then, not merely emaciated but non-existent. Early Friends wrote, nevertheless, a great deal of theology but did so, as I have tried to show, in a different "way and method of his Spirit"—as Penn called it.[18]

Making Theology Quaker

But what then makes Quaker theology "Quaker?" Does starting from and in the Spirit? That is a *sine qua non* but other kinds of thinking can start from a tacit indwelling of reality, which, however similar, would not be Quaker. I would suggest that to be Quaker, theology must not only work from and with the principle of the life (the divine presence experienced in the present amidst our relatedness to the community of being), but must work from and with our Quaker heritage—its historical writings, practices, and actions. The greatest richness of our heritage—both in expression and in potential meaning—is in our beginnings in the middle of seventeenth-century England. To be "Quaker" theology, then, our thinking should start from the divine reality experienced in the present—from being in the life—and work consciously amidst the metaphors, methods, anecdotes, and principles of our historical origins.

Finally as theology, it must not simply be a historical study of the past but must seek to make sense of the meaning—especially that which is deepest and most significant—of our contemporary existence through the use of the past and whatever means at hand in the present can be vehicles of the life—"to answer," as

Fox would say, "that of God in everyone."[19] The purpose is not to describe the characteristics of an object, whether God or self, but to bring the reader to an experience of the divine—as Sarah Jones says, to "sink down into that measure of life"[20]—in the depths of the self's being, situated in this moment and this place in the world.

The Need for Quaker Theology

But if that is how Quaker theology can be done in our day, why would anyone want to? The answers are different for liberal and evangelical Friends. For liberals "theology" means systematic theology, which typically obstructs the mending of the world by its exclusivism, political conservatism, and rational abstraction from the real needs of people. Many convinced Friends are refugees from such dogmatic traditions of Christianity and want no truck with them. Others enter Quakerism from secularism; lacking any theological heritage to react against, they do not expect to encounter theology in their search for spiritual nurture. Birthright Friends, on the other hand, in part define themselves as not engaging in things that other Christian groups do, such as the physical sacraments or theology. Hence, whenever they reflect on the meaning of existence, such thinking is by definition not "theology."

I remember a close birthright Friend—who had a significant hand in founding the Friends Association in Higher Education—whenever engaged in intellectual articulation of the religious life, would always resist calling what she was doing "theology." When confronted with this, she would always respond: "What I am thinking and writing about is not 'theology,' because I don't like theology but I do like what I am doing." In a similar vein of serious playfulness, she was known to say of jazz that she liked, that it was not jazz because she didn't like jazz but she did like this.

The answer to liberals, why do theology, is, in Socrates' words, that "the unexamined life is not worth living," and in John's words, "you will know the truth, and the truth will make you free."[21] Reflection on our commitments, making them explicit, can focus, develop, enrich, connect, and transform our lives. While theology was the coin of the realm in seventeenth-century England, the ethical was present in it. Today the liberal Quakers' language is ethical, but within it the theological is implicit. To make it explicit — in a Quaker manner of doing theology — would enable us: to understand better who we are, to show the connection between our "doing good" and "being in the Spirit," to create a common realm of dialogue for Quakers within which our disparate views can be shared and be made more responsive to the life, and to communicate with non-Quakers what we have to offer and to learn from them what they can contribute to us.

Evangelical Friends, on the other hand, are not afraid to articulate their beliefs and to do so in consciously theological language. The question for them is not whether to use theology but how. Do they begin from an objective concept taken from scripture or do they begin from experience of the divine life within? Do they move so as to conform to an outward doctrinal structure or do they move in the creativity and novelty of the Spirit? Are they seeking certainty or the fullness of life? The answer to evangelicals, why do theology, is ever to think how to use that theological language so it can speak with freshness and depth to our condition in the modern world.

Evangelical Friends keep alive the importance of the Christian language of our Quaker heritage. From them the liberals can learn, since there is a wealth of spiritual wisdom inherent in that heritage that can nurture our souls. Liberal Friends keep alive the search for new ways in our culture of engendering and deepening the spiritual life, from which evangelicals can learn to find Christ in unanticipated ways in unexpected places. I would offer a query to both evangelical and liberal Friends in the form of a passage to meditate upon. For the evangelical I suggest Isaac

Penington's:

> For, Friends, there is no straitness in the Fountain. God is fulness: and it is his delight to empty himself into the hearts of his children: and he doth empty himself, according as he makes way in them, and as they are able to drink in of his living virtue.[22]

For the liberal I suggest George Fox's:

> being renewed up into the image of God by Christ Jesus,... [g]reat things did the Lord lead me into, and wonderful depths were opened unto me, beyond what can by words be declared; but as people come into subjection to the spirit of God, and grow up in the image and power of the Almighty, they may receive the Word of wisdom, that opens all things, and come to know the hidden unity in the Eternal Being.[23]

Thinking about the meaning of such passages for our life so as to make sense of the ultimate meaning of our lives in ways that fit our condition—which includes, for example, the otherness of diverse peoples and systems of oppression, opening to the former so as not only to tolerate but to honor and learn from these differences, and transforming the latter—is the doing of theology.

Theological Reflection on Faith and Practice

This question of the need for theology is implicit in the discussion of faith and practice by Rupert Read and John Miller in an issue of *Quaker Religious Thought* (December 1995). In search for what is common among Friends, Read identifies practice alone—the practice of waiting in silence—apart from faith. Miller responds that faith is central for Friends both within and outside of practice. Implicit here are the opposite views that theology is not needed because practice is the only essential element and that theology is indispensable because we need to reflect upon and articulate our faith. While I agree with Miller on the indispensability of faith and therefore of theology, and appreciate his narrative theological perspective (being shaped myself by many of the same theological influences he mentions[24]), I want to engage him as well as Read in dialogue. To Read, I suggest that faith is implicit in practice, which a certain kind of theological reflection can uncover and usefully articulate. To Miller, I suggest that this uncovered faith is deeper than—and indispensable to—his meaning of faith. Hence Miller's view of faith can be enriched by theological reflection on practice, even as Read's view of practice is enriched by theological exploration of faith.

I value Read's efforts to locate a commonality among Friends and have myself investigated practice in the search for commonality in Quaker education. As far as I know, all Quaker schools, colleges, theological schools, and study centers use Quaker business procedure. It is here, if nowhere else, that the students (both the many non-Quakers and few Quakers) experience the Friends' spiritual principles, faith in practice.[25] While I honor Read's efforts, the silent meeting for worship cannot, of course, be this point of commonality since it is—as he acknowledges—only central to unprogrammed Friends; while some evangelical meetings use some silence amidst a prepared liturgy, most of them do not.

For Friends worshipping in this traditional way, I would not, however, define their commonality by saying that "what we do in Meeting" is simply "constitute meeting." We both experience and expect much more than "*demand*[ing] nothing more nor less of each other than a sincere and non-hostile effort at so constituting Meeting, at being Friends." [26] In the language of H. Richard Niebuhr—whom Miller acknowledges as important to him, as he is to me—this is an "external" rather than an "internal" account of waiting in silence.[27]

What happens in inwardness, in the silence? We in fact do not constitute the meeting, except in the sociological sense of getting ourselves there to sit together in the same room. Rather we are constituted into a meeting. While there is considerable diversity now among silent Friends how this would be expressed, the traditional phrase is "gathered" by the Holy Spirit, Light, Life, or eternal Christ into a "meeting with" the divine and each other. To be so gathered is our constant hope and, from time to time, our experience. Yet Read says:

> I have contended that there are no principles which are central to Quakerism any more, save for principles of practice. That is, socio-ethical-spiritual principles of action outside of Meeting, and the action, the practice, of sitting and waiting in silence, inside Meeting."[28]

But what I want to call his attention to are not the "principles *of* practice"; I want to uncover the principles *in* practice. What these are is faith as the experience of the divine—whether we call it Christ, God, the Self, the Whole, the Way, or Gatheredness (not that these words are identical, but they are all expressing our experience of a More, a Beyond, in the midst of those sitting together in silence).

The practice for traditional Friends of sitting in silence is, as Read says, something like scientists practicing their craft; there are probably as much difference in how the silence is used as in the different ways in which scientists do their work. But one can reflect on what commitments they hold in their diverse yet scientific work, as one can reflect on what these are in the practice of silence. These take the scientist, as it does the worshipper, beyond the mere demand to constitute a group. They both are passionate about the realities they are encountering, even if some scientists speak not of realities but only observations, and even if some worshippers do not speak of Christ and God. Within the common practices, they do argue, though not just at the point of shift from one paradigm to another — witness Einstein's ongoing debate with quantum mechanics. But I would agree that their arguments go on within an accepted general way of doing things. Perhaps, rather than jettisoning ideas of faith, there is a model here of dialogue — "that makes Friends keep talking to and being with and doing what we call worshipping with Friends"[29] — that could be useful to us all as we seek commonality by reflecting on what is going on in practice — which is, faith in the sense of experiencing a More we are inherently related to in the silence.

Miller articulates in a fruitful way this principle of faith within practice. He expands the meaning of "faith," used by Read, as belief (i.e. explicit conceptual affirmation), to include "trust." When he reflects (theologically) on the principles in practice both of worship and life, he locates faith in experience, "in the intersection between my Encounter with God and my Story." He goes on:

> I seek to understand the Encounter in the light of my Story, and this understanding produces one dimension of faith; we often call it religious belief. I seek to live out my Story in the light of the Encounter, and this provides the other dimension of faith; we often call it trust in God.[30]

Telling one's own story can be a powerful expression of the meaning of one's life and of the realities one is connected with — as I find it to be in Miller's own account. Here is an internal account for which I was asking. In our practice there is a story that we are living and that we can, through reflection, make explicit. To see one's own story within a larger Story is to grasp its greater symbolic import, since all meaning is contextual, and to understand our larger context illuminates the parts and partialities of our individual story.

What I find limiting, however, in Miller's narrative theology is the location and definition of faith. I would not locate faith as trust only in the living out of my story; is it not as well central to my understanding of God as it underlies faith as belief? Moreover, I would not locate faith only "in the intersection between my Encounter with God and my Story." Is not faith as trust directly involved in that divine encounter on the basis of which I tell my/our story, which in the telling expresses that trust? Finally, I would suggest that the faith as trust involved in "my Encounter with God" is underlain by a deeper faith of trusting commitment within an ongoing relatedness to God.

Encounters are episodic, as Miller recognizes; but they are momentary occurrences within ongoing relatedness to God dwelling at the roots of our being. Such encounters can be pivotal life-transforming experiences that function as the interpretive moment by which all relatedness and other moments are understood in our life. But the moments of faith in encounter rest upon the deeper faith within our constitutive relatedness to God and all of creation, which they bring to focus. To distinguish this kind of trust from the trust involved in a momentary encounter, we might call it "tacit commitment" (Polanyi). We all, I am suggesting, exist in a largely unconscious reliance upon the divine in our inward depths. Many ignore or deny this; many seek to control others to defend against this uncontrollable dimension at our foundations; some erect beliefs as protection against it; some have life-transforming encounters that reveal it.

Practice can be enriching to Miller's definition of faith, as belief and trust between encounter and story, for in theological reflection on practice we find, not only moments of encounter, but our ongoing experiential reliance on God. The waiting in silence is practicing the presence of God, that is, becoming aware of (listening to, being challenged and guided by, celebrating) indwelling divinity. Quaker spirituality is the calling not only to constitute a meeting, nor only to tell our story of the divine encounter, but to live in constant awareness of divine presence, which underlies such moments of encounter. In our ongoing experience of the divine life in this inherent relatedness—in its feeling, fullness, fruits, and fittingness—is our measure of truth. The danger in narrative theology is that the larger story will become abstract and hegemonic, absorbing our own story, so that we measure our lives by an objective standard—narrative though, not dogmatic—rather than by our sense of the spirit in our present life, out of which the narrative of encounter has come and on the basis of which it is sustained.

We in fact are living several stories at once; the particulars of our life can be ordered in various patterns. The big Story takes elements of our story and puts them into a certain pattern. If this pattern becomes hegemonic, we lose sight of the various elements in our life that do not fit and thus obscure the transformative efforts of the whole-making as well as holy-making spirit—who is bigger and deeper than any story, who "searches everything, even the depths of God"[31]—who seeks ever to expand and deepen our being to include these alien particulars. We may also be living the same story but telling it differently. What then constitutes it as the same? Is it the same telling, the same words recounting the same events, or the same spirit in relation to whom we render it in different words illuminated by different moments of experience?

Our need for theology is evident in the telling of our stories— which Miller embraces—and in making us aware of the dangers in that story-telling. It is evident as well in thinking about the meaning and realities encountered in the practice of waiting in silence—which Miller and I are suggesting Read consider. And it is evident in the effort to find a commonality among Friends, for to think about the meaning of our meeting together is to ask after the ultimate significance of humans being with each other, as part of our being in the world, which is what Quaker theology reflects on—through the language of our Quaker, biblical, and secular heritage.

If the search for commonality is a theological undertaking, how can theological reflection help us along? It can investigate both our practice and our faith. We can describe our different practices—whether as waiting in silence or praising Christ—and look for the common spirit at work within it. We can tell our own stories and the bigger Story we see it as part of and listen to the different contents and styles of others' stories, and through these seek for the common holy spirit. I do not think we can find our unity on the explicit level. I agree with Read we do not find it in belief; but Miller would agree. I do not think we can find it in looking for a uniformity of plot or of narration. Our unity, I believe, is rather in God and in relatedness to creation beneath all explicitness in our tacit commitments and connectedness. We do approach these within the Quaker context, present and past. However little or much is known and however differently it is understood, we have chosen to join or to continue as part of this particular conversation on faith and practice rather than some other Christian or non-Christian one.

What I am suggesting is that our unity is ultimately found through the "spirit of God" in "the hidden unity in the Eternal Being" which "opens all things" to us, within us, whose "wonderful depths" are, however, "beyond what can by words be declared."[32] Penultimately, our unity is in dialogue amidst our Quaker context. The theological question then becomes what will facilitate such dialogue? The need for theology becomes evident in finding a way to speak and to listen to our stories, beliefs, practices, and understandings of our Quaker, biblical, and secular contexts, that sustain, enrich, illuminate, and make problematic this dialogue. Such dialogue can be life-giving, edifying, and community-building if we approach one another knowing that our meeting is in this hidden unity beneath words which enables us to accept, and even to learn from, our differences. Drawing upon the more inclusive, caring elements in our diverse practice, faith, and stories—as the spirit opens us—we can be graced by otherness. Then we can live in the "love and unity" of which Isaac Penington speaks:

> For this is the true ground of love and unity, not that such a man walks and does just as I do, but because I feel the same Spirit and life in him, and that he walks in his rank, in his order, in his proper way and place of subjection to that; and this is far more pleasing to me than if we walked just in that track wherein I walk.... The great error of the ages of the apostacy hath been to set up an outward order and uniformity, and to make men's consciences bend thereto, either by arguments of wisdom, or by force; but the property of the true church government is, to leave the conscience to its full liberty in the Lord, to preserve it single and entire for the Lord to exercise, and to seek unity in the light and in the Spirit, walking sweetly and harmoniously together in the midst of different practices.[33]

The Quaker Vision's Contribution to the Field of Theology

What can we say, then, in conclusion, to the question of the conference, in what ways has the Quaker vision contributed to the discipline of theology. The answer is "not a wit," judging by the Protestant scholar's remark. There was a vigorous theological exchange between Quakers and other Protestants in the seventeenth century. Samuel Fisher, in his eight hundred-page *Rusticus Ad Academicos*, answers point by point the written attacks on Quakers by such leading Puritan theologians as John Owen and Richard Baxter, and contributes to the beginnings of higher biblical criticism through extensive arguments about the sources and formation of the biblical canon, with the purpose of refuting their identification of scripture with the Word of God. But his efforts are forgotten in biblical scholarly history with the passage of time.

Significant writings of Penn and Barclay also exhibit this Puritan-Quaker dispute, but Penn is remembered for his contributions to the making of modern government rather than to theology. Barclay's *Apology* may, however, make it into a syllabus for a course in the History of Protestantism, but it is without effect on the wider field of theology. While Fox's *Journal* has had a profound effect on Quaker life and thought through the centuries, it has not contributed to the larger field of theology—although it has surprisingly touched non-Quaker intellectuals, such as, of all people, Ludwig Wittgenstein. With recent interest in story-telling, the *Journal* has come into the non-Quaker purview of some but is categorized as autobiography rather than theology.

The places to look for the influence of Quaker theology is not in the field of theology but rather in such practical effects as the seventeenth-century formation of modern democratic institutions—as Penn wrote the first two frames of modern government and as colonial Pennsylvania contributed to the formation of the U.S. Constitution; the eighteenth-century creation of the abolition movement—as the Quaker commitment to perfection here and now, and thus to the possibility and imperative to transform society, according to the non-Quaker historian David Brion Davis, initiated the anti-slavery movement; and the nineteenth-century beginnings of the feminist movement—as Lucretia Mott, Susan B. Anthony, and others organized Quaker and non-Quaker women and men.

Because Quaker theology is inherently integrative, rather than pure thought, we should not be surprised at theology having practical effects. But we have lost today the recognition that these practical outcomes have issued from theological commitments and expressions, and think to pursue further practical outcomes but without the unnecessary baggage of theological thinking. Yet such effects in the world were incubated within the minds and hearts of Quakers seeking, as they understood it, to sink down into the measure of the life and to manifest that life as led into both word and deed. To the degree that liberal Friends do not reflect on their commitments in doing good, and to the degree that evangelical Friends do reflect on their commitments but do so not in the life but adhering to objective forms, the scope of action is curtailed and the depths of spirituality are restricted in energizing, sustaining, and imagining such ways of being in the world.

If our theology has in fact been so potent in its impact on social life, even though having no noticeable effect on others' theology, perhaps there is further socially transformative potential in Quaker theology. In any case, there are contemporary theologies that, like Quaker theology, are focused on doing theology so as to overcome social oppression. From these Quakers can learn— such as how to do systemic analysis of social oppression—but can also contribute insofar as our theology is grounded in a spirituality of divine presence—in a sinking down into the measure of life from which comes both action and words, and their integration.

Reflecting Theologically from the Gathered Meeting: The Nature and Origin of Quaker Theology

To speak of the nature and origin of Quaker theology is to raise the question of how systematic we should be in our theological pursuits as Quakers. As a Quaker theologian and postcritical philosopher, I am drawn to systematic theology because I am interested in how intellectual principles structure our thought and life; in how doctrines carry within them a wisdom about life; and in how a tradition is a forest for exploration and a well for sustenance. But I am pulled two ways. If systematic theology means conquering the absolute and bringing it home; if it means explaining the inexplicable so as to eradicate mystery; if it means a place for everything and everything in its place; if it means finishedness and the end to creativity—I reject it.

I am repelled when the principles are dogmatic rather than experiential; when doctrines dominate, demanding logical connections and subsuming all truth under logic; and when the tradition, rather than our contemporary needs and experience, sets the agenda. Yet I am drawn to it because I discern within its hard shell of thought a seed of life that can help make sense of my and our life, and a comprehensiveness that attempts to relate the many parts to each other and to the whole. In particular Tillich's *Systematic Theology* has been and continues to be an exciting venture in making sense of my own life and of my relation to the larger world I inhabit even as I have become more critical of his underlying mind/body dualism.

My current assessment is that what I have said not only negatively applies to systematic theology but applies to much of mainstream theology as well, inasmuch as it employs principles, doctrines, and tradition in intellectualistic ways detached from and imposed upon the lived meaning of our ordinary lives. Thus even though Quaker theology can reach for comprehensiveness, can use traditional theological words, and should have a clarity, coherence, and interconnectedness—as systematic theology does—it is not, nor can it be, "systematic." But if we cannot call our theology systematic, what kind of theology is it that we do as Quakers? Let's just call it "Quaker theology"—*philosophical* in getting at the principles that shape our faith and practice, *historical* in working with and from both principles and images embedded in the origins of our heritage, and *socially transformative* in starting in a deep place from which arises the imperative to achieve justice, peace, and mutuality. As such, may it become an opening way that "allows so much to Love" that "there's no lack of grace."[1]

Do we even dare, though, to speak of "Quaker theology?" Do Quakers write, have Quakers done, "theology?" In the beginnings of Quakerism in the second half of seventeenth-century England, there is a voluminous wealth of theological writing which, I believe, emerged from life in the Spirit. The language is laced with traditional biblical and Protestant concepts, yet they are employed in the service of metaphors that emerge from and give shape to the spiritual depths of early Friends' lives. So, if we take "theology" not in its normal meaning, but as the *logos* of *theos*—as thinking and speaking of divinity—we can affirm "Quaker theology." While it might be still better, drawing upon the existentialist and phenomenologist Gabriel Marcel, to call what Quakers did and do "religious reflection," yet I want to retain the word "theology" to maintain some link, however problematic, with the religious thinking of others within and beyond the Christian tradition.

But who is the audience for Quaker theology? Among American Quakers theology is suspect. For many liberal Friends you ought to do and be—let your lives so speak—but not think about it. For many evangelical Friends you should celebrate and witness to Jesus Christ but not engage in thought that might deviate from tried and true biblical expressions. I do want to write for Quakers—as an enterprise of faith seeking understanding, attempting to raise our commitments to a level of articulateness that can enrich our lives, our self-understanding and our socially transformative work. But I also want to write for non-Quakers. However small and young we are, I believe we have some important things to offer the wider world—Christian, inter-faith, and secular. Quakerism offers a tradition committed to radical social action that is grounded in a life of spirituality. It has provided in the twenty-first century a refuge from dogmatic Christianity for those interested in the spiritual life within a Christian context. It maintains a serious religious community without hierarchical authority that is ethically engaged for those seeking to go beyond the impoverishments of secular life. And to the many searching for a deepening of spirituality, it offers a meditative tradition, in fact the sole meditative tradition within Christian denominations outside of monastic orders. Whether or not it entices into convincement, it can be a means of enrichment to other Christians, a place of dialogue with other meditative traditions of the world, and a springboard for social transformation.

The Need for Life

The need in our time around the world is for life. Many people are starving and are without adequate clothing and shelter. They need physical necessities to sustain life. Many people suffer under oppression—military, racial, gender, socioeconomic. They need liberation from and transformation of those social structures that so diminish life. All are suffering to some degree under the effects of our exploitation of the earth. We need a new way of relating to the environment that will both free us from the effects of our exploitation on soil, air, water, which are polluting our bodies, and open us to the qualities of nature that nourish our vitality. We are witnessing and are caught up in the encounter with otherness which is occurring in the global context. We need a way of life that will get along with people very different from ourselves, so that we not merely can tolerate but grow from the encounters. We are becoming aware of our own cultural hegemony, the expansion of our ways of thinking around the globe, just at a time when we are becoming aware of the inadequate foundations of modern thought as we continue to grope for ways of making sense of our lives under the impact of modern science and technology. We need a new paradigm in cultural life that can enable us to live beyond the fragmenting dualisms that set in opposition science and spirituality, technology and morality, and body and mind. Many people are living spiritually impoverished or diminished lives. We are in need of a greater fullness of life here and now.

Theology may strike some as an unlikely perspective from which to address these many levels of life's needs. Theology deals with our fundamental consciousness of self, other, and world. Understood as the quest for meaning, the effort to understand the ultimate context of our orientation in the world, pursuit of self-transformation, reflection upon God or the sacred—it can contribute to the recovery and enhancement of life. In speaking of God, Christ, freedom, new life, integration, theology must deal with what really matters to us and with the way we relate to everything in terms of what matters. What "matters" is not only what is important to us but the material shape things take in our lives. Theology is able, not only to listen to and articulate what we say matters, but is able to discern in the matter of our lives what meaning we are in actuality living.

It matters to all of us to meet our need for life, on whatever level that we experience that need as acute. There are many answers to our needs on the different physical, social, cultural, and spiritual levels of life—and in different places and situations different answers to the same need—but overall we are all in need of a change in consciousness (of our explicit but much more of our unconscious attitudes) that will enable us to create and live into new patterns of being. To be more fully human with ourselves, with each other, with the cosmos, with that which is ultimate, we need Quaker theology. Along with other disciplines, it can contribute to understanding our present consciousness and can imagine new ways of being that can sustain life and realize its abundance.

To move ahead in hope, we often draw upon ingredients that are buried in our past or that are marginal, hidden, inchoate in our present. In embarking upon a theology of what matters in life, I write from being situated within the Quaker heritage, which is oriented towards life. While many metaphors are used by the first generation of the Religious Society of Friends for the divine and for their way of being responsive to it—such as light, seed, and truth—life is a central one. Without disregarding the others or the importance of employing multiple metaphors, I am presenting this theology of life in the hope, not only of drawing out ingredients in my and our past into greater visibility, but of opening up possibilities inchoate in our present that may contribute towards the engendering of life.

Throughout three hundred and fifty years, Quakers have been involved with every level of nurturing life. From its beginnings in the English Civil War of the 1640s, Quakerism has been committed to the struggle for justice—political, social, and economic. They were the major agent in achieving religious toleration in England. Constitutional government of the United States was fundamentally shaped by William Penn's Pennsylvania "Frame of Government" and commitment to religious toleration. Quakers have consistently opposed war and worked for peace. From the American Revolution to Viet Nam they have provided medical assistance to the wounded on both sides of military conflicts. They fed and clothed many Europeans after World War I and II. In recent times they have provided aid to people suffering from natural disasters. At the beginning of the nineteenth century they sought to provide an economic basis for sustainable life to Native Americans; after the American Civil War to areas in the war-torn South; and in the twenty-first century to many people in need around the world. Amidst its active concerns to meet the physical, social, and cultural needs of many people around the globe, Quakerism has sustained a life of worship centered in communal meditation and the deepening of the spiritual life.

While not unique in any one of these concerns, Quakerism is unique in its integration of physical, social, and spiritual concerns. Not that parts of other religious traditions do not achieve an interconnection between these dimensions—from which Quakers can and do learn—but the Society of Friends as a whole is unique as a religious movement in how it unites these different dimensions by being engaged in worship and living shaped by silence. While this uniting of many levels of concern is not true of every Friend, since some focus their energies upon one area of concern rather than another, it is true that each Friend carries the weight of a tradition which addresses the conscience to realize the wholeness of life.

The theological expression of this wholistic perspective, its principles and roots, is one area to which twenty-first-century Friends have given scant attention. The feeling is often: do not think and talk about it, live it and benefit humanity. There has, in fact, been a wariness of theology since the beginnings of Quakerism. Yet, while objecting to the dogmatic views of Puritan and Anglican seventeenth-century England and the nonexperiential ways in which theology was done, the first generations of Friends were engaged in developing a different way of doing theology. Through journals, letters, essays, books of discipline called "faith and practice," and queries (which is probably the only new genre created by Friends), early Friends sought to speak out of the silence, to manifest intellectually their experience of, and the principles involved in, their rootedness in the indwelling presence of the divine.

Seventeenth-century Friends often used the phrase "in the life" or "out of the life." People's actions were judged as "in" or "out" of the life, in or out of accord with divine leadings. So also the social structures of oppression and as well the speculations of dogmatic theologians. Because the theology early Quakers wrote was "in the life," the theological task for Quakers in our own day is to figure out how to write "in the life." The importance is that life in our day is under threat at every level. Theology written in the life about what matters in life can contribute to contemporary Friends' own understanding of self and the principles upon which we act, and can model for a wider audience a wholistic religious tradition that carries power and hope for meeting people's physical needs, transforming our social structures, and deepening the spiritual life.

The Gathered Meeting

What is the starting point for Quaker theology? I have learned from a variety of liberation theologies how necessary it is to unmask the systemic oppressions we all participate in, from which older white straight economically-advantaged academic males, such as myself, are benefitting, even when critical of them. The perfectionistic strain that has led Quakers into social action to establish equality, justice, peace, and community is the very thing that makes it difficult for us to acknowledge how we are entrammeled, like others, in these systems of destruction. Yet Quaker theology is grounded in something more primal in human experience than suffering and more immediate than the words of scripture, and so I do not begin theology from oppression or "God's preferential option for the poor," as many feminist and liberation theologians do.

The experienced depth of divine mystery is the place wherein resources lie for recognizing and overcoming oppression and affirming and developing life toward mutuality amidst the otherness of humanity and the entire community of being. I am aware that I am writing from within a tradition that from its outset has affirmed that spiritual development and social transformation are inseparable. The experience of sacred depth can whelm within us in any moment—in private meditation, the meeting for business, education, social action, the experience of oppression, a conversation with another, artistic creation or scientific discovery, a walk in the woods in solitude. Still, I find myself writing Quaker theology from the starting point of the gathered meeting, as the most intense form of communal experience of sacred mystery.

The life of Friends is founded and formed in silence. In worship we gather in silence. People quietly enter the plain meeting house, unadorned with sign or symbol, and take a seat, finding a comfortable position for their body and closing their eyes. From the surface of our lives, filled with the momentary involvements of the morning and the week, we descend into the meditative depths. We call it "centering down." There in the silence we expect to meet the divine mystery. Always there, yet we live so much of our lives on the surface, we are unaware of it, disconnected from it, not living consciously out of its energy and insight. Silence provides the context for awakening, connecting, envisioning, revitalizing. While our modern culture treats silence as a vacuum, an emptiness, the absence of sound, Friends experience it as a fullness: a richness of inchoate tacit connectedness with reality (natural, human, and divine) and a well of potentiality—of insight and action, and of new ways to relate to self, world, and God. Silence is the unifying depth beneath our seemingly disparate surface preoccupations; the whole which encompasses and sustains the parts of our being— our thoughts, words, deeds, artifacts, and conscious self; the mystery in which we live and move and have our being.

As we sit in the silence, we may be assailed by clamoring monkeys in the branches of consciousness that insist we deal with the particular demands of the day and week. Or we may encounter a dry nothingness untouched by anything vital, a spiritual torpor that at best can be thought of as a quiet space shared with others after a hard week. But sometimes, perhaps often, after centering down we encounter an unencumbered calm and then a dynamic that moves us into unanticipated regions. Entering such stillness we may find rest and rejuvenation; we may feel our connectedness with those present, other humans, or the natural world living and inanimate; we may discover our present moment lengthening to encompass the remembered past or anticipated future; we may sense the presence of that which is more than self affecting us. Beyond our possible doubts about how to interpret what is happening, we know experientially that we are in touch with that which is really real, because we are brought into a transformed state of momentary peace and relatedness.

It happens miraculously, from time to time, that a meeting moves as a whole into deep stillness and vibrant creativity in which all feel bound together with each other, with the wider world, and with the divine. Friends call this a "gathered meeting." There may be no speaking yet people feel this *religere*, this binding of each to each and to the whole, and emerge from the meeting knowing they have been together in deep places. Or speaking may occur; if it does, it nurtures the gathering. A theme may be sounded which others are ripe to hear and work with or already have been meditating upon. In my own experience there have been moments when the exact idea or biblical passage I have been led to meditate upon is expressed by another in vocal ministry. We come to know that in depth we are not alone but connected as something more than the ego self is at work there. In a gathered meeting we thus experience the sacred binding us together in community, what Catholics and Anglicans have traditionally recognized in the sacrament of Eucharist as "the real presence of Christ," although we as Friends stress the experiential aspect of this and the free movement of the Spirit creating it in its own particular way in that moment.

Inward and Outward: Theological Structure and Process of the Gathered Meeting

Reflecting on the structure and process of the gathered meeting, we can get at the theological principles at work within it. Experiencing a gathered meeting is a descent from the surface of our ordinary lives into the depths of stillness, and a return at the end of meeting back to the surface. Friends from the beginning of Quakerism have spoken of surface as "outward" and depths as "inward." The process in this structure is then a movement from outward to inward and a return to the outward. Inward and outward are not opposites but are interrelated as different levels of awareness of reality, each having their own important meaning, and each gaining in meaning through openness to the other.

Within such depths we experience a connective creativity which moves us into a felt knowledge of our relatedness to that which is present—divinity, fellow worshippers, other humans, fellow earth creatures, the cosmos. We discover that we are parts of a divine whole. George Fox, in his visionary return through the flaming sword back into Eden, discovered this cosmic connectedness as the context of his encounter with the Christ within. The process then is not only descent and return but movement into the breadth of relatedness with all reality. So far then, we can discern in the gathered meeting theological principles which are experiential, dimensional, and relational.

Fullness of Life: The Rule of Christ

While I have begun with the gathered meeting, corporate worship is not the authority in Quakerism but only a context for it. Any other time and place in a Quaker's life could offer other contexts. The authority is not the gathered meeting but the Life experienced in inwardness. The Life is but one of many metaphors that focuses the central authority as the divine presence experienced in its connectedness—illumining the meaning of our lives, guiding us into speech and action, uniting us with others and with the world.

In his first book after convincement, Isaac Penington calls this authority the "rule of Christ." He asks: "What is a Christian's rule, whereby he is to steer and order his course?" and answers with a simple definition of a Christian: "A Christian is to be a follower of Christ, and consequently must have the same rule to walk by, as Christ had. A Christian proceeds from Christ, hath the same life in him, and needs the same rule." What is the rule of Christ but "the fulness of life":

> Christ had the fulness of life, and of his fulness we all receive a measure of the same life.... Yea we came out of the same spring of life, from whence he came.... Now what was his rule? Was it not the fulness of life which he received? And what is their rule? Is it not the measure of life which they receive?[2]

To take up this rule of Christ is to be transformed, to be made a new creature by the Holy Spirit: "The Spirit forms the heart anew, forms Christ in the heart, begets a new creature there,... and this is the rule of Righteousness, the new creature, or the spirit of life in the new creature."

He then goes on to quote 2 Corinthians 5:17, "If any man be in Christ, he is a new creature [or "new creation" in RSV]," and Galatians 6:15, that what counts is "a new creature" ["new creation," RSV].[3] The rule is the new creature in the sense that only the transformed self has access to the rule which dwells within as divine spirit. In the language we have been using above, we are only in touch with the rule of Christ when we have entered into the depth of inwardness. In the language of

Paul, and his metaphor of the law of the spirit and of the flesh, and John's metaphor of Light, Penington goes on:

> And as any man walks according to this rule, according to the new creature, according to the law of light and life that the spirit continually breathes into the new creature, he hath peace; but as he transgresses that, and walks not after the spirit but after the flesh, he walks out of the light, out of the life, out of the peace, into the sea, into death, into the trouble, into the condemnation. Here then is the law of the converted man, the new creature; and the law of the new creature is the spirit of life which begat him, which lives, and breathes, and gives forth his law continually in him. Here's a Christian; here is his rule: he that hath not the new creature formed in him, is no Christian; and he that hath the new creature, hath the rule in himself.[4]

The central authority for Friends is whatever measure we have of the fullness of life, the divine presence known in the inward depths of our relational being, which we open to in a gathered meeting but can experience in any other moment. Truth in theology can be measured, then, by our sense of the life and fullness in it.

Quakerism is unequivocally Christian in its origins, emerging out of left-wing Puritanism, i.e., mid-seventeenth-century English Protestantism, and its context which includes strains of experiential and meditative religion from the Radical (or left wing) Reformation of the sixteenth century on the continent and from Catholic spirituality of medieval England. Through its affirmation of the indwelling presence of Christ in all peoples, Quakers have been unusually open to other religious traditions (including secularism), and have been nurtured by them to such an extent in the twentieth century that some Friends resist the title "Christian." Quakerism can offer to other Christian groups a companion in dialogue as they also explore their Christian identity and roots in the light of our contemporary crisis. To paraphrase John Woolman's statement about why he felt led to visit Native Americans in the wilderness during the French and Indian War, we can say that in such dialogue Quakers can learn by feeling and understanding the life and spirit another Christian group lives in, while being able perhaps in some degree to help them forward on their way.[5]

Life and Form: The Emergence of Inwardness

From the beginning Friends spoke of inward and outward as "life and form" or "spirit and form." The energy and reality of inward life and spirit would emerge in the outward forms of word and act, ritual and things made, the shape of an individual life and of our lives together. Once emergent, however, the forms do not by themselves preserve the life and spirit. Only in an ongoing interactive process, where people descend into inwardness and bear this life with them in a return to the forms, are they vital. If a form has lost its connection with inwardness, it must either be revitalized, transformed, or "laid down." Hence early Friends' attack on the sacraments and church liturgy as empty forms perpetuating themselves rather than opening people to the indwelling presence of God.

The separation of outward from inward that Friends attacked in Puritan and Anglican England of the seventeenth century became problematic later in the history of Quakerism itself. Most notably in the American conflict in 1827 between Orthodox and Hicksites, an outward objectivism was opposed to an inward subjectivism. In this conflict, an outwardness severed from depth led to a dogmatism of belief and practice, demanding conformity to explicit objective standards, while an inwardness disjoined from outward expression led to a quietism of the spirit, demanding conformity to a form of rigid subjectivity. From the originating seventeenth-century Quaker perspective of the interaction of inner and outer, we can see that both sides of the nineteenth-century split are self-deceived: dogmatists in thinking their objective forms are true and the only truth; quietists in thinking their subjectivity is free from all forms; and both in thinking that either the outer or inner can exist separated from interdependence with the other. Both assume a superiority, whether of correct belief or spiritual purity. In either case the individual's creativity of living in and from the divine source is undercut as new forms or deeper levels are not tolerated.

Even though there have been times in Quakerism when inner and outer have been rent apart, the experience of early Friends and of much of Quaker history down to the present has been to affirm and depend upon the existence of an intimate and inextricable relation between them. Most evidently in the gathered meeting, but throughout our lives, we move from the outward to the inward and back again. The inward emerges into outward forms which are sustained by a continual openness to the inward source from which they come.

Feeling the Life—Beyond Dualism: Philosophical Innovations in Homespun

Although Friends are not inclined to think of inward and outward as having a philosophical dimension, its epistemological and metaphysical implications are startling. In mid-seventeenth-century England the philosophical and cultural direction of modernity had not yet congealed. Many elements were in solution that could have been configured differently from the way they in fact came to be. Under the impact of Galileo and Descartes, who conceived all reality dualistically as separated into either subject or object, feelings came to lose any bearing on truth, displaced by the subject's mathematical reasoning that attended to the measurable qualities of objects. At the same time that this view was becoming the precipitate of modernity, Quakers in their simplicity were developing a method of worship, decision-making, and knowing God that depended fundamentally upon feelings.

Over and over again George Fox, the founder of Quakerism, speaks of feeling the Life or Light or Seed or Truth: "Live in the Life of God, and feel it"; "feel the Seed of God"; "feel the presence of God in you and with you."[6] He does this because it is through feeling that we are aware of inwardness. Whether outer forms are filled with inward life is discerned, therefore, by feel. Life shows itself in the form of a life lived, a meeting gathered into genuine worship, the fitting word spoken, acts establishing justice and nurturing love. It is through the intuitive sensitivity of feeling that we become aware of the presence or absence of inwardness, and the degree of its fullness.

Within the gathered meeting, therefore, an epistemological perspective is implicit that, contrary to modernity's grounding knowledge upon reason itself, conceives of knowing as affectional. Reality is known through the feel of it in the depths of inwardness. After three hundred and fifty years of Cartesianism, developed in either a rationalistic or empiricist manner, some philosophies in the twentieth century have explored a similar alternative orientation that grounds our knowing upon non-rational factors; hence my interest in "background" and "pre-reflective awareness" in Merleau-Ponty, "tacit knowing" in Polanyi, and words as "forms of life" in Wittgenstein. It is by no mere chance that I see similarities between "postcritical" philosophies (to use Polanyi's word) and Quaker thought, because it was my pre-reflective Quaker commitments that first drew me to them.

The inward life that is felt in outward forms is, as we have said, emergent. The emergence of form from life offers an alternative to the traditional western metaphysical dualistic conception of being as divided into spirit and matter. Influential upon Greek, medieval, and modern thought, Aristotle conceives reality as the result of the formative agency of spirit imposing form upon formless matter. For originating Quakers, form emerges from, rather than being imposed upon, matter. The matter of our lives has a fullness within it which can arise in meaningful forms. The silence entered in worship is a formlessness that is a divine fullness pregnant with the possibilities of new words, new ways of being, new life, and old ways and words freshly invigorated. While none to my knowledge have said so, Friends' experience illuminates how matter is implicit spirit and how spirit is explicit matter—a radically different notion from the dominant western tradition.

The inwardness of silence we enter in our descent into depth is an experience of formlessness—of the inchoate, of mystery. In this formlessness we experience presence, the felt presence of others—divine, human, and fellow creatures—and the creative process that carries us into words to be spoken or deeds to be done. The inward is not "subjective" nor is the outward "objective." Inwardness is not my own private individuality separating me from the multiple objects of the world but is rather a relational level of consciousness in which I know myself in relation to divinity and world. Nor is outwardness objective as the Cartesian tradition develops it—as quantitatively measurable and unambiguous (an "object" is what it is and that's all that it is)—since the meaning of an outer form depends on its authenticity: whether it is presently bearing inwardness or has been severed from it.

In this simple practice of descending over and over again into formlessness—in worship, transacting the meeting's business, and daily living—we are trusting, without knowing how or what, that divinely shaped forms of knowing and doing will arise. In this we have a profound manifestation of the traditional Christian affirmation of "faith seeking understanding." Not faith as conceptual belief in something, but faith as trust—Friends pursuit of what, from the outset, they called "Truth" is grounded in this experiential reliance on mystery at the bottom of the self. The inchoateness of inward silence does not have to be controlled by an external agency—whether reason, scripture, or tradition; the mystery can be trusted and, in gathered meetings, is trusted again and again.

The Way of Words

Words that often arise in this practice of descent into inward mystery and reemergence into outward life, whether in worship or daily living, are metaphors. Quaker theology is rife with metaphors as they emerge out of the inward depths. A wealth of metaphors is used for God. While Light (and Inward Light) is the most pervasive image used by Friends today and has been consistently used since Quaker beginnings, it co-exists from our beginnings with many others, such as Life, Seed, Spirit, Truth, Power, Presence, Wisdom, Way, Inward Teacher, That of God in Everyone. As we have seen above, religious talk has a metaphoric abundance, such as in speaking of "the same spring of life" existing in Jesus as in us; "feeling" the Life, Seed, Presence, Fullness; becoming a "new creation"; "the law of spirit and flesh."

Metaphors in the way they relate disparate aspects of experience carry the richness of our lives into theological reflection. Beyond conceptual control, using them is an act of trust. As metaphors are better able to reach for the unsayable depths of inwardness, we are beyond the conceptual boundaries of doctrine and systematic theology.

Quaker thought, emerging out of experiencing God in the depths of a gathered meeting and of our solitary meditation, is therefore metaphoric theology. Through the metaphoric presencing of God, it engages philosophical and historical exploration and socially transformative action.

Rather than traditional theology seeking cognitive clarity, comprehensiveness, and certainty through propositions based on scripture and reason, Quaker theology seeks, through waiting in silence and its emergent metaphors and subsequent ideas, to evoke the experience of Divine Mystery, the seed bed for creative thought and responsible action, transformation of self and society, lived confidence and compassion, and feeling the whole-making and meaning-giving Reality, the fullness of Life, in which we dwell.

Conclusion

So what is Quaker theology? I am a Quaker doing theology but is what I am doing here Quaker theology? In reflecting on what I have said, and even more so on how I have said it, perhaps I can see and say what I believe Quaker theology is. I have spoken in the first person from the beginning. I have spoken not only of specific experiences but of the experiential. This is the realm of the personal, of my relating and responding to the multifarious phenomena in my world, my awareness tacit and explicit, my sensitivities, memories, anticipations, feelings, fears and hopes, defenses and vulnerabilities, and thinking and willing in certain ways.

Within this realm of the personal I have sought a level of depth in which I am ongoingly in touch with mystery felt as sacred. The place in which I have found this and chosen to start my reflection from is the communal space of a gathered Friends meeting. What I am finding in general, but specifically here in the gathered meeting, is that the principles for theological work in Quakerism are: *experiential*—starting from experience of divinity; *dimensional*—sensitive to the different levels of meaning experienced on surface and in the depths; *relational*—aware that experience of the divine carries with it a sense of our relatedness to being; *vital*—using the fullness of life as a measure for truth; *affectional*—knowing that life and truth through feeling; and *non-dualistic*—affirming that the forms of our intellectual, social, and religious lives emerge from and are sustained upon formlessness we indwell beneath our knowing and control.

Starting with this waiting together in silence, structured ritually as the way of Friends worship, I have drawn into my reflections thinkers, images, concepts from the Quaker heritage. To write theologically from the divine within without drawing upon the Quaker heritage would not be Quaker theology. Or perhaps, more accurately, it would be "latent" but not "manifest" Quaker theology. Not that Quaker theology must start with meeting for worship; it can start from any place in which I am aware of sacred mystery. But the meeting for worship dramatizes for me "persons in relation" (to use a word from the Quaker Edinburgh philosopher John Macmurray[8]), and the gathered meeting focuses that communal experience in depth. Quaker theology, situated in its heritage, is a reflective enterprise that reflects on what *is*. It is not principally a thinking about the past—as other parts of Christianity do in starting from tradition or scripture—nor is it a judging by some ethical standard what ought to be done, since oughtness is derived from isness of the indwelling present divine.

From what is in inwardness, from what is in the deepest reaches of our being—the divine Life—we begin to reflect on the meaning of our lives in the world shaped by the Quaker ethos rooted in the Christian and biblical heritage, speaking in the first person from the here and now, though informed by past and future. Such it seems to me, as I have so far discovered through reflecting on my and our dwelling in the Life, is the nature and origin of Quaker theology.

III. Quaker Thought as Theopoetic: Christ, History, and Biblical Interpretation

As I have long thought about the nature of language, and Quaker language, drawing on the insights of various contemporary thinkers, my involvement with the writings of Stanley Romaine Hopper (professor and dean at Drew Theological School), collecting his best essays for publication,[1] slowly converged with my inquiry into the nature of Quaker life and language. I belatedly came to realize I am dwelling in a theopoetic tradition. We are clothed in a rich weave of metaphors, symbols, and ideas—drawn from nature, scripture, and ordinary life. We comport ourselves differently, therefore, from other Christians garbed in a logical mesh of doctrine and scripture.

Hopper's word "theopoetic" attends to our participation in divinity (*theo*) through figural language (*poetic*). He introduced this word into the American theological conversation in 1970 as a fecund alternative to "theology."[2] The difference in etymological roots of *poiesis* and *logos* is between creativity and rationality, since *poiesis* (from which "poetry" comes) means "making," whereas *logos* (from which "logic" and "study of," as in "biology," come) means "word" and "structure." By making this switch in the connective with God, Hopper called attention to creativity in our inward depths rather than logic in our thinking. His focus was on the making, in how metaphors work in inwardness to evoke meanings and participation in divine reality that logic does not.

While the word "theopoetic" does not occur in the essays below, since I only recently began to use this word for how Friends speak, Quaker theology is a weave of metaphors that arise from and evoke the depths of inwardness. We enter the inward Silence in worship, do business, and seek guidance for actions *in metaphor*—the metaphoric Light, Seed, Truth, Life,

Presence, Power, Wisdom, Inward, Way, Teacher, That of God in Everyone. The essays below speak of this inwardness as a dimension in our ordinary lives beneath belief and critical reason, underlying thought and ethical action, the source of our efforts to speak of Christ, to understand history, and to do biblical interpretation.

Recognizing Quaker thought as intrinsically theopoetic—as words rising from the Silence of inwardness and coming much of the time into play in metaphors—I look at Christ through the lens of theo*poiesis* rather than theo*logos*. The word "Christ" is itself a metaphor, although it has been dogmatized as a concept and elaborated logically by the Church. The meaning of Christ from the beginnings of Quakerism has its abundance of meanings from its use in a dense web of interwoven metaphors. These create a sense of meaning different from Church doctrines as it engages the user and (hopefully) the hearer in personal awareness of the presence and stirring of the divine within our own inwardness.

In my search for the historical Jesus in the Holy Land and my search to understand Christ's resurrection, I wonder what has the Church done to the inward experience of Jesus as he lived his life in Palestine and to the inward experience of those who experienced the risen Christ? The Church has objectified both life and resurrection by applying logic to scripture resulting in the fixedness of doctrine obscuring the inwardness of Jesus and ourselves, and eliminating the play of metaphors in our personal existence which can evoke experience of the divine and be transformative of self and world.

Christ in the Mesh of Metaphor

Christ is the great connector in the Christian tradition, the mediator between humanity and divinity, and the one who calls us to love of neighbor. Yet within Quakerism today, Christ is the cause of division rather than of unity. Is it possible to attend to Christ in Quaker experience so as to discover why Christ divides us and whether, beneath this divisiveness, we can find unity with each other and, in George Fox's words, "unity with the creation?"[1]

While it will take a degree of grace-given openness to difference at both poles of belief, I believe it is possible. If we return to the origins of Quakerism, each belief will find endorsement of some of its views but will also encounter that which is significantly other. Such richness can engender humility and encouragement to grow. But perhaps even more importantly, it can show us a way to experience and express Christ that leads us into unity — not into a uniformity but into a felt sense of belonging amidst diversity to one another. Engaging early Friends, the "liberal" will have the opportunity to wrestle with the centrality of Christ as a well of wisdom for the spiritual life, and the "evangelical" will find a different way in which Christ was and can be central.

The way in which early Friends express Christ is through a multiplicity of metaphors. Christ is Light, Seed, Truth, Life, Inward Teacher, Power, Wisdom, Spirit, Way, That of God in Everyone. These multifarious metaphors for Christ are part of an entire language pervaded by metaphor that early Friends used to describe and nurture the religious life. In early Friends' use of metaphor, we can discover a way of speaking of Christ that elicits unity with others and all of creation.

We do not have to adopt this way just because it is that out of which our Quaker tradition has come, but it can henceforth stand as a query to us as we seek to deepen our life with God.

To understand Christ as the metaphor for God, we will need to understand how metaphors work and see them at work in early Friends, especially in Fox our founder. But first we need to understand better the problem Christ poses for Friends today in order to see more clearly why and how this metaphoric way matters.

The Problem with Christ

Evangelical Friends are committed to Christ in a manner that shapes all aspects of life. Their lives have been saved from sin, death, meaninglessness, and uncertainty, and given present direction and future hope through Christ's crucifixion and resurrection. God's sacrificial action in Christ is a free, loving gift to creatures beyond help from anything in this world. How, they ask, can others claim to be Quaker and live a spiritual life apart from the grace of Christ which has changed them in this life and guarantees a life everlasting?

Liberal Friends, on the other hand, see Christ as the symbol of exclusion and domination. Christ is used to demarcate clear boundaries of an inside and outside group, distinguished in terms of formulations of belief. This either/or thinking delimits a superior and inferior, and endorses the right of the superior to dominate the inferior. Christ has been used to justify war against Muslims, pogroms against Jews, conflict between Catholics and Protestants, the colonization of native peoples, the enslavement of Africans, the denigration of people of color, the subordination of women, the economic subjugation of the poor, the dehumanization of homosexuals, and the exploitation of the environment. Christ is a defense against the strangeness of others and the ambiguities of existence. Christ is a way to control our bodily desires and the bodies of others, a demand for conformity of belief and action rather than an encouragement to creativity, and an assurance of rational certitude rather than a deepening of trust. How, these liberal Quakers ask, can others claim to be Quaker and live a spiritual life devoted to such a Christ of constriction and oppression?

Faced with such an opposition, the question is whether there is another way of approaching Christ that will interest liberals in the positive importance of Christ and that will interest evangelicals in other ways of speaking centrally of Christ. Among early Friends, I am suggesting, we find another way as they express the meaning and reality of Christ as metaphor and through multiple metaphors. What then is "metaphor" and how does it function for early Friends?

The Nature of Metaphor and the Quaker Way

The Quaker way with metaphors is evident in an early letter from Fox:

> And Friends, though you may have tasted of the power and been convinced and have felt the light, yet afterwards you may feel winter storms, tempests, and hail, and be frozen, in frost and cold and a wilderness and temptations. Be patient and still in the power and still in the light that doth convince you, to keep your minds to God; in that be quiet, that you may come to the summer, that your flight be not in the winter. For if you sit still in the patience which overcomes in the power of God, there will be no flying. For the husbandman, after he hath sown his seed, he is patient. For by the power and by the light you will come to see through and feel over winter storms, tempests, and all the coldness, barrenness, emptyness. And the same light and power will go over the tempter's head, which power and light were before he was. And so in the light standing still you will see your salvation, you will see the Lord's strength, you will feel the small rain, you will feel the fresh springs....[2]

Here Fox uses a density of metaphors to speak of God — as power and light—and of the religious life—as winter and summer, a waiting for plants to grow, and a sensuous life that tastes, feels, and sees. Amidst this rich play of metaphors, Fox enjoins us to be still in the power and light, suggesting a connection between metaphor and silence.

The Quaker way is epitomized in traditional worship as a descent into silence within which the divine presence is experienced and from which words may arise as a message to be shared in Meeting or as a leading for future action. So also in solitude, decision-making, acts of creativity, relating to others, or social action, Friends seek to enter the silence from which will come word or deed. Silence is the source of metaphor and metaphors have a peculiar capacity to carry such stillness within them.

The appropriateness of metaphoric language for a religious way rooted in silence becomes evident in considering the nature of metaphor. Perhaps the shortest (and certainly least adequate) definition of metaphor is that it is an "implied comparison." A metaphor suggests what something is *like*. In Fox's quote God is like power and light; the religious life is like wintry storms and summer freshness. The reality experienced by Friends in silence is deeper than words so that the words we use to speak of it cannot say what it *is* but only what it is *like*. Hence Fox speaks of God as like a force that moves things around or a light that illumines the dark. In the use of metaphoric likeness there is an implicit acknowledgement of the mystery of the divine that transcends our comprehension of what something is. Metaphors bear stillness within them because they arise from silence and suggest such mystery through expressing likeness.

To use multiple metaphors, as Fox invariably does (as evident above), is to suggest likeness from several angles. Each metaphor for God manifests, therefore, an aspect of our experience of divine reality: Light illumines and purges; Life engenders vitality; Seed grows down into darkness and up into light;

Spirit energizes; Truth draws us into knowing reality; Power makes things happen; Wisdom orders our being in the world; Way leads us forward in our living; Inward Teacher guides and instructs; That of God in Everyone calls attention to the interiority and universality of divine presence in human selves. Together these metaphors express a richness of multi-faceted reality simultaneously grasped from multiple perspectives.

As a likeness, a metaphor is more readily recognized as a human construct and is less easily confused with the reality it is symbolizing. It thus reinforces our sense, and signals to others, that the divine forever extends beyond our verbal reach. Nevertheless, while it resists identification with reality, it brings us into contact with it. The etymology of metaphor (*meta*: beyond, and *pherein*: to bear or to carry) means to bear beyond or to carry beyond. Metaphor bears us beyond the words to the reality itself. In metaphor an aspect of reality is manifest, becomes present to us. Yet the reality can never be known in that way apart from those words. Hence, likening the spiritual life to winter cold and summer freshness puts us in touch with this aspect of our lives. Always there implicitly in our experience, this aspect enters into consciousness through this focusing by the seasonal metaphor.

This consciousness involves a feel for the aspect it brings to focus. Winter and summer elicit certain feelings from us; conjoined with the spiritual life, they elicit similar feelings for it: we feel our spiritual life as we have felt winter and summer. Weaving several metaphors together, as Fox does above— tasting the power, feeling the light and the winter storms, being and standing still in the power and light, being patient like the farmer after sowing the seed, feeling the small rain and fresh springs, and all of these signifying our spiritual lives—creates a density of feeling that moves us to open to a reality of our lives and the presence of God active within it.

Metaphor connects us with reality because it is itself a phenomenon of connection. A metaphor is always a meaning constructed of at least two terms joined together. The terms are from different realms of discourse (such as taste and power or feeling and light) so exist in tension as they interact with each other. In knowing through a metaphor we are always therefore put into touch with at least two things; in knowing one thing we always know another. Indeed, we know each thing from the perspective of the other, so we experience taste in terms of power and power in terms of taste, feeling in terms of light and light in terms of feeling, or the spiritual life and winter/summer simultaneously in terms of each other. This interaction is of course going on beneath explicit notice but we feel it, are drawn in by it into contact with both realities. Metaphors are, therefore, a relational way of knowing. They are especially apt to catch up and show forth the relational character of our being—our relatedness to divinity, humanity, and cosmos.

At the same time we are brought into relation to our own self as the user of metaphor, so that in connecting with two things simultaneously we are also connecting with a third, ourselves. Words from different regions of our experience, when connected, bring together these different regions within ourselves; or rather, make us aware of their underlying connections in ourselves. We are changed in using metaphors; we are carried beyond our previous awareness into a sense of further connections within ourselves.

One of the connections the Fox quote above makes, and that is made in much of early Friends' extensive use of metaphors, is between sensuality and spirituality. The spiritual life is like light or like growing things or like the seasons. There is a natural welcome in hearing such metaphors, not only because of the familiarity of light, seed, and summer, but because of their draw; they affect us—we are attracted by the pleasures of summer or of light or of plants growing, or we are repelled by the winter's cold and storm. In either case, metaphors connect our spirituality with the particulars of our sensuous experience as we feel the presence of spiritual meaning embedded in the things of nature. By discovering the sensible world in the middle of our spiritual lives, and reciprocally the sensuous in the middle of spirituality, we are changed.

Not that all metaphors, natural or otherwise, change us all the time; there is a range in metaphoric power from "dead" metaphors to whose tension we are dead (such as in the use of "God the Father," until the recent feminist critique), through conventional connections (such as in calling someone a "pig"), to surprising ones (I remember, during a summer of much writing on my dissertation, telling my little daughter goodnight once again and saying she was a gem, when she turned on me and said "Good night, Daddy. You are a typewriter.").

At the far end of this spectrum, surprising metaphors can get deep. When metaphors function symbolically, they manifest a richness of hidden meaning. When Gerard Manley Hopkins says "The world is charged with the grandeur of God," we sense such richness in our bewilderment about his meaning, focused on the word "charged." Is it a financial verb, or a military, ethical, electrical one? It is, of course, all of these. Amidst the ambiguity we begin to get a glimmer of what he means by "the grandeur of God." The world in some way—in fact, in many ways—is intimately tied up with divine glory. Bombarded from many angles we are opened to the depth of the divine in nature, as he in fact claims in the next stanza: "nature is never spent;/There lives the dearest freshness deep down things...."[3] Drawn into such depth through metaphors, we feel in touch with that which is really real. Such a metaphor may be a passing one in a poem or may be a central archetype or paradigm for my life or for our culture or perhaps for humanity as such.

Our speaking and thinking and living are unfinished. This is part of the meaning of Quakerism being a non-creedal church. We have no systematic framework or set formula to adhere to, conform to. Rather we live in those connections of which metaphors make us aware. We are bound together historically as a people through various metaphors. Seeing things, from shifting perspectives, as aspects of reality, being borne again and again into the silent depths to experience that evocative mystery, feeling the world and our lives afresh as pervaded by divinity, as sacred—is the Quaker way, the metaphoric way, of words.

Christ as Metaphor

Remembering silence as the source that metaphors come from and carry with them, along with these functions of metaphor we have delineated, we now turn to Christ. The word itself is a metaphor. "Christ" from the Greek and "Messiah" from the Hebrew mean "the Anointed." This religious leader in Jewish expectation and in Christian experience is identified as like a king who is given royal authority by a ritual marking of the head with oil (although the earliest Jewish meaning was literal, a hoped-for successor to King David). To recognize that the word "Christ" itself is a metaphor is to see that at the foundation of Christology is an effort to speak of Jesus through likeness. Jesus is like an anointed king or emperor, anointed by God, the divine king or emperor. This metaphor of royal power, the greatest human power known at that time, carries within itself the silence of what God is beyond this likeness.

Of course, the metaphoric meaning of Christ is lost in the first few centuries of the church as the councils of Nicea and Chalcedon set conceptual boundaries around the word and attempt to name what God and Christ are, rather than what they are like. While concepts can be invaluable in picking out characteristics of things or in distinguishing things, they can also be used, and were used, to deny the silence carried within metaphors and thus to deny their elusive and resonant meaning which overflow any definitive designation of what the divine is.

While Fox nowhere indicates his recognition that "Christ" is a metaphor (although his convincement discovery of "Christ Jesus" rather than "Jesus Christ" suggests "Christ" is a title rather than a last name), nevertheless, his and other early Friends' use of multiple metaphors for Christ recovers the fundamental Jewish and Christian metaphoric meaning of Christ. Thus, to speak of Christ as power and light, seed and inward teacher, is to recover the metaphoric nature of Christ-language in Christian origins. What early Friends experienced of the divine in the inwardness of worship and active living is like these phenomena, yet is richer than any designation. We gain a better sense, I believe, of what it is by speaking, as they did, of more rather than fewer likenesses. Thus, Christ is like light who inside the self shows up the dark places of unresponsiveness to God and illumines the direction it should take. But Christ is also like a seed that germinates out of sight nurtured by darkness and dampness. Christ is also like a person who teaches, although from within. And Christ is like wisdom by whom the world was created and structured with whom we need to be brought into harmony.

The metaphoric character of Fox's speech sheds light on his constant interchange of words for God and Christ. In the quote above Fox speaks of God as power and light, yet many other places he uses these metaphors for Christ. He does not draw sharp boundaries between God and Christ: God is present within us, Christ is the light and seed within, the Holy Spirit moves within us. The reason is that he is speaking metaphorically rather than conceptually. The church's efforts to define the doctrines of the trinity and the two natures of Christ is a conceptual effort. Fox is trinitarian because he speaks of Father, Son, and Holy Spirit, but he is not trinitarian in the usual doctrinal sense because he uses these words, amidst many others, as metaphors rather than restricting their meaning to certain set acceptable ideas. The divine within us is thus like a father, a son, and a spirit, but is also like light, seed, power, and a teacher.

Metaphoric Truth

What then is the truth about God and Christ? The truth is reached in the midst of such a mesh of metaphors. But it is not a concept, not an idea, doctrine, or belief. Rather it is a reality we experience. These metaphors evoke the divine presence; they open us to this reality which is always present but of which we are not always (not usually, for most of us) aware. They bear (*pherein*) us beyond (*meta*) to this reality in the silent depths of ourselves. But they always bear us to some aspect of the divine; through multiple metaphors we are borne into contact with several aspects simultaneously. Without these particular metaphors we would not be in touch with these particular aspects of the divine.

The truth is the reality we experience beneath words (not a correspondence of idea to thing). We can only express it and think about it, however, through words. Our tacit experience of the divine emerges into consciousness as taste, feeling, image, and word. While our experience in the depths is unmediated, our conscious awareness is mediated through these forms, even though the reality cannot be captured within these forms.

The metaphor, for example, of Christ the seed involves the interaction of the divinity of Christ with the naturalness of a seed. In using this metaphor we experience Christ under the aspect of a seed, and a seed under the aspect of divinity, simultaneously. Tension exists because the divine is not really a seed nor is a seed really divine. Nevertheless, we experience the divine as like a seed and a seed as like the divine. In the interaction between these two terms or regions of discourse, we are drawn into this tension, which opens us to two disparate realms of our experience—divinity and seeds—and brings them together within us, or rather makes us aware of their underlying connectedness within us.

In this tension the meaning of a metaphor originates below consciousness; in our being drawn into this tension we have a tacit grasp of its meaning. The meaning enters consciousness, therefore, at first as a feeling or a sense. The very fact it speaks of likeness rather than literal attribution (i.e. of a divine seed rather than a little or black seed) is at first felt intuitively. It may only be through conceptual analysis of the nature of metaphor and how divinity and seed are each being experienced under the aspect of the other that we are able to express in words what is going on in what we originally intuited. The criterion for the truth of such a metaphor is not, however, this conceptual understanding but lies at the level of feeling. There is a feel of fittingness and fruitfulness about speaking of Christ as seed.

This sense comes from our experience of various attractive elements of a seed: its potentiality of growth, smallness, rootedness, beauty of mature growth, and organic wholeness as it draws water out of soil and sunlight out of air. When joined with divinity, we sense the likeness of these characteristics to the divine and feel an aptness and potency in them to express ways in which we relate to the divine. Fox and early Friends spoke of this criterion as life in the spirit rather than adherence to a form, and therefore judged by it whether a person's words or deeds were "in the life" or "out of the life," and thus gone off into forms and notions. The criterion is not an explicit concept (such as the two natures of Christ or justification by faith) to which the term should conform, but is a sense of hidden meaning that can move us and open out to the enriching and transforming of our lives.

Metaphors connect. Through Christ as seed, not only are divinity and nature connected, but I am connected with them, and therefore I am connected with myself through them. I can experience myself under the aspect of both. I am natural as the soil within which the seed Christ dwells and germinates. And by the relational logic of a metaphor's interactive dynamism, I am also a seed dwelling and growing within Christ—within the "hidden Womb of Wisdom," as Isaac Penington put it.[4] But I am also divine as birthed by Christ ("sons" and "children of God" as in Romans 8:14–17 and in John 1:12), or as birthing Christ. Hence Fox and others spoke of themselves as sons and daughters, as children, of God, and of "that of God in everyone,"[5] to indicate a dimension of divinity inherent in our humanity.

The user of metaphor is metamorphosed. I am changed as I connect with the divine and seed-like parts of myself as they interact within me. Experiencing myself as soil for Christ's seed and as seed within Christ's womb, I am changed in my relation to others and to the whole world. Moreover, through metaphoric extension I can experience society and nature as the soil of this seed or as seeds within the divine womb.

Through the interaction of divinity and nature in Christ the seed, this metaphor endorses the interrelation between spirituality and sensuality. They are drawn together by using a natural phenomenon to speak of the divine: a seed can become a vehicle for experiencing the divine. The physical senses are endorsed as the means to know this metaphoric Christ, as Fox eludes the conceptual alignment of one sense with one kind of object (e.g., of sight with the seen) so that, in the passage I quoted in the beginning of this essay, the power is tasted rather than felt, light is felt rather than seen, and winter storms and emptiness are seen through and felt over rather than simply seen and felt. This mixing of the senses (technically called "synaesthesia") expands their capacities beyond objective physical receptivity to their experiential use to discern spiritual presence in others, nature, and within our own embodied selves.

Fox speaks early on in his *Journal* of the corrupt senses—"the false hearing and the false seeing, and the false smelling which was atop, above the Spirit"[6]—and of their renewal in his visionary return to the new creation in which "creation gave another smell unto me than before."[7] This is not a literal but a metaphoric smelling of the divine creation, yet a discerning of the spiritual through the actual use of the physical senses of smelling, seeing, tasting, hearing, and feeling. In his metaphoric approach to Christ and the senses, Fox is eluding the mind/body dualism that was beginning to congeal in the mid-seventeenth century.

Quaker Christology

The truth about God and Christ is the reality we dwell within, or that dwells within us, beneath our awareness, yet which we consciously sense as presence and image in metaphors that feel appropriate and full of life. Through images drawn, like seed, from nature, and, like the anointed king, from society, we are borne by metaphoric movement into contact with the divine deep within. Living by such metaphors, we re-orient our lives towards world, self, and God so that we respond in new ways. Through the seed, for example, we experience self and world in their potentiality of what they might yet grow into. We similarly experience the divine in its potentiality of how it may yet disclose itself in what Friends have called "continuing revelation."

Not only is our living and talking unfinished but our theologies and Christologies are unfinished which the metaphoric way of early Quakers both signals and enables. To maintain and symbolize this unfinishedness, we worship in plain meetinghouses without any traditional Christian symbols. It is not the Spirit's meaning for yesterday as contained in historical signs but the meaning of today that we seek. It is our experience to find it by descending into the silence to discover emerging there new images or old images re-energized. Old metaphors can die by losing their tension. The silence can reinvigorate them and open us to their dynamic resonance that brings us into new connections.

Metaphors are erotic. In Freud's sense of eros, metaphors connect and go on connecting more and more. To the dogmatic spirit this is problematic if not terrifying. The connecting exceeds the order of a rational mind, fusing and confusing things that should rationally be kept separate. Most especially, the self is pulled into the interaction so that it cannot maintain a position of detachment, objectivity, and certainty. A metaphoric approach slips the leash of control. While doctrinal concepts attempt to control meanings, metaphor complexifies and ramifies meanings and touches the user and hearer in unexpected ways. It promotes discovery and creativity rather than conformity and obedience.

The Christ we encounter in Fox and early Friends is metaphoric and metamorphic. It is not dominating and exclusive but welcoming and explorative, not constraining but transforming. The point of the metaphoric Christ is to bear us into the divine presence, not to achieve a right and certain formula about the divine. It is possible to do a conceptual analysis of Christ metaphors as they are used within the Quaker ethos to inquire further what they mean and how they work—as I have attempted here. But such conceptual work should acknowledge the primacy of metaphors and ideas' dependence upon them, as well as the rootedness of both concept and metaphor in our experience in the silence.

To the liberal then, I would offer that Christ can be a major vehicle into the presence of the divine and has been the fertile source for engendering a tradition of images, ideas, stories, and acts that are a way of wisdom from which our life with God can be deepened and broadened. To the evangelical, I would suggest that in this metaphoric way of understanding Christ, one can hold to Christ's centrality for oneself while recognizing that other aspects of the same multi-faceted metaphors or other metaphors altogether may express more fittingly other people's relations to the divine.

The basic criterion for Christological language is the sense of fittingness and fruitfulness for fullness of life that we discover in our ongoing relation to the divine in silence and the other endeavors of our lives. But there are further criteria we can conceive from the way metaphors work and the way Quakers work with metaphors. Speaking of Christ in the Quaker way should connect with, rather than detach from, our multifarious relatedness to all of creation; it should affirm and liberate, rather than dominate and control, life in others and in ourselves; it should enhance, rather than reduce, the fullness of being; it should include, rather than exclude, others and otherness; it should evoke, rather than ignore or obscure, mystery; it should engender, rather than constrain, dialogue of shared experience; and it should elicit trust in, rather than defense against, our being in the world.

We have only spoken of the metaphoric method of Quaker Christology and of a few metaphors used for Christ. There are many more metaphors within the Quaker tradition, as well as within the biblical tradition. Moreover, there is the question of the metaphors and parabolic method that the historical Jesus used, which scholars are working to identify, and those the church attributed to him in the Gospel accounts. And there is the question of what would come from the encounter of Christ's metaphoric approach with the doctrinal approach of the Christian church and evangelical Quakerism. We have not addressed the question of whether the trinity still retains a usefulness within such a metaphoric approach, how to talk of the two natures of Christ, what to say about the substitutionary atonement (rejected by early Friends but so important to evangelical Friends).

Nor have we pressed further into the relationship between word and silence. We need the forms of word, image, and metaphor to focus and give structure to our lives. At the same time we need to acknowledge the formless mystery in which we live and move and have our being out of which these forms emerge. Christ can give a concreteness and shape to our lives through our relating to him as a personal companion. Yet, on the other hand, such companionship can grow too familiar, comfortable, and ego-enhancing so as to deny our commonality with others, our own implication in social injustice, and the vast and often terrifying mystery in which we dwell. Yet, I believe, we as Friends in dialogue can hold together Christ the concrete companion and the unnamable Presence—through the mesh of metaphor.

Meaning in Historical Existence: Modern and Quaker Perspectives

What meaning is there in historical existence and how do we understand it? How do the study of history and the living of spirituality relate? Is there, or should there be, a distinctive approach to the study of history by Quakers?

Jeffrey Dudiak in his address to the Friends Historical Association, "The Meaning of 'Quaker History,'"[1] raises these issues by focusing on the difference, as he sees it, between a modern approach to history and a Quaker approach. A modern approach presents facts; a Quaker approach should explore the meaning in those facts. Facts are accessible to reason used by anyone. Meaning in the facts involves the reality of the inward lived experience of whomever is being studied. The modern approach aspires to an objectivity of what happened detached from the historian's own inwardness, and disregarding the inwardness in the object of study.

A Quaker approach aspires to an understanding of the meaning of what happened by participating in the historical agents' inward experience through being aware of this dimension of inwardness in one's own experience, and how it connects, or doesn't, with the experience of the object of study. The modern approach wants to present the truth without any personal bias distorting it. The Quaker approach recognizes that truth can only be reached through a personal grasp that invariably comes from within a particular perspective that is background to all knowing. One way Dudiak puts what he wants is that Quaker historians should look not merely at *what* happened but *why*?

The example Dudiak gives of a Quaker approach to history is of George Fox, the Younger, finding the meaning of God acting in history in his contemporary events of the Protectorate and Restoration. Dudiak says that Fox "demonstrates to the king how, external appearances notwithstanding, current events were in fact the very arena of God's actions and purposes—something that the Quakers, by means of their exposure and attentiveness to the Light of Christ, were in a unique position to understand … [which] was available to anyone and everyone…."[2]

Responses to Dudiak's address by modern historians, who are Quaker, reject using God as a causal agent in historical explanations. Larry Ingle in "One Historian's Reflections on Philosopher Jeffrey Dudiak's Search for the 'Meaning of Quaker History'" and J. William Frost in "Revealed Truth and Quaker History"[3] both say talk of God acting in history belongs in Quaker meeting for worship not in historical explanations.

Dudiak provides context for their critique. In the seventeenth- and eighteenth-century Enlightenment, philosophers realized that adhering to Reason could transcend the bloody conflicts between Protestants and Catholics. They used critical reason to unhinge facts from ideology, religious belief structures that involved superstition and adherence to traditional dogma, which were at the root of the violent conflict. God acting in history is an idea drawn from scripture and church tradition which Reason shows is not factual and is therefore to be discarded in historical work. Facts and ideas (as interpretations of experience), are put in opposition. Personal experience and theology are therefore excluded from historical explanations.

How then does the person doing history and the person participating in silent meeting for worship connect, especially if it is the same person? Frost provides a clue how to understand this conflict. He refers to H. Richard Niebuhr's distinction between "outer history" and "inner history" in *The Meaning of Revelation*, one of the great theological books of the twentieth century. He refers to Niebuhr's example of the "difference between saying the U.S. was founded 87 years ago and 'our forefathers brought forth a new nation conceived in liberty….'"[4] This distinction between inner and outer, fundamental to early

Friends' writings, Niebuhr encountered in his serious study of seventeenth-century Friends in his first post-conversion book *The Kingdom of God in America* (and as well in his reading of nineteenth-century Lutheran Sören Kierkegaard). He recast this distinction into the language of history pressing to its limits the Kantian dualism between pure (outer) and practical (inner) reason.

How then do inner and outer history relate? Niebuhr suggests several ways in which inner and outer interact.[5] External views can, and should, be *internalized,* so the outer is integrated into the inner view. An example of this is that the painful fact that some Quakers were slave-holders needs to be accepted as part of the historical description of Friends and embraced therefore as part of our Quaker identity. Niebuhr goes on: what truth we know in our inner history can be *an impulsion* towards doing external history, to look for what we know to be true in our experience in the experience of others. Recognizing our own inner history makes us aware of our own *limited perspective* in all knowing and that the reality studied as outer history is richer than it can grasp. Finally, Niebuhr says that all inner history is *embodied* in external history; inner history is not some transcendental realm separate from what is happening in the world.

In conclusion, Niebuhr acknowledges, however, that his "two-aspect theory of history," while affirming "intimate relations of subjective and objective truth," does not resolve the problem of a dualistic split between them. It is only in his final book, *The Responsible Self,* that he resolves it, but not in the language of history but of responsiveness in the relatedness of our being. The outer is underlain by, and emergent from, the unconscious relatedness we exist within as selves and knowers.

Niebuhr's solution is consonant with, and I think influenced by, the thought of Michael Polanyi, whom Niebuhr was reading and teaching in his last years. Polanyi was a physical chemist turned philosopher of science and epistemology. His Gifford

Lectures, *Personal Knowledge: Towards a Post-critical Philosophy*, argue that all knowing, including all scientific knowing, is personal, because all explicit knowing emerges from a creative integrative activity in an unconscious tacit grasp of reality. How he would say this in terms of historical study is that historians immerse themselves in an event they want to understand, tacitly indwelling the various aspects of the event and following clues to how the parts fit together in an explicit pattern.

Niebuhr's thought is also consonant with the philosophy of Merleau-Ponty (whom he was becoming aware of at the end of his life), who in his *Phenomenology of Perception* uses the metaphor of figure and background to understand both our perceiving and knowing. We always focus on a figure against a background, within a context, of which we are pre-reflectively (not explicitly) aware. We inhabit the background unconsciously from which we draw out the figure into visibility. We thus always view historical events against a particular background that provides a certain perspective on the reality.

Niebuhr at the end of his life and these two philosophers in their mature thought are all affirming an experiential base which underlies and enables all knowing. They point a way to combine outer and inner history. Dudiak says that this combining existed among early Friends but has been lost over our three hundred and fifty year history to a one-sided modern approach looking only at the outward facts. It would help if Dudiak could provide a brief history of who these modern historians are who have lost a Quaker lens. I think of two recent outstanding historians among Quakers who explore the inward experience of early Friends as well as the outer events. Both Howard Brinton and Hugh Barbour get at the inward experience (the why) as well as the facts (the what) of early Quaker development.

I am surprised towards the end of his address that Dudiak says that this sharp distinction between objective and subjective rendering of history is "undertaken for heuristic purposes," and "is foreign to the integrated spirituality of Quakerism itself."[6] What he suggests immediately after this confession is that the subjective and objective are held together by what he calls "the story" and its truth. The story for Quakers that continues through the changes from Protectorate to Restoration of monarchy is that "the Kingdom was 'come and coming.'"[7] He says early Friends thought that the establishment of a republic under Cromwell would be the mechanism for this coming, but under the Restoration had to adjust to the facts that the republic would not be the means. He writes:

> As the experience of being in the "end time," with its promise of the immediate return of Christ as king, gave way to that of being in the "mean time," where this promise was put on hold, and Friends had to settle into an arrangement of rightly waiting, there was no immediate abandonment of the conviction that the Kingdom was "come and coming," even if the mechanism of this would, over the next century, increasingly come to be seen as a holy communion built in isolation from (rather than as a conquering of) the impure world.[8]

Dudiak is here making several outer historical claims. He is referring to what modern historians have substantiated as a shift from the original public efforts to transform British society to Quietism at the end of the seventeenth and into the eighteenth century where they withdrew into themselves to lick their wounds, the persecutions having stopped in 1689, and to raise up the next generation of Quakers educated about their own identity.

He interprets the beginning and subsequent shift in traditional Christian apocalyptic terms. As with the early church so with the beginnings of Quakerism, he says, it was believed that Christ would come again in a literal, physical, outward event, that

199

would be the end of history. When this did not happen, a shift occurred in both early Christianity and early Quakerism from living in the "end time" to living in the "mean time," waiting expectantly for the event of Christ's coming to happen in the future.

This is a modern outer historical claim of what early Quakers believed. The textual evidence I am aware of suggests that early Friends did not believe in the literal appearance of the risen Jesus. Rather they emphatically believed that the eternal Christ was present in all hearts as a Seed and that many were opening during the Protectorate to this indwelling presence and learning to live in this dimension of inwardness, the kingdom of God. Their hope was that this transformation would overtake all of Britain, which had some realism about it since by the 1680s one in a hundred in England were Quakers. While we can disagree about what early Friends believed, it is outer history in which we need to look at the evidence in what they said and did.

Similarly, it is an outer historical claim that Friends withdrew into themselves when the republic was replaced by monarchy. Again, I don't see the textual evidence that they reinterpreted the expectation from "now" to living in the "mean time." They continued, as they withdrew from the public arena, to believe that "Christ is come to teach his people himself" — in their hearts, in their individual and communal inwardness, while recognizing all of Britain in the Restoration was not going to dwell in this dimension of the kingdom come. Another outer historical claim: Friends became a "peculiar people," withdrawn from public activism, yet they were, as is evident, very much involved in the eighteenth-century world of business and science.

Making such outer historical claims elicits modern historical responses arguing from the evidence. More specifically, however, what is this story that has continued? Is the essence of Quakerism a story? To raise the question about the essence of Quakerism is to dive into the inward experience of Friends, into inner history. Here the historian's own inwardness comes into play. I think this is one thing Dudiak is recommending to modern Quaker historians: to descend into your own inwardness in order to be able to understand the inwardness in the object of historical study. Do I experience Quakerism as a way of being, and what is at its center? Do I find this dimension of inwardness and the same center in what I am studying, or is it different?

When I enter into my own inwardness as a Quaker, I do not find a story at its center but an experiential depth of reality. When I open to it, dwell within, and act from it, (and here early Friends used many metaphors that are helpful to me), I am illumined about my condition by this reality as Light, transformed by it as Truth, guided by it as Spirit, comforted and shaken by it as Presence. Other Friends today looking within themselves and then looking at early Friends see liberal concerns enacted in seeking peace and justice, or given the post-Reformation Christian language, see evangelical assertions of orthodox belief.

What we have entered into here, however, is no longer outer history by modern historians. We can argue about the center of Quakerism then and now but we have entered into theology, which can argue from textual evidence but is not modern history that focuses on the outer social, political, economic aspects of people and events. The truth modern historians argue about for the most part is not on this theological level, although the inward experience, as Niebuhr says, is embodied in this outer history, from which the inward-looking thinker can benefit. I think Brinton and Barbour both do argue for the inner experiential meaning in the outer aspects of Quaker history, so it has recently been done. They both give textual evidence for the center lying in the dimension of transformative experience, so claim this to be historically true. They also believe it to be truth in their own experience. That is not, however, part of their historical argument, although it could be of a theological argument.

While merely heuristic, I find Dudiak opposing inner and

outer history provocative of my thinking. He says in conclusion that his model for doing Quaker history is Fox's approach to scripture, to read it in the spirit in which it was written. For Fox, it meant living in the Holy Spirit in order to see the Spirit's meaning in the words. This would mean doing Quaker history with an awareness of the Spirit in me and discerning its presence in early Friends.

To resolve Dudiak's heuristic opposition—with Niebuhr, Polanyi, and Merleau-Ponty in the background—I draw from his suggestion for Friends doing Quaker history the following. One is for modern historians to acknowledge that objective history is from a perspective that grasps true aspects of reality but not all aspects of an historical event. An objective description, while avoiding personal bias in getting at the facts, is a personally creative act as committed to its certain methods against a background framework of understanding with certain interests that direct one's attention. Other perspectives discover other aspects of historical truth.

Secondly, to combine outer and inner history, involves descending into one's own inwardness to be able to discern what is going on in the inwardness of the objects of historical study. Recognizing how my own interests shape my outward action, I can be sensitive to what interests (the why) are motivating my historical agents because we really do not understand what the facts mean without understanding persons' and a historical period's interests.

As an example of discerning the inward spirit in an historical complex, consider Niebuhr's distinction between facts about America and the experience of America. Digging into my own orientation, I can discern a spirit in which I live as an American that is the spirit of domination. Sensitive to this spirit I can interpret the facts of American history as an Anglo landgrab from Natives and a building of its wealth upon the free labor of enslaved Africans. Without looking into my own condition, infected as well by this spirit, I so easily stand in judgment of previous periods, while oblivious of my own blind use, or acquiescence to others' use, of power to dominate. Revisionist modern historians might call such a landgrab a fact, but it is clearly an interpretation of, an idea-laden (ideological) take on, the fact of Euro-Americans' western expansion.

Thirdly, while you can challenge modern historians who are Quaker to reflect on the inward dimension of historical existence, that may not be their passion nor their tool set. So it is up to the Friend with the concern to act on it. Do the publicly verifiable factual history and embark on its inward meaning, being honest about the lens you are using.

To do inward history really involves a shift in the language historians use. Outer history is done in the third person. Events and people presented objectively, verifiable by other historians using rational arguments from public evidence, are approached in the third person as he, she, they, its. To go deeper into the inward meaning of events requires shifting to the first person. In the first person it is clear that the historian is personally involved and speaking from a certain perspective shaped by tacit commitments. In the third person such tacit commitments are hidden. To speak in the first person is to leave the apparent certainties of modern history to engage in the acknowledged uncertainties and ambiguities of experiential reflection.

The attitude is different. In the third person I am arguing what is the case, hoping to demonstrate I have it right, and you should succumb to my superior rationality because the way I have organized the facts is the way it really is. In the first person, I am sharing rather than arguing, asking the reader to reflect on their own inwardness to confirm what I say or provide new insight about it from which I can learn. This could be called theological history, although modern theology is usually done in the objective mode to establish objective truth. Quaker historians who are combining inner experiential and outer modern history would be doing this kind of personal theological history. Only the factual part of a theological historical argument can be verified by organizing publicly available evidence. The inward part can be communally confirmed by others who have the same experience and use the same lens. While confirmable as truth of existence, which matters to our very being in the world, it is not factual truth.

What then do we do with the idea of God acting in history? Frost applies the theological word *Heilsgeschichte*, which means salvation history, to Niebuhr's inner history. This mistaken application shows his lack of understanding of what Niebuhr means by inner history. Salvation history is presented by Christian theologians as the objective facts of God's action in history—creation, redemption, and consummation of the world. Making such truth claims as factual is what modern historians rightly reject using the tools of historical rationality because these claims are not publicly verifiable (that is, rationally accessible to anyone using reason). In the modern perspective these are unsubstantiated beliefs, which are merely subjective and do not carry the weight of truth that verifiable facts do.

Niebuhr says God acting in history is not evident in outer history. That is his way of saying God is excluded as a cause in modern history. Revelation is not a factual event. Had we been there when God spoke to Moses, we would not have heard anything. It was an experience in inner history. God works in our subjectivity. We experience things deep in our personal being; some interpret them as divine action in us. That is what early Friends were doing as they discovered themselves searched and guided by what they named, from the Gospel of John, as the Light. Discovering such reality in themselves, they looked to see it in the world around them. This is what George Fox, the Younger, was doing as he appealed to the newly restored Charles II to understand the inner meaning of what was visibly happening in outer history. Fox was urging a particular religious interpretation of events that the king and others were interpreting only in social and political terms. It was a conflict of interpretations.

While communally verifiable by others who are similarly aware in their inwardness of such action, divine action is not publicly, empirically verifiable, which reason requires. No doubt one can be deluded about what one is finding in one's experience, which critical reason happily points out, and of which history is rank with examples. And one's whole community can be deluded. The European community was deluded at the beginning of the twentieth century using reason to set up a rational system of alliances that would protect them from violence, which when activated precipitated World War I. Similarly, the European community was deluded by the Ptolemaic explanation of the universe.

In any case, what is happening in inwardness is always being interpreted. So also is outer history interpretive. Both kinds of interpretation are grounded in our personal capacities, interests, methods of approach, and frameworks of understanding to which we are tacitly committed.

While seventeenth-century Friends were using Protestant biblical language to present their experience, they were developing an epistemology, theology, and spirituality divergent from the direction modern thought was taking. Whether scientific, historical, or theological, the direction of modernity was to embrace Cartesian dualism that separates and subordinates the subjective to the objective. Early Friends chose rather to hold the subjective and objective, the inner and outer, together as the outer emerges from and is grounded in the inner. They did this by speaking in the first person.

What this meant about God acting in history is that for early Friends God was real as they experienced God acting in their hearts and potentially in the hearts of all the historical actors. The modern dualism of objective and subjective was being put in place but was not yet set so that Friends would not have distinguished between outer and inner historical truth. From my perspective, inheriting this dualism, I would say that God for early Friends was not an objective Entity whose factuality could be argued for or against through reason appealing to empirical evidence or scripture. God was the Mystery they encountered in their own inward experience as they lived in the world which was a presence that illumined their condition and that of the world, transformed them from ego-dominated lives, and guided them into challenging the oppressive social hierarchy (religious and political) of their time and speaking to the inward dimension of depth in those they met.

From my Quaker philosophical perspective, I would say everyone was responding to underlying Mystery in their individual, political, economic lives and the structures they set up. George Fox the Younger was not writing history but addressing his contemporary situation as biblical prophets did, saying what was really happening (that means in the depths of experience) in his present situation. Modern historians may be iconoclastic but they are not inclined to be prophetic. Modern historians could reflect theologically on how historical events are a manifestation of some way of relating to Mystery (usually as defense and denial). This cannot happen, however, without letting go of their detached approach and opening to their own inwardness to become aware of how they relate to Mystery. In that light they can then explore how God was acting in history by exploring how the Protectorate and Restoration responded to Mystery in what they did and said.

This, however, is theological not modern history. So what is the problem with modern historians doing what they do, which is often invaluable in opening our eyes to aspects of reality of which we were not aware or intentionally overlooked and denied? The problem I think Dudiak is concerned about is that the objective picture of modern historical writing, and of modern scientific thinking, can lead to a sense that the real context of our lives is meaningless or overwhelmingly oppressive as we identify only with the facts of our existence, rather than the richness of our experiential knowledge, as definitive of who we are.

If only the objective is true, then we had better seek to satisfy our desires by creating meaning by controlling as much of our lives as we can. To control others leads into domination and violence. There is a greater richness in our historical existence than the factual account portrays. To open to the richness of our inward lives as a true part of reality can engender learning to live humbly with uncertainty, to feel and inhabit our relatedness with all of being, to trust our capacities of creativity to carry us further into truth in thought and action, and to make us aware of our limited perspective on reality — that is, to make us feel at home in the world.

What is the meaning of our historical existence is a burning issue today as everything seems to be commodified, the purpose of life seems to be to satisfy my desires and defend against the Other's restrictions on me, as we live in America which seeks to dominate the world militarily and economically as the latest and greatest empire of all time. How then do we get at what is really true about our world and ourselves, what are the factual and personal realities we are living within? Why else engage in historical study but to know more of the breadth and depths of who we were, of the history from which we have come, and thus who we are? To engage our whole self and our whole world, outer and inner, will give us a fuller view of the reality, the truth, of our existence that can enrich and transform us.

To See Jesus in Holy Land Travails

We traveled to Israel-Palestine at the end of September 2009 for three weeks to see the situation ourselves, to show our caring for the people we would meet, and to see the sites where Jesus had (most likely) been.

But Jesus was hard to see, as churches had been built over many of the sites. After trying to wrestle through the overlay unsuccessfully to see how the terrain would have appeared to Jesus, I finally relaxed and enjoyed the ancient structures: the Church of the Nativity in Bethlehem, considered to be the site of Jesus' birth; Church of the Holy Sepulcher in Old Jerusalem, presumably over Golgotha; and Church of the Annunciation in Nazareth, one of the two spots (Catholic; the Greek Orthodox have another site) where Gabriel brought Mary news of her pregnancy.

In the north around the Sea of Galilee, I could get a better sense of Jesus having been there. Peter's house in Capernaum, where Jesus stayed and healed Peter's sick mother-in-law, could well be historically accurate. The beautiful modern church built over it is elevated so you can see the results of the archaeological dig. I could easily imagine Jesus living in this village, boating on the big lake, and walking from there across Galilee to preach and heal.

Jesus came from Nazareth, a town of 200–400 people, not big enough to have a synagogue building. A poor carpenter, he obviously made a tremendous impact on the residents of Galilee. Mark's Gospel, which I read as my wife and I traveled (or "travailed," the word is the same in mid-seventeenth-century Quaker English), speaks repeatedly of people being "amazed."

It came to me, however, as I looked at this semi-arid, rock-strewn landscape and beautiful lake, that it could have been different. Other peasant leaders had arisen and died in obscurity, and it could have happened to Jesus. He was human, like us (the creeds say "fully human"). And his life, like ours, was chancy.

Yet his contingent life has been transformative for many, and so he has been remembered and honored by the construction of churches over the places associated with his life. I understand that impulse, but to me these architectural structures obscure the concreteness and contingency of Jesus, freezing him in stone. Similarly, dogmatic structures have been erected over the contingent Jesus. They claim that what Jesus did was all part of God's eternal plan. God foresaw and willed it all: birth, life, crucifixion, and resurrection.

These impositions of architectural and doctrinal structures over Jesus' chancy existence are intended to make us feel secure in the divine inevitability of a cosmic plan. But such certitude of divine manipulation obscures the spontaneity of Jesus' decisions and interactions with God and the context that made up the weave of his life.

It is as though Jesus could not be as significant as he is, the Savior for millions, unless what happened was planned. But why is something only of eternal importance if it is the result of a plan? Are not our lives of eternal moment, even though our being born and how we have interacted with our human and natural environment consist of considerable chance? Is not my meeting and marrying my wife, Beth, of eternal value even though there was no cosmic plan? Is not the beauty of this autumnal day refulgent with divine presence even though it is the result of meteorological concatenations? Even if my parents planned to have a child, they did not plan to have me, and yet I experience my life as rife with meaning.

The need for a plan to justify significance is similarly at play in the Creationists' view of evolution. The creation of our world could not hold the value it does for us without God's plan and manipulation.

Why do we fixate on being and control? Can we fully feel and celebrate the wonder of becoming human in our world, of our emergence out of the mystery of being?

Waiting in silence in a Quaker meeting is an event of contingency par excellence. Without a plan or guiding structures of liturgy or symbols, we open to the sheer chance and spontaneity of what will emerge out of the formless depths. Friends should be experienced with the plan-less contingency of divine agency.

Jesus' life was similarly contingent and spontaneous, and he used his own Jewish heritage and God-given capacities to interact with what was given. What a wonder that such beauty and power should exist, and take fire among so many. That the power we know in our depths should be shaped by what we know about him in and outside the New Testament is cause for wonder—without recourse to a plan that explains it.

In our travels, we not only encountered structures of architecture and dogma imposed on the simple and amazing transformative life of Jesus, we also felt the travails of those living under political imposition. Palestinians living in Bethlehem (whether Christian or Muslim) are not permitted to travel the ten miles to their holy city of Jerusalem. Palestinians living in Old Jerusalem cannot leave without being forbidden to return. The Wall (or "Security Fence") divides families from each other and farmers from their farmlands. An Israeli citizen, upon returning to Tel Aviv after seeing her new grandson in Houston, was body searched—including between her toes—because she was Arab. When she asked the guard, "Is this a matter of security?" the woman replied, "We don't argue." She then asked, "But how does this make you feel?" and was answered, "We don't feel."

Soldiers with rifles standing in clumps around the Old City may feel to Palestinians the way 2,000 years ago Roman soldiers with spears standing around the same city may have felt to the Jews of that time. The occupation of, and building settlements in, Palestine makes me think of what our Euro-American ancestors did to Native Americans through "manifest destiny" in the nineteenth century.

We looked for Jesus in these travels and travails. Jesus drew heavily upon the "law and the prophets" in his understanding of love of God and neighbor.[1] The words of an earlier inhabitant of Jerusalem, a prophet with whom Jesus was no doubt familiar came to me: "Do justice and righteousness, and deliver from the hand of the oppressor him who has been robbed. And do no wrong or violence to the alien, the fatherless, and the widow, nor shed innocent blood in this place."[2] In Torah (the law) God says: "The land is mine; for you are strangers and sojourners with me."[3] The Jewish people after all, long before Jesus took up the theme, introduced justice as a divine mandate to the world.

While my seeing Jesus was obstructed by the overlay of architecture, dogma, and politics, I could feel his spirit shaped by his Hebraic sense of justice and the presence of God. I could feel the contingency of this unique—and for many centrally significant—revelation of divine love, creativity, and justice. In his experience of God he knew that no structure—especially the political—is permanent. His spirit speaking within my spirit drew me down into the depths of love and held forth the potential for these travails and hardheartedness to change towards the inclusion of the "other" within a shared existence. Sinking into silence beneath all these structures (what early Friends called "forms"), I know the power—whether given Christian, Jewish, or Muslim names—that can transform individual and social structures, making us all Children of Light.

Resurrection for Paul, Mark, and Friends

Traveling once again in England, to places we had lived and loved, visiting old friends, my wife and I found ourselves on Good Friday spending time at Durham Cathedral where we had been able to spend only two hours long ago. On Easter Sunday afternoon we were back in our neighborhood minster in York. Between these on Easter Morning we were again worshiping at our "home" York Friends Meeting, no longer "Clifford Street," now "Friargate." Prior to Easter weekend, staying with friends on their dairy farm we inhabited thirty-five years ago, we met new f/Friends, through an American Friend, who invited us to worship-sharing in their home on the theme of resurrection. Amidst the warm hospitality of Roswitha and Peter Jarmin, the Friends gathered were focused by Peter on the question: What does the resurrection mean to you?

An important and difficult subject I have wrestled with through the years, what emerged for me then, reflected upon further in the intervening year, speaks to my own condition, and hopefully to others', of a Friends way to embrace resurrection and to understand it in Paul and Mark.

The earliest written account of the resurrection is Paul's in Galatians. He says he experienced Christ "*in* me." Invariably this is translated as "*to* me": God "was pleased to reveal his Son to me,"[1] even though footnotes now appear in translations that brazenly say the Greek is "in." Which preposition makes a big difference. If "to me," then the appearance is external and particular to Paul. If "in me," then the appearance is available to all in each's own inwardness. If Christ's risen appearance is in inwardness, then there is no need for the mediation of, nor control by, the Church. Nor is it a matter of belief, to get right, but of experience, to open to.

I am aware reading New Testament scholarship[2] that the

representations of Jesus' resurrection become increasingly physical, as we move from early to late. Paul, in his own account in Galatians of Christ "in me" sees no visible figure appearing to him as the risen Christ. The earliest canonical Gospel, Mark, coming some thirty-five years after Paul's experience, like Paul, does not have a visible appearance but only an empty tomb. Scholars are clear that the appearance of the risen Christ in Mk 16:9–20 is a later addition. By the time you get to the Gospel of John, we have Thomas sticking his hand in Jesus' side. The more material, substantial, the more the Church controls the event, its meaning, its effects, because it only happened to these followers, and we only know about it because the Church records and owns it.

Who is this risen "Christ" whom Paul experiences in inwardness? As a title applied to him, what after all is Jesus' view of "Christ"? In working on the Gospel of Mark, I find it significantly different from the later gospels. Mark's Jesus seems to have real ambivalence about this title of "Christ." In fact he gets mad at Peter after he identifies Jesus as the Christ. Jesus immediately responds after Peter's confession by speaking of the suffering that will be endured by "the Son of the man." Mark's Peter responds with shock and anger at the suggestion that Jesus, the Son of the man, will suffer, to which Jesus responds with even greater anger, calling Peter "Satan."[3]

Matthew's Jesus, contrary to Mark's, does not get angry at Peter nor speak of suffering, but affirms Peter's identification of Jesus as the Christ, and expansively endorses Peter as the foundation of the church and wielder of the keys of the kingdom.[4] Matthew's Jesus does not have the ambivalence that Mark's does about "Christ." Where Matthew has Jesus institute the Church with Peter as its leader, Mark's Jesus strangely diverts Peter's designation of Christ to talk, not about the Church, but about the Son of the man, a phrase Matthew's Jesus does not use here, and about this Son's death and resurrection.

Jesus in Mark would seem to have ambivalence about this title, "the Son of the man," as well, though less so than about "Christ." Strange to ask someone who you think you are, and then when you get an answer, "Christ," to talk about "the Son of the man," and in such a way that suggests this Son is other than yourself. Jesus, it becomes clear by the end of the Gospel, is obliquely referring to himself with this title of Son of the man, but why such obliqueness, if not some ambivalence?

Once again, the translators have left out a Greek word, for Jesus' use of this title throughout the canonical gospels has "*the* man." Walter Wink argues persuasively this refers to Ezekiel's vision of God as "the man."[5] Ezekiel sees God in human form. If God appears imaged as human, then humanity is revelatory of divinity. "Son of the man" is a way then of saying simply human being, son of "the man," that is child of God. We Friends speak similarly of humanity as revelatory of divinity by speaking of "that of God in everyone" and the Light within. Perhaps Ezekiel's vision of God imaged as human is the basis of the subsequent P author of Genesis 1 saying we are made in God's image.[6] Jesus would then be referring to himself as a human being, a child of God, an actualization of the *imago dei*, the epitome for Mark of what it is to be fully human. In his reply to Peter, Jesus links suffering, death, and resurrection with being human. His talk then of death and resurrection of this seemingly other being, the Son of the man, is not only about himself but about divinely revealed humanity, what authentic humans undergo, such as what Paul will experience in the death of his old self and birth of new being.

Jesus predicts in Mark at Peter's confession that the Son of the man will be killed and raised.[7] In the Garden of Gethsemane Jesus anticipates his own death and resurrection: "But after I am raised up, I will go before you to Galilee."[8] Then at the empty tomb the three women are told by a young man that "Jesus of Nazareth ... has risen" and "is going before you to Galilee, there you will see him, as he told you" (Mk 16:6–7). Not seen in Mark, the risen Jesus, who is Son of the man (no mention of Christ), it is promised, will be seen when you get home to Galilee. Home is then the place to experience resurrection, not at a tomb.

In the Hebrew Bible there is no indication that the Son of man (no "*the* man") or the Christ will suffer. Isaiah speaks of the Suffering Servant but Isaiah does not connect this with the Son of man. Christ, of course, means "the anointed one," which is applied to various kings and prophets, some of whom suffer, but the word itself does not carry the meaning of suffering. In Mark, Jesus does seem to be making these connections. Perhaps Jesus' seeming ambivalence about the title "Christ" is because he wants to redefine these terms in order to connect them with suffering, or because, like Friends, he rejects all titles. Something else is more important than titles, than who Jesus is. But what?

Jesus at his baptism in Mark experiences in inwardness, without public display reported in later gospels, the Spirit entering his life. What ensues in the Gospel shows Jesus as living in and guided by Spirit. If in his own mind (according to Mark), Jesus manifests the essence of human being as Son of the man, then his life, death, and resurrection are a model for all human beings: to live in the Spirit that has filled him.

Jesus' message with which he begins his ministry in Mark is not, however, it would appear, a call to live in Spirit but a call to repentance, as the kingdom of God is near now in the fullness of time. "Repentance" is rightly translated as renewed or transformed mind, but a deeper meaning lies in its literal components: *meta* beyond and *noia* mind. Jesus proclaims a life that is "beyond-mind": that lets go of what we call ego in order to be filled with and led by Spirit. Letting go of ego is a death, and living in Spirit is a resurrection. This is coming home to authentic human being-ness, a child of God.

Mark's Jesus models what Paul experiences of Christ "in" him: to die to his old self and be filled with the Holy Spirit as a new way of being. The Spirit that fills Jesus in living and dying to an unexcelled fullness—as early Friends would say—confronts, transforms, fills, and guides Paul as he is drawn beyond mind, letting go of his framework of understanding and action, to discover in his depths of inwardness Christ "in me." "Christ in me" is not an appearance "to me" of an external divine figure but is indwelling Spirit; as Paul says: "Now the Lord is the Spirit."[9] Experiencing death of his old mind-controlled life, what he calls "flesh," Paul is raised to new life beyond mind in the Spirit: "But you are not in the flesh, you are in the Spirit, if the Spirit of God really dwells in you."[10]

Whatever else the empty tomb means, it is emptiness without the figure of Christ to look at. The condition of beyond-mind is similarly an emptiness that has slipped beneath all figures. The empty tomb terrifies the two Marys and Salome. The Gospel ends with them fleeing with "trembling and astonishment," the last word being fear: "and they said nothing to any one, for they were afraid."[11] This fear is the overwhelming sense of awe that comes in encounter with the sacred beyond mind. Before this sacred emptiness, they can only be silent. It is this same overwhelming sacred silence *in* Paul in which he encounters, and is shattered by, the risen Christ as Spirit within. Just as the disciples must go home to Galilee to experience the risen Christ, so Paul discovers Christ as he comes home to his true self in his depths. The "good news" he preaches is the availability of what he has experienced within: resurrection by divine agency into new life in the Spirit.

"Resurrection" is a big theological term that can carry us away into strident arguments. I see early Friends, unafraid of such doctrines, approaching them to discern experiential depth in them. If we get pulled away into questions of belief—such as did Jesus rise bodily (which Paul denies in affirming resurrection of a spiritual not a physical body,[12] as he knows from his own experience)—we are diverted from the real issue for Jesus, Paul, and Mark: to let go of our ego control and open to living in the depths of our spirit in which dwells the Holy Spirit as Inward Teacher.

To live beyond-mind, is this not at the heart of Quaker spirituality, as George Fox enjoins us: "Be still and cool in thy own mind and spirit from thy own thoughts, and then thou wilt feel the principle of God to turn thy mind to the Lord God ..."?[13]

Resurrection, Roswitha and Peter, is then for me, as far as I have come after a life-time of search and a year of seasoning my words spoken in your living room, the new life of ongoing transformation that opens as I let go of my mind-controlled life and "sink down to the seed," as Isaac Penington would say,[14] as I come home to the depths of my life in the world, in which the Spirit confronts, fills, and guides me. This is resurrection, it strikes me, as Jesus lived it, Paul experienced it, and Mark represents it. Here is a way Friends can speak of it, and the way that is opening for me: the Spirit of Jesus, the Spirit in which Jesus lived, is that resurrection reality I find "in me."

"I Knew Him Not but by Revelation": A Hermeneutics of Inwardness and the Ethics of Same-Sex Love

Early Friends were clear that scripture is a secondary authority dependent on the primary authority of the Spirit. This subordination of scripture has resulted, however, in an uncertainty in the subsequent history of Quakerism of how to approach scripture. Evangelical Quakers in the nineteenth century responded to this uncertainty by moving into the mainstream Protestant approach that conceives scripture as the primary and objective authority. Liberal Quakers in the twentieth century have responded by discarding scripture altogether as any kind of authority.

In our current engagement with controversial social issues, such as same-sex love, evangelicals claim the Bible as an objective authority to support their exclusivistic judgments. Liberals concede the biblical terrain to the evangelicals and assert their inclusive judgments without recourse to the formative texts at the spiritual foundations of the west. We could be helped by finding another approach to scripture that would draw upon its resources but in a non-objectivistic and secondary way for ethical decision making.

The real, though secondary, authority of scriptural texts depended for early Friends upon the primary authority of the Holy Spirit. Words issue from Spirit, as the biblical writers wrote as they were led by the indwelling Spirit. Being led to speak by and in the Spirit resulted in words bearing and expressing this Spirit. In order to interpret these words aright it is necessary to be in that Spirit in which they were written, since their meaning is not only their explicit content but their spirit. To use these words but to be in a different spirit was to have missed their true meaning. George Fox and other early Friends spoke of this problem of the relation between spirit, word, and interpreter generally in the language of "inward" and "outward."

To understand the early Quaker approach to the Bible, we must understand the meaning of inward and outward. Their meaning is made more difficult, however, by the fact that Fox and other Friends used various word pairs—such as spirit and flesh, the law of God and the law of sin and death, spirit and letter (or light and letter), life and form (or power and form)—to express different aspects of this distinction, yet the words are often used interchangeably. Nevertheless, even though a word pair does not consistently mean one aspect, we can use these word pairs to get at the different aspects of inward and outward. To understand the early Quaker approach to the Bible, which took it with seriousness but not as primary, we must explore the meaning of the inwardness of the spirit and the outwardness of the word, as the outward word issues from and is rooted in the inwardness of spirit, and as the same outward word, if rooted in some other spirit, is rejected as an empty form. In such a "hermeneutics of inwardness"—an interpretive approach in and about inwardness—I believe, we find an alternative approach to the Bible which helped sustain early Friends spiritually in their work for justice and which can similarly assist us in our efforts to overcome the social system that oppresses homosexuals.

The Experiential Basis of Quaker Hermeneutics

In Fox's account of his convincement in his *Journal* he makes it clear that his discovery of Christ within came only when he despaired of outward help. He says: "And when all my hopes in them and in all men were gone, so that I had nothing outwardly to help me, nor could tell what to do," then he hears a voice that says "There is one, even Christ Jesus, that can speak to thy condition." "Inward" here simply put means what is going on in the psyche of the self, while "outward" means other people and things which are outside the self. Inwardness is, therefore, experiential. He concludes this account by saying of his new knowing—"And this I knew experimentally."[1]

Immediately following, Fox distinguishes his experiential knowing of Christ from scriptural knowledge of him:

> My desires after the Lord grew stronger, and zeal in the pure knowledge of God and of Christ alone, without the help of any man, book, or writing. For though I read the Scriptures that spoke of Christ and of God, yet *I knew him not but by revelation*, as he who hath the key did open, and as the Father of life drew me to his Son by his spirit. And then the Lord did gently lead me along, and did let me see his love, which was endless and eternal, and surpasseth all the knowledge that men have in the natural state, or can get by history or books; and that love let me see myself as I was without him. And I was afraid of all company, for I saw them perfectly where they were, through the love of God which let me see myself.[2]

Now this is an extraordinary passage and central to our exploration, and obviously important to Fox because he reiterates it immediately after his experience of the cosmic implications of his convincement a year later in his return to the New Creation:

> Now the Lord God hath opened to me by his invisible power how that every man was enlightened by the divine light of Christ; and I saw it shine through all…. This I saw in the pure openings of the Light without the help of any man, neither did I then know where to find it in the Scriptures; though afterwards, searching the Scriptures, I found it. For I saw in that Light and Spirit which was before Scripture was given forth, and which led the holy men of God to give them forth, that all must come to that Spirit, if they would know God, or Christ, or the Scriptures aright, which they that gave them forth were led and taught by.[3]

What is extraordinary about this is that Fox is saying he knew Christ through revelation but not through scripture, and that what he had known before of Christ through scripture was not revelation, even though he later could find in scripture what he had experienced. The distinction he is making is between revelation as inward (an experience of the divine reality within the psyche) and scripture as outward (an entity outside the self). Inward and outward involve two different kinds of knowing. Quaker hermeneutics has to do with this dimension of experiential knowing within and its relation to the outward words of scripture.

Revelation in Inwardness

But what does Fox mean by "revelation" and what does he realize in and through revelation? While "revelation" in mainstream Protestantism means divine truth disclosed by God in the scriptures, here it means the presence of God within Fox's own inward experience — opening the meaning of scripture, drawing into more intimate contact with divinity, leading into awareness of the loving nature of God, and bringing into an understanding of self and others.

Within this divine immediacy Fox becomes aware of things about God, self, Christ, and others. He realizes about God that the divine is present in his living, acts on him as "the Father of life" drawing him "to his Son by his spirit," speaks to his condition, empowers him, and is unchangeable and endlessly loving in his nature. About himself he realizes that he "was in the deep, under all shut up,"[4] on the verge of despairing of ever overcoming his troubles and temptations. He discovers "two thirsts" within himself, "one after the creatures, to have gotten help and strength there, and the other after the Lord...." Then he finds that he has been joined to the Lord in letting go of his search for help outside—"my inward mind being joined to his good Seed" so that "this inward life did spring up in me," enabling him to answer his opponents and "bring in Scriptures to my memory to refute them with."[5]

About Christ, Fox realizes how Christ opened him to light and life. In Christ being "tempted by the same Devil" and overcoming, Fox received confidence of similarly overcoming. Christ enlightened him and gave him faith, hope, spirit, and grace—belief in the light that was enlightening him, "hope, which is himself"[6] (i.e. hope which is the substance of Christ's presence within), spirit as Christ's Spirit "revealed himself in me," and grace which he "found sufficient in the deeps and in weakness."[7]

About others he realizes how "all are concluded under sin,"[8] how "people's minds do run in the earthly, after the creatures and changeable things, and changeable ways...."[9] This is the life of "fleshly things or words,"[10] the life of death that "had passed upon all men and oppressed the Seed of God in man and in me...."[11] Inward revelation means, then, the divine presence within the psyche issuing in insight that comes in the midst of our relatedness to self and others as we open ourselves to immediate experience of this presence.

The Phenomena of Outwardness: Flesh, Law, Letter, and Form

Inward revelation is set over against the phenomena of outwardness. In order to understand the hermeneutics of inwardness we must understand what Fox means by outward. While he often speaks of flesh, law, letter, and form interchangeably, he uses them to get at four distinguishable aspects of outwardness: *flesh* (self-will resulting in conformity), *law* (an external commandment or standard), *letter* (words detached from self and God), and *form* (any objective pattern not seen as part of a larger divine whole).

The *flesh*, he says, is the self "that could not give up to the will of God," that "could not give up self to die by the Cross."[12]

This uncrucified self is a "veiled" self, clouded both from itself and from the presence of Christ within the self: Fox says that the flesh "did veil me ... from the presence of Christ."[13] The fleshly self is a self enclosed upon itself, directing itself out of its own ego-consciousness, and not open to its own depths, within which it could find the presence of Christ. Its life is impatience amidst "all trials, troubles and anguishes and perplexities"[14] of existence. And its knowing is conformist: "And while there is this knowledge in the flesh, deceit and self-will conform to anything, and will say, 'Yes, yes,' to that it doth not know."[15]

Most especially what it does not know because it is veiled from within, and yet says "Yes" to, are self and Christ without as represented in the scripture. Such knowledge of scripture, while veiled from the human and divine depths within, is "fleshly knowledge": "The knowledge which the world hath of what the prophets and apostles spake is a fleshly knowledge...."[16] Rather than grounding itself in the presence of Christ in the self's own depths, fleshly knowing seeks its security in conforming to something outside itself, and thus ends in "deceit." We are deceived in mistakenly thinking Christ is an external entity when it is an inward reality.

The result is confusion and lust—a life in conflict as it seeks to satisfy the desires of its own will: "And so they all lie in confusion and are making provision for the flesh, to fulfil the lusts thereof, but not to fulfil the law and command of Christ in his power and spirit...."[17] Having drawn boundaries around the self so as to locate the divine outside the self rather than in its depths, the self is separated from the power of God so that it cannot fulfill the law of Christ. Separated from the divine power within, it operates out of the power of this surface self, "to fulfil the lusts of the flesh ... with delight."[18] Alienated from the divine within, the self lives a life of desire for what it does not have outside itself.

The discussion of flesh easily moves into discussion of *law*, but law is not simply allied with flesh since Fox speaks of two kinds of law: the law of sin and death (which is bondage to the flesh) and the law of God (or the law of the Spirit). Law as such means a standard to obey, an external commandment to conform to, and hence a means by which to judge this conformity. While the law of God for Fox has obligatory and judgmental functions, it is not a commandment but an active reality—the reality of love. Fox says: "I saw this law was the pure love of God...."[19] God's nature is love and because God indwells the self, this love resides within selves, setting up a resonance between God and self: "the law of God that is perfect answers the perfect principle of God in every one."[20]

This law of God as the reality of divine love, nevertheless, by its nature has the consequence to oblige and judge. Fox's view of God's law has the same three functions of law that John Calvin delineates. In agreement with Martin Luther, Calvin speaks of the first two uses of the law to condemn and to constrain, to which he adds his own "third use of the law"—to transform. Fox experiences divine love, in his struggles just after his convincement, in its condemning function of law:

I saw this law was the pure love of God which was upon me, and which I must go through, though I was troubled while I was under it; for I could not be dead to the law but through the law which did judge and condemn that which is to be condemned.[21]... Though they may have his light [like God's law of love] to condemn them that hate it....[22]

He realizes, as well, its constraining nature: "The pure and perfect law of God is over the flesh to keep it and its works, which are not perfect, under, by the perfect law."[23] And he knows its transforming character:

And as you are brought into the law, and through the law

224

to be dead to it, and witness the righteousness of the law fulfilled in you, ye will afterwards come to know what it is to be brought into the faith, and through faith from under the law. And abiding in the faith which Christ is the author of, ye will have peace and access to God.[24]

The difference between Calvin and Fox on the meaning of these three uses of the law lies, however, precisely in Fox's advocacy of inwardness. While the law for Calvin is outward as explicit standard and verbal commandment to which we are to conform, the law for Fox is inward as the love of God dwelling in our depths. Hence it is the loving presence of God in the self that is condemning, constraining, and transforming. By transformation Calvin means that real progress is made, individually and communally, in becoming righteous, but we still continue to sin, because the redemptive power is in the objective event of Christ's crucifixion, to which we are not wholly conformed.

By transformation Fox means, on the contrary, that the indwelling redemptive power pervades our lives changing all of it so that we live with a moment to moment responsiveness to the divine reality within, which is "perfection." If we experience the presence of divine love, not as an external standard, but as an inward reality, we become aware of the contrast of our life with this reality—thus being condemned and constrained—but in this very act of awareness we can open to this reality and be transformed into a love-responsive being so that, as Fox says, "the righteousness of the law [is] fulfilled in you."[25]

We can see then how talk of flesh is closely related to, yet distinguishable from, talk of law. The flesh is outward in seeking to conform to external words, inasmuch as it grounds itself, not in the self's own inward depths, but in an encapsulated self-will which in its lusts is constantly looking outside itself. The law is outward when interpreted as an external standard demanding conformity to divine righteousness. Rather than seeing the law as the internal possibility of divine love in our being, the self projects this reality outside turning it into an external obligation.

Letter as a third aspect of outwardness is about words that are detached from either actions or a spiritual source. Words that are mere talk without action and without appropriate action are the simplest exemplification of the letter. Fox speaks of people who "lived in their airy notions, talking" of Christ,[26] who "lived in words but that God Almighty looked for fruits,"[27] and who "hold a talk of the Lord's words but [do not] practise them."[28] Some of these talkers do in fact act but their actions are not in the spirit of the words they speak; rather their words accompany beatings, persecutions, and unjust imprisonments. As Fox says: "they that had not the life, but the words, persecuted and imprisoned them that lived the life...."[29]

Letter, more profoundly, means words separated from a spiritual source. A letter is outside one's own experience: the "talking of other men's words,"[30] the "knowledge that men have in the natural state, or can get by history or books,"[31] and the speaking of "a notionist ... [who is] not in possession of what he talked of."[32] As such, the letter is detached from one's own spiritual source—the presence and power of God within. The Ranters and their speech, for Fox, illustrate this detachment:

[T]hey did not wait upon God to feel his power to gather their minds together to feel his presence and power and therein to sit to wait upon him, for they had spoken themselves dry and had spent their portions and not lived in that which they spake...."[33]

But so also do those in the established church illustrate it: they are "apostates from the life in which the prophets and apostles were, [and] have gotten their words, the Holy Scriptures, in a form, but not in their life nor spirit that gave them forth."[34]

To adhere to the letter is, therefore, to relate to biblical words in such a way that they are not grounded in the divine presence within one's own self and do not issue from this Spirit from which they originally came forth. Rather they express some other spirit. If propelled by the flesh, the words will be used in such a way as to manifest self-will in pursuit of satisfying its lusts for what it has not. If propelled by the law of sin and death, the words will turn our attention to an external standard and motivate efforts to conform to it. In either case these spirits draw us away from the divine reality in our depths.

The words may still have the same content, may still be about God and Christ; but expressing a spirit other than the Spirit of God, they can lead into the inaction of mere talk or the action of violence towards others. Fox speaks of having a sense of discerning whether religious words are spoken in the Spirit of God or another spirit: "I had a sense and discerning given me by the Lord, through which I saw plainly that when many people talked of God and of Christ, etc., the Serpent spoke in them...."[35] The letter means, therefore, biblical words severed from their spiritual origins of the indwelling presence of God, which are being used in some other spirit than the original Spirit—which, as we shall see, is the spirit of love.

The fourth aspect of outwardness, a *form*, draws our attention to any objective pattern—whether biblical words, a worship service, an appearance of godliness—not seen as part of a larger divine whole. Inwardness is not an object but a way of being. All human forms are explicit manifestations of ways of being. Scriptural words are forms which were written from within a way of being that was open to the divine coming to expression from the writers' inward depths. This way of being, which is expressive of the divine, Fox calls the "life" and the "power." As we have seen, "the apostates from the life ... have gotten their words ... in a form, but not in their life...."[36] The form is that of godliness but it lacks the way of being godly. Fox says:

> They that could speak some experiences of Christ and God, but lived not in the life, these were they that led the world after them, who got the form of godliness, but denied the power; who inwardly ravened from the Spirit, and brought people into the form but persecuted them that were in the power....[37]

The forms Fox objects to as outward, which lack the life and power, because they have lost connection with their inward way of being and therefore with the divine—for example, as the letter is detached from the spirit—are treated as ends in themselves. But the end of spiritual meaning is beyond all forms: it is the divine presence, which is infinite. Fox speaks of the end of words—"end" both in the sense of limit and purpose:

> They could not know the spiritual meaning of Moses', the prophets', and John's words, nor see their path and travels, much less *see through them* and *to the end of them* into the kingdom, unless they had the Spirit and the light of Jesus....[38]

Words have a limit, an end, beyond which they cannot go. But they have a purpose which is to see through them beyond their limit so as to participate in the kingdom. This reality beyond the limits of words is infinite and thus cannot be captured in words. It is the divine presence of love. Fox writes:

> And I saw into that which was without end, and things which cannot be uttered, and of the greatness and infiniteness of the love of God, which cannot be expressed by words. For I had been brought through the very ocean of darkness and death, and through the power and over the power of Satan, by the eternal glorious power of Christ.[39]

Fox's frequent word pairs of form and life, or form and power, is the distinction between part and whole. The inward loving presence of God is a whole. Any words I speak that issue from it are parts of it, bearing with it a sense of the whole. So also with godly living and worshipping; where they are particular forms issuing from the divine presence within, they are parts expressive of the divine whole. But where these are merely outward forms, they do not bear the divine whole as the end to which the words intend, but present themselves as ends and thus do not represent themselves as parts of a larger whole. Inwardness is thus a way of being that is participative in the divine whole, the infinite love of God. The result of participation in the divine whole is to be brought, as Fox says, "into unity and fellowship in the Spirit, which was before the Scriptures were given forth."[40]

> For all people had the Scriptures, but were not in that same light and power, and spirit that they were in that gave forth the Scriptures and so they neither knew God, nor Christ, nor the prophets, nor the apostles, nor Scriptures, neither had they unity one with another being out of the power and spirit of God.[41]

We can see then that while outwardness means in its simplest sense things outside the self, that at a deeper level, as seen through these four aspects, it means circumscribed phenomena cut off from the divine depths in the self—whether the encapsulated self of the flesh operating out of its own will rather than out of the divine reality; or the externalized law commanding conformity from outside rather than transforming the self from within through the indwelling actuality of divine love; or detached words being received in some spirit other than the Holy Spirit; or any objective pattern being understood to have its meaning in itself rather than as part expressive of a larger divine whole.

The Language of Inwardness and a Right Sense

How then does language work in relation to inwardness when it is not objectified as outward words separated from the divine within? The language of inwardness is symbolic. Language that is in, and filled with, the life and power unveils our inner being and the divine presence within it. Fox speaks of receiving a "spiritual discerning [which] came into me, by which I did discern my own thoughts, groans and sighs, and what it was that did veil me, and what it was that did open me."[42] What he discovers about biblical language in his struggles just after his convincement is that it is to be read as symbolic of his inward condition:

> [T]he Lord shewed me that the natures of those things which were hurtful without were within, in the hearts and minds of wicked men. The natures of dogs, swine, vipers, of Sodom and Egypt, Pharaoh, Cain, Ishmael, Esau, etc. The natures of these I saw within, though people had been looking without.[43]

Thus using biblical language symbolically, he can say: "I had been in spiritual Babylon, Sodom, Egypt, and the grave...." And using natural metaphors symbolically, he can speak of the inward condition of people in the surrounding territory: "And I saw the harvest white, and the Seed of God lying thick in the ground, as ever did wheat that was sown outwardly, and none to gather it...."[44] As symbolic, whether biblical words or natural metaphors, the images do not point to an objectified entity but rather unveil aspects of our own inward condition.

It takes, what Fox calls, "a right sense"[45] to read scripture in this way: "I saw also how people read the Scriptures without a right sense of them, and without duly applying them to their own states."[46] To have this right sense one must be in the spirit in which the Bible was written. Hence to understand Moses' depiction of Paradise in Genesis "none could read Moses aright without Moses' spirit."[47] So also to understand John the Baptist: "none could read John's words aright and with a true understanding of them, but in and with the same divine Spirit by which John spoke them, and by his burning, shining light, which is sent from God."[48]

With this right sense, filled with the Spirit, not only is the inner condition of the self unveiled, but the divine reality is known. Drawing upon traditional typological thinking, Fox affirms that it is "Christ who fulfils the types, figures, shadows, promises, and prophecies that were of him."[49] That is, reading the Hebrew Bible typologically, various things are said and done that are understood to be anticipations and prophecies of Christ. Catholic and Protestant thought often make Hebraic figures fit into and support an abstract Christian theological system, whose truth is doctrinal. But Fox shifts it so as to talk about Moses' own experience for whom these types unveiled to himself Christ's reality: "And both Moses and the prophets saw through the types and figures and beyond them, and saw Christ the great prophet that was to come to fulfil them."[50]

Types in Fox's hands are not pointers to an external reality but are vehicles to the experience of the inward reality of God. They bear one beyond the symbol itself to Christ and the kingdom. Typological symbols unveil both the human situation and carry us through to the spiritual end: "They could not know the spiritual meaning of Moses', the prophets', and John's words, nor see their path and travels, much less see through them and to the end of them into the kingdom, unless they had the Spirit and the light of Jesus...."[51] The "end" is Christ, "the substance." Through using these types with "the right sense" we not only "see" Christ but are "sitting down in him," that is, participating in his reality:

But as man comes through by the Spirit and power of God to Christ who fulfils the types ... and is led by the Holy Ghost into the truth and substance of the Scriptures, sitting down in him who is the author and end of them, then are they read and understood with profit and great delight.[52]

The language of inwardness is, therefore, symbolic—unveiling the depths of human experience and the divine reality within it, carrying us across to the end of all words and symbols into the reality of ourselves and of the divine these words manifest.

The divine is "without end" and "cannot be expressed by words"[53] because it is infinite love. In Fox's convincement it is remarkable how much talk there is of God's love. When he says "I knew him not but by revelation,"[54] he says that this inward revelation led him to see God's love—how it was endless and surpassed any knowledge from books; how he came to understand himself and others by comparison with this love;[55] how this love transforms the self: "It is the great love of God to make a wilderness of that which is pleasant to the outward eye and fleshly mind; and to make a fruitful field of a barren wilderness;"[56] and how he experienced this love over and over again: "And one day when I had been walking solitarily abroad and was come home, I was taken up in the love of God, so that I could not but admire the greatness of his love."[57] The right sense he receives in opening himself to the divine depths by which he interprets scripture "aright" is a sense of divine love.

A Hermeneutics of Inwardness

Quaker hermeneutics approaches scripture as symbolic but the symbols are not taken as referential, pointing to some outward reality of an external God or Christ, but are evocative of reality of the depths both of self and of God. Interpreting biblical words aright gets at both the meaning of words and beyond words. Put another way, the true meaning of words is to be in touch with the reality they bespeak which is itself beyond words. This is done through "a right sense" which is activated when one is participating "in the spirit"[58] which engendered the biblical words in the first place. Such a right sense comes then from within a way of being. It is the way of divine love.

Fox's approach to scripture recognizes that we all bring a perspective to bear in our reading. We read it in one spirit or another. This is part of the meaning of saying the Bible is a secondary authority. Its words can be taken to mean certain things from one orientation and other things from a different one. Biblical words, then, do not have an objective meaning independent of a perspective we bring to the text.

This acknowledgement of the perspectival nature of our understanding of scripture freed up Quakers to contribute to the beginnings of higher biblical criticism. Samuel Fisher, in *Rusticus Ad Academicos or The Rustick's Alarm to the Rabbies: or The Country Correcting the University* (1660), carries on a lengthy argument with John Owen, Richard Baxter, and two other Puritan theologians about the biblical canon, showing how the biblical words we have are the result of a long process of literary formation by many people and how the canonical boundaries have been drawn differently at different times so as to include texts that are not currently in our Bibles.

The theological argument that Fisher is waging is that the scriptural word cannot be the primary authority, as Owen and others claim, since the accuracy of the words and legitimacy of whole texts is something we can never be certain about. If your theology is dependent upon the accuracy of the word as the final authority, then you do not have the flexibility to explore the process of textual and canonical formation. In recognizing the Spirit as the authority, one can have such flexibility, for what matters is not the accuracy of the word but the right sense of the Spirit's meaning through whatever words are there.

While most Christian interpretations assume an objective framework of meaning that is independent of self and its experience, such a framework in fact rests upon some kind of inward sense. The Fundamentalist has a sense of being saved from destruction, which underlies the doctrinal affirmation of sacrificial atonement; Martin Luther had a sense of unmerited forgiveness, which underlies the doctrinal affirmation of justification by faith; the liberation theologian has a sense of being empowered, which underlies the idea of God's preferential alignment with the poor. In stressing the Spirit as the primary authority, Fox calls our attention away from looking in scripture for a concept to expecting an experience of the divine. God speaks to us through scripture by manifesting divine presence, if we are open to the symbolic power of the biblical language that opens us to our own depths and the divine within them. We can meet God in any biblical text because any text can become the means to open us to—become a chute into—such depth.

But how do you know that it is God who speaks and not some other spirit. Much fanatical destructiveness has been born of people thinking God is speaking to them. But then much destructiveness has also been unleashed by adherence to objective principles. In Fox there are three criteria I see: feeling, fruits, and fittingness. The right sense is a *feeling*. Over and over again Fox says to "feel it in the life."[59] The feel is a sense of divine love; it is like a taste of honey, you know it when you taste it. But one can and should query the feeling: what *fruits* will it bear? Does it result in humility or domination of others, the enhancing or destroying of others or of oneself, the freeing up from self-will or subjugation to it?

Finally, for Fox the feeling of God speaking through a certain text, which has intimations of fruitfulness, must have a *fittingness* with my own immediate condition—it must, as Fox says, "speak to thy condition"[60]—and my community. Early Friends frequently checked their leadings with each other, so that the feel one had of God speaking to him or herself was corroborated by others' intuitive sense of that leading. Such inward revelations felt and shared carry one into unity of fellowship in the life of the Spirit:

All my dear Friends in the noble Seed of God, and who have known his power, life, and presence amongst you, let it be your joy to hear or see the springs break forth in any, through which you have all unity in the same feeling, life, and power.[61]

And such unity is ultimately a "unity with the creation" which is "the hidden unity in the Eternal Being."[62]

Reading scripture looking for a sense of divine presence is different from bringing an objective framework to apply to any text in order to confirm one's doctrinal or ethical beliefs. The latter draws boundaries and emphasizes conforming to the external standard. Sensing the divine, on the other hand, emphasizes creativity. The framework that emerges from getting a right sense by being in the true spirit of the text is a gestalt, a pattern that emerges in the given moment that may present us with something new, a new leading or insight. That is what Friends mean by "continuing revelation."

Today's Challenge to Interpreting the Bible

The challenge for our reading the Bible today is how to use it positively when it poses so much of a negative threat—probably more so now than in any earlier time. A hermeneutic of suspicion has delineated the extensive patriarchal character of the whole Bible and the anti-Judaism of the New Testament. We know how the Bible has been used to justify domination over and exclusion of others different from ourselves through colonization, enslavement, and religious wars. And we know how it has fostered our exploitation of the natural environment. Once we have become sensitized to all these biblical strands, how can we still find it a spiritual resource and ethical guide? If we discard all tainted parts, our Bible becomes exceedingly small. Some seek for a pristine rule either within or beyond the scripture by which to interrogate it. The feminist theologian, Letty Russell, distinguishes her own approach from that of Elisabeth Schussler

Fiorenza's in these terms. She says: "Fiorenza moves the locus of revelation beyond the text itself to the reconstructed ministry of Jesus and the life of the early church."[63] For herself she says: "The particular interpretive key that assists me in continuing to give assent is the witness of scripture to God's promise (for the mending of creation) on its way to fulfillment."[64]

The alternative Fox's hermeneutic of inwardness poses is first to recognize that principles, whether devised through theological conceptualization or historical reconstruction, are done from a perspective grounded in a sense we have of the divine. We have said that for Fox this is a sense of divine love that brings us into unity with others and with the creation. But how does such a hermeneutic of inwardness fit with a hermeneutic of suspicion?

What we have seen is that experience of the divine reality in its infinite love is a measure of how far out of it we are. There is a critical edge to love; we have seen in our discussion of law that love can condemn and constrain as well as transform. That is what Fox meant by the Light illuminating and eliminating the places of darkness within us where we have not yet given up self-will. The criticism does not come, however, from applying an external standard but rather from experiencing a reality. A hermeneutic of suspicion based on a hermeneutic of inwardness recognizes that our criticisms are grounded in our involvement with reality rather than in detachment from it—our involvement in everyday life with others and the world, our involvement in the systems of social oppression, and especially our involvement with the divine in the depths of self and world.

The Ethics of Same-Sex Love

What light then does Fox's approach throw on ethical issues and the use of the Bible? Let us begin first with an ethical command by God in the Hebrew Bible that is uncontroversially immoral. There are places in the Bible where God commands the Israelites to enact holy war, that is to wipe out every man, woman, and child of an opposing group—and their cattle too. If we can figure out how to approach such scriptural texts, then we may see how to deal with anti-Judaism, sexism, and homophobia.

What do we do with holy war? Ignore it, I suppose, for the most part. Or speak, as early twentieth-century liberalism did, of this as a stage of growth that was transcended by later maturity. But what if someone says scripture is the truth and this is part of scripture, therefore this is now for us a command from God? Fox's approach would suggest we consider the sense underlying our organizing our lives around holy war. What spirit is it in? It is not the spirit of love; it does not bear the fruits of humility and enhancing the well-being of others, and it does not bring into unity with others and with the creation. But if it is true that God can speak through any biblical text, what do we discover when we experience God here?

If we read these texts in the spirit in which the Bible was written, that is in the Spirit of love, we can feel God's love in and through these texts—but as the basis for criticism and judgment. The life that speaks to us through these texts may be of the single-minded loyalty to God these Israelites exhibit in their understanding of their relationship with the sacred. But at the same time, in the spirit of love, we can feel how narrow the scope was in which they exercised this loyalty. The divine love draws us to such unequivocal fidelity but also opens us out to the breadth of our fundamental relatedness to others and to all of creation, and beckons us to affirm and enhance the community of being.

The spirit of love can unmask the spirit of holy war as a purist spirit that has erected an external form of purity, calling it God's command, with which all is to be brought into conformity. For someone so committed to wreak holy war upon another group, Fox would turn that person's attention to the spirit they dwell within. Does it have the feel of the divine, of that which is really real, of depth, of the *mysterium tremendum et fascinosum*?

Secondly, does it bear the fruits of the Spirit? Thirdly, does it bring into unity with our fellows and with creation?

If such questioning about the spirit which is embodied in the objective principle of holy war can be done successfully, the person can come to see that they had objectified a spirit, they were in, into an external form that they represented to themselves as a commandment from God, and relinquish it, let it dissipate, by returning to the source from which it came. Then one is in the position to query whether the purist spirit is the deepest spirit one knows within oneself, whether it is in and from the Holy Spirit. If it is not, one can open to that deeper Spirit that speaks to us through scripture and in rounds of our everyday lives.

What I am suggesting is that Fox's approach draws us away from outward forms, principles, ethical injunctions to the inward reality of the divine manifesting itself through biblical words and the events of our lives. Humility and empowerment come from realizing that truth is not in conformity to some outward form but is in dwelling in the Life and being responsive to it from moment to moment.

What then of same-sex love? We know this is controversial within the Society of Friends and outside in our larger society. Because it is sexual and because it is unconventional—and perhaps because it is mythic, as well—it touches us deeply where we live in our fundamental identities. It thus generates a lot of feeling. We know about the arguments from nature, about what is and what is not natural. We know the arguments from scripture, which select and elevate certain passages as rules for behavior. And we are learning about the history of compulsory heterosexism in the history of the Christian West that has leant cultural support to the conventional view so as to make same-sex love feel both unnatural and a violation of divine will.

Many good things have been written exploring the biblical passages cited as God's condemnation of same-sex love. I commend to you one of Pendle Hill's own pamphlets, Walter

Barnett's *Homosexuality and the Bible: An Interpretation* (1979). I find the careful, logical explanations of what was really meant by Deuteronomy and Leviticus or by Paul very useful. But I do not want to focus on any of those passages to show how they do not mean a universal condemnation of homosexuality by God. Rather, following Fox's lead, I want to turn rather to what spirit it is that leads one to fasten upon a few idiosyncratic texts and elevate them to objective ethical principles. We know scripture says things that even the most biblicist devotee ignores, such as forbidding wearing mixed fibers or forbidding men wearing their hair long. And most people disregard Jesus' own proscription against divorce. So it is not that the Bible says various things that matters, it is what spirit we are in that grasps certain of these and makes them defining principles.

What Fox's hermeneutics of inwardness suggests is that as we read these apparently condemnatory passages, we query the feel of the divine in them. Do they speak of the life and in the life? If we can get a right sense of divine love in these passages, it becomes a measure, as in the case of holy war, of how far out of this spirit such condemnation and exclusion is. Does the spirit, which asserts the divine condemnation of homosexuality, lead into the fruits of the Spirit, to humility and compassion and engendering the well-being of others? Does it open us to unity with others and with all of creation? What is the feel, the fruitfulness, and the fittingness of such destructive exclusions?

We are all embrangled in the systems of modern day oppression. It took many Friends a long time to come to the truth grasped by some Friends that slavery was immoral and out of the spirit of God, whatever support Paul leant to it. We are in the middle of one of those lengthy struggles. What do you do if you are one of those so embrangled that you feel the divine reality demands the rejection of same-sex love? Here is where dialogue is so important, not so much a logical argument as a sharing with one another of what we each discern of the divine presence.

Confronting the otherness of someone different from me provides me with the opportunity to descend deeper into myself to discover what divine love really means, released from the objective law, letter, and form which I have set up in the passions of my fleshly self-will to conform to, as I have cut myself off from divine dwelling within. The task is to speak to that of God in others, to open them to these depths we experience as love's affirmation of being. And if it be in ourselves, our task is to wait upon such opening from God to reconfigure our explicit commitments so as to make them manifest with the life. In this struggle and this waiting, the presence of others who body forth the divine possibility of a greater inclusive love is indispensable.

Yet it is finally within the inwardness of our own self that we can be liberated from the oppressive systems that are so much a part of our make-up. It is finally not the outward word but the inward sense, that orients us toward outward words, that illumines and elevates certain words for guidance, to which we must turn if we are to know the divine presence, as Fox did, "not but by revelation." Fox's hermeneutics of inwardness calls us to interpret the scripture in the Spirit in which it was written.

In this Spirit certain passages become luminous as words filled with life. The dying words of James Nayler are this for me, as he gives expression to the divine he has found in the depths: "There is a spirit which I feel that delights to do no evil.... Its hope is to outlive all wrath and contention, and to weary out all exaltation and cruelty, or whatever is of a nature contrary to itself.... Its crown is meekness, its life is everlasting love unfeigned; it takes its kingdom with entreaty and not with contention, and keeps it by lowliness of mind."[65]

So also are the words of First John: "God is love, and he who abides in love abides in God, and God abides in him."[66] But these words are not objectively true. Their truth is only known in the Spirit which dwells in the depths of everyone. And so also with the goodness of same-sex love, in the contentiousness of our times, we who are obstructed from divine inclusiveness can come to affirm that goodness only in inwardness where we meet the Spirit who affirms all love, because it is the Spirit of love who will gently lead us into the unutterable "infiniteness of the love of God."[67]

A Theopoetic Concluding

Prolegomena to Any Future Systematic Theology

"You must include all this," the voice said:
"Hemlock, earth, and mosscovered rock;
Branches reaching like sustaining arms into the gorge,
Cleaving the air, caressing the water course;
Modulating the greening light gliding on the surface of things;
Stone walls in shelves of shale deepcut
Descending to the boulders below
Awash with the boisterous gaiety of mountain stream
Astir from the cataracts' precipitous plunge,
Broad glistening like the white ruff of a dun deer;
And the departed but still palpable presence
Of buffalo, elk, wolf, and Native wooddweller."

"But in theology?" I replied.
"Our lives are in fragments, the gods have fled,
And meaninglessness mewls at the door,
Sifts in our pores, and rots in the bonemarrow of our minds;
We must be up about our Father's business,
Creating value in a valueless world,
Saving souls by turning inward, or eastward,
Engineering and capitalizing comforts in a homeless world,
Proclaiming the Word of a world to come
Where we shall no longer be stranger sojourner in an alien space
And our time of dwelling will no longer be longing but now."

After I fruitlessly awaited further reply
As my voice rang on the rock into echoes of nothingness
The silence gathered and deepened:
Roots upheld the light swaying dance of trees
Gripping hard the jagged shelves of stone;
Moss drew my hand to feel its cool soft plush;

Light thickened, achieved weight,
As it soaked up green life and brown earth,
Took on the density of situation,
Momentary configuration—
"Voice of a gentle stillness."

.

Abbreviations

Apol – Robert Barclay. *An Apology for the True Christian Divinity*. Philadelphia: Friends Books Store, 1908.

Descartes – René Descartes. *Descartes: Philosophical Writings*. *The Modern Library*. Trans. Norman Kemp Smith. New York: Random, 1958.

Experiences – Mary Penington. *Experiences in the life of Mary Penington (written by herself)*. Ed. Norman Penny. Philadelphia: The Biddle Press; London: Headley Bros., 1911; rpt. London: Friends Historical Society, 1992.

Fell – Margaret Fell. *Womens Speaking Justified, Proved and Allowed of By the Scriptures, All Such as Speak by the Spirit and Power of the Lord Jesus*. 1666. London. Reprinted Amherst, Massachusetts: Mosher Book & Tract Committee, New England Yearly Meeting of Friends, 1980.

IP – Isaac Penington, *The Works of Isaac Penington: A Minister of the Gospel in the Society of Friends, including His Collected Letters*, 4 vols. Glenside, PA: Quaker Heritage Press, 1995-1997.

Journal – George Fox. *The Journal of George Fox*. Ed. John L. Nickalls. London: Religious Society of Friends, 1975.

KMLW – R. Melvin Keiser & Rosemary Moore, eds. *Knowing the Mystery of Life Within: Selected Writings of Isaac Penington in their Historical and Theological Context*. London: Quaker Books, 2005.

Phen – Maurice Merleau-Ponty. *Phenomenology of Perception*. Trans. Colin Smith. London: Routledge & Kegan Paul; New York: The Humanities Press, 1962.

PI – Ludwig Wittgenstein. *Philosophical Investigations*. Trans. G.E.M. Anscombe. New York: The
Macmillan Company, 1953.

Notes

I. Silence as Origin
Waiting in Silence: The Metaphoric Matrix of Quakerism

1   *Journal* 251.

2   *Journal* 25.

3   T.S. Eliot, *East Coker, Four Quartets*, (sec. III, lines 123–128), 28.

4   Thomas Lurting, "The Fighting Sailor Turn'd Peaceable Christian," 212.

5   Lurting 218.

6   *Journal* 11.

7   *Journal* 8; cf. 7.

8   *Journal* 11.

9   *Journal* 4.

10   *Journal* 12.

11   *Journal* 1.

12   *Journal* 4 & 10; cf. 1.

13   *Journal* 1.

14   *Journal* 3.

15   *Journal* 7.

16   Journal 9.

17   *Journal* 10.

18   *Journal* 11.

19   *Journal* 13.

20   *Journal* 11 & 13.

21   Journal 1.

22   Journal 11.

23   Journal 11-12.

24   *Journal* 14.

25   *Journal* 14.

26 *Journal* 13.

27 *Journal* 10.

28 Journal 13.

29 *Journal* 14.

30 *Journal* 15.

31 *Journal* 2.

32 *Journal* 27.

33 *Journal* 19.

34 *Journal* 284.

35 *Journal* 283.

36 *Journal* 283.

37 *Journal* 283–284.

38 *Journal* 175 & 184.

Inward Light and the New Creation: A Theological Meditation upon the Center and Circumference of Quakerism

1 James Nayler, *Love to the Lost. A Collection of Sundry Books,* 271.

2 *Journal* 144.

3 *Journal* 11.

4 *Journal* 27–28.

5 *Journal* 11.

6 *Journal* 12.

7 *Journal* 19.

8 *Journal* 25.

9 *Journal* 25.

10 See Hugh Barbour, *The Quakers in Puritan England,* ch. 4.

11 *Journal* 14–15.

12 IP – "Short Catechism," v. I, 120–122.

13 For discussion of "original righteousness," see Reinhold Niebuhr, *The Nature and Destiny of Man: A Christian Interpretation,* v. I, ch. X *"Justitia Originalis."*

14 On this Irenaean tradition, see John Hick, *Evil and the God of Love*.
15 IP – "The Way of Life and Death," v. I, 36.
16 *Journal* 32.
17 William Penn, *No Cross, No Crown* 53.
18 *Journal* 18.
19 *Journal* 2.
20 *Journal* 263.
21 *Journal* 65.
22 *Journal* 353.
23 *Journal* 205–206.
24 *Journal* 36–38.
25 *Journal* 520.
26 Fell 3.
27 Fell 5.
28 Fell 11.
29 Fell 5–7.
30 Fell 4.
31 Fell 10–11.
32 In her handling of Paul's expressions of patriarchal subordination of women, Fell assumes he is for sexual equality and so we have misunderstood his meaning. She does not consider the possibility that he is exhibiting the sexism of his culture. Since her argument turns on locating equality in the New Creation and inequality in the fallen condition, she has restricted herself to arguing for women's equality only within the church (understood in the broadest terms as wherever the Spirit is poured out upon people). Since only those who have opened to the Light live now in the New Creation, those who have not opened to Light and Spirit are caught in the inequalities of the fallen world. She is not able, then, to argue that all women have innate equality with men.
33 Fell 12.

Two Lads in Front of a Fire: A Seventeenth-Century Tale

1 Descartes 101.

2 Descartes 101.

3 Descartes 102.

4 Descartes 102.

5 Descartes 102.

6 Descartes 102.

7 Descartes 103.

8 Descartes 103.

9 Descartes 104.

10 Descartes 103.

11 Descartes 104.

12 Descartes 103.

13 Descartes 115.

14 Descartes 106–107.

15 Descartes 116.

16 *Journal* 25.

17 *Journal* 25.

18 Descartes 119.

19 Descartes 118–119.

20 Descartes 119–120.

21 Descartes 119.

22 Descartes 120.

23 This has been overlooked, however, by some Quaker scholars. See Mel Endy's insistence on divine/human and spirit/body dualisms in early Friends in his otherwise fine treatment of *William Penn and Early Quakerism*, 68, 75.

24 See William Hardman Poteat, *Pascal's Conception of Man and Modern Sensibility*.

25 Stanley Romaine Hopper, "The Literary Imagination and the Doing of Theology." 1972. *The Way of Transfiguration: Religious Imagination as Theopoiesis*, 207.

26 Hopper, "The Literary Imagination," 219.

27 Stanley Romaine Hopper, *"Le Cri de Merlin!* or Interpretation and the Metalogical." 1971. *The Way of Transfiguration*, 198; cf. 194 – 199.

28 Michael Polanyi, *Personal Knowledge: Towards a Post-Critical Philosophy*, 269. See also Michael Polanyi, *The Tacit Dimension*.

29 Polanyi, *Personal Knowledge*, 269.

30 Norman Malcolm, *Ludwig Wittgenstein: A Memoir*, 70–72 (his italics).

31 While I am contrasting the Enlightenment rational tradition of natural rights and establishing democracy with the Quaker way of depending on resources in inwardness beneath and infusing reason, through waiting in silence, some Friends have combined natural rights with their basis in silence as a way to "apologetically" find common ground with civil society, e.g., William Penn in the seventeenth century and Lucretia Mott in the nineteenth century. William Penn also made significant contributions to American democracy with his "Frame of Government" establishing democracy in Pennsylvania which became something of a model for the Constitutional Convention meeting in Philadelphia.

32 Rosemary Radford Ruether, *Sexism and God-Talk: Toward a Feminist Theology*, 102.

II. What Is Quaker Philosophical Theology?
A. *Becoming Quaker: Doing, Speaking, Thinking*

Felt Reality in Practical Living and Innovative Thinking: Mary and Isaac Penington's Journey from Puritan Anguish to Quaker Truth

1 Acts 17:6; see Christopher Hill, *The World Turned Upside Down: Radical Ideas During the English Revolution*.

2 Isaac Penington, *Expositions with Observations Sometimes on Severall Scriptures*, 18, 51; also in R. Melvin Keiser, "From

Dark Christian to Fullness of Life: Isaac Penington's Journey from Puritanism to Quakerism," 53.

3 *Experiences* 19.

4 *Experiences* 28.

5 *Experiences* 33–34.

6 *Experiences* 35.

7 *Experiences* 41.

8 *KMLW* 28–29, 109–113.

9 *Experiences* 48.

10 *Experiences* 42.

11 *Experiences* 42.

12 *Experiences* 43–44.

13 *Experiences* 44–45.

14 *Experiences* 46.

15 See Carla Gerona, *Night Journeys: The Power of Dreams in Transatlantic Quaker Culture*, esp ch. 2.

16 *Experiences* 32–33.

17 *Experiences* 35–36.

18 *Experiences* 36–7.

19 *Experiences* 37–38.

20 *Experiences* 49–50.

21 *Experiences* 50–51.

22 *Experiences* 51–52.

23 *Ezekiel* 1:26–28.

24 IP – "An Examination Of the Ground Or Causes Which Are Said To Induce the Court of Boston In New England To Make That Order Or Law Of Banishment, Upon Pain Of Death, Against The Quakers," v. I, 388; *KMLW* 165. Cf. "To His Children," *KMLW* 61.

25 *Experiences* 52.

26 I. Penington, *Expositions* 592–593; also Keiser, "Dark Christian" 45.

27 Isaac Penington, *The Great and Sole Troubler of the Times*, 25; also Keiser, "Dark Christian" 46.

28 Isaac Penington, *Light or Darknesse,* 31; also Keiser, "Dark Christian" 48.

29 Isaac Penington, *Severall Fresh Inward Openings,* 1; also Keiser, "Dark Christian" 48–49.

30 I.Penington, *Light* 8, 14, 19–20; also Keiser, "Dark Christian" 49–51. Isaac anticipates the nineteenth-century rise of historical consciousness, recognition of "God" as a projected image, and creative role of imagination; also Keiser, "Dark Christian" 49–50.

31 I.Penington, *Light* 8–9; also Keiser, "Dark Christian" 51.

32 I.Penington, *Divine Essays or Considerations about Several Things in Religion,* 9; also Keiser, "Dark Christian" 51. See Boehme's influence, in Keiser, "Dark Christian" 52–53.

33 I.Penington, *Severall ... Openings* 28–29; also Keiser, "Dark Christian" 52.

34 I. Penington, *Divine Essays* 9–11; also Keiser, "Dark Christian" 52. On Isaac's relation to Ranters, see *KMLW* 8–10; and Douglas Gwyn, *Seekers Found: Atonement in Early Quaker Experience,* 269–279.

35 I. Penington, *Expositions* 18, 51; also Keiser, "Dark Christian" 53.

36 IP – "The Way of Life and Death Made Manifest and Set Before Men," 89; *KMLW* 131.

37 IP – "To All Such As Complain That They Want Power," v. II, 289; *KMLW* 154.

38 IP – "A True And Faithful Relation, In Brief, Concerning Myself, In Reference To My Spiritual Travails," v. I, 9–11; *KMLW* 15–17.

39 IP – "True ... Travails," v. I, 7–11; *KMLW* 17, 24–25.

40 *KMLW* 134, 276.

41 IP – "Way," v. I, 90; *KMLW* 131.

42 IP – "True ... Travails," v. I, *KMLW* 17.

43 See Rosemary Moore on Isaac's relation to Perrot, *KMLW* 39–42, 57, 65–66, 68–69, 104–105, 159.

44 Romans 2:28–29, 2 Corinthians 3:6, 2 Timothy 3:5, respectively; *KMLW* 133–134.

45 IP – "The Axe Laid To The Root Of The Old Corrupt Tree," v. I, 229, 257; *KMLW* 245, 140.

46 IP – "To Catharine Pordage," v. III, 484; *KMLW* 135.

47 IP – "Reply To Queries And Animadversions," v. IV, 176; *KMLW* 183.

48 IP – "Axe," v. I, 256; *KMLW* 140.

49 IP – "The Flesh And Blood Of Christ In The Mystery And In The Outward," v. III, 357–358; *KMLW* 192.

50 IP – A Treatise Concerning God's Teachings, And Christ's Law With Some Other Things Of Weighty Importance," v. IV, 259; *KMLW* 181.

51 IP – "To Friends Of Both The Chalfonts," v. II, 494; *KMLW* 181.

52 IP – "To___," v. III, 458; *KMLW* 217.

53 IP – "Flesh," v. III, 358; *KMLW* 182–183.

54 IP – "Some Of The Mysteries Of God's Kingdom Glanced At," v. II, 343; *KMLW* 249–250.

55 IP – "Flesh," v. III, 368; *KMLW* 167.

56 IP – "The Seed of God And His Kingdom Treated and Tested Of According To The Scriptures Of Truth And According To True Experience Felt In The Heart From The God Of Truth," v. IV, 341; *KMLW* 217.

57 IP – "Flesh," v. III, 358; *KMLW* 182.

58 IP – "The Scattered Sheep Sought After," v. I, 117–18; *KMLW* 267.

59 IP – "Mysteries," v. II, 343; *KMLW* 249.

60 IP – "A Question To The Professors Of Christianity Whether They Have The True, Living, Powerful, Saving Knowledge of Christ, Or No," v. III, 49–50; *KMLW* 249.

61 IP – "Life and immortality Brought To Light Through The Gospel Being A True Discovery Of The Nature And Ground Of The Religion And Kingdom Of Christ," v. IV, 166; *KMLW*

249.

62   IP – "Examination ... Boston," v. I, 380; *KMLW* 162.

63   IP – "The Jew Outward Being A Glass For The Professors Of This Age," v. I, 206, 202; *KMLW* 251.

64   IP – *"Concerning Persecution Which Is The Afflicting Or Punishing That Which is Good, Under The Pretence Of Its Being Evil,"* v. II, 188–189; *KMLW* 215.

65   IP – "Short Catechism for the Sake of the Simple-Hearted." In "The Scattered Sheep Sought After," v. I, 120–121; *KMLW* 233.

66   IP – "To My Friends at Horton And Thereabouts," v. II, 469–70; *KMLW* 206.

67   IP – "Some Misrepresentations Of Me Concerning Church-Government Cleared And The Power And Authority Of God's Spirit In Governing His Church Testified To," v. IV, 334; *KMLW* 247.

68   IP – "Reply To Queries," v. IV, 182.

69   *Experiences* 47.

70   IP – "To ... Chalfonts," v. II, 495–496; *KMLW* 144–145.

"Gathered Inward to the Word": The Way of Word and Silence in Quaker Experience

1   *Apol* 340.

2   *Phen* 3, 13, 101.

3   Michael Polanyi, *The Tacit Dimension*.

4   Ludwig Wittgenstein, *Tractatus Logico-Philosophicus*, 149, 151 #6.44–45, 6.522.

5   Wittgenstein, *Tractatus*, 151; #6.522, 4.1212.

6   *Apol* 335.

7   *Apol* 337.

8   *Apol* 336.

9   *Apol* 337.

10   *Apol* 336.

11 *Apol* 336–337.

12 *Apol* 336.

13 *Apol* 336.

14 *Apol* 337.

15 *Apol* 335.

16 *Apol* 337.

17 *Apol* 338.

18 *Apol* 336.

19 *Apol* 337.

20 *Apol* 337–338.

21 *Apol* 340.

22 *Apol* 338.

23 *Apol* 340.

24 *Apol* 336.

25 *Apol* 338.

26 *Apol* 338.

27 *Apol* 339.

28 *Apol* 340.

29 *Apol* 336.

30 *Apol* 336.

31 *Apol* 336.

32 Robert Barclay, "Quakerism Confirmed: Or a Vindication of the Chief Doctrines and Principles of the People Called Quakers," in *Truth Triumphant*, v. III, 128.

33 *Apol* 336.

34 *Apol* 338–339.

35 *Apol* 338.

36 *PI* #19.

37 *PI* #23; his italics.

38 *PI* 204e.

39 *PI* #43.

40 *Apol* 37–38.

41 *Apol* 38.

42 *PI* #19.

43 *PI* #7 & 23.

44 John Woolman, *The Journal and Major Essays of John Woolman*, 133.

45 Paul Ricoeur, *Interpretation Theory: Discourse and the Surplus of Meaning* 16.

46 Ricoeur, *Interpretation,* 17.

47 *Phen* 179; his italics.

48 *Phen* 180.

49 *Phen* 180.

50 *Phen* 182; cf. 193.

51 *Phen* 180.

52 *Phen* 180.

53 *Phen* 193; his italics.

54 *Phen* 193.

55 *Phen* 182.

56 *Apol* 364.

57 *Apol* 337.

58 *Apol* 336.

59 *Apol* 364.

60 *Apol* 364.

61 *Apol* 341; cf. 364–365.

62 Barclay, "Quakerism Confirmed," 124.

63 Barclay, "Quakerism Confirmed," 122.

64 Barclay, "Quakerism Confirmed," 125.

65 Robert Barclay, "R.B.'s Apology for the True Christian Divinity Vindicated," in *Truth Triumphant,* v. III, 314.

66 Barclay, "Quakerism Confirmed," 128.

67 Barclay, "R.B.'s Apology," 492.

68 Barclay, "Quakerism Confirmed," 151.

69 *Apol* 337.

70 *Phen* 193.

71 *Phen* 184.

72 *Phen* 194.

73 *Phen* 194.

74   *Phen* 182.

75   *Phen* 194.

76   *Apol* 337–338.

77   *Apol* 339, 336.

78   *Phen* 196; Merleau-Ponty is quoting; his italics deleted.

79   *Phen* 183.

80   *Phen* 184.

81   *Quaker Faith & Practice: The Book of Christian Discipline of the Yearly Meeting of the Religious Society of Friends (Quakers) in Britain,* #27.27.

82   Martin Heidegger, *An Introduction to Metaphysics,* 124.

83   Heidegger, *Intro,* 130.

84   Rumi, *The Essential Rumi,* 30.

85   *Apol* 343.

B. Quaker Thought: Relational and Emergent in Robert Barclay

Touched and Knit in The Life: Barclay's Relational Theology Beyond Cartesian Dualism

1   Margaret Fell, "The Testimony of Margaret Fox Concerning her Late Husband George Fox," in Mary Garman, Judith Applegate, Margaret Benefiel, Dortha Meredith, eds., *Hidden in Plain Sight: Quaker Women's Writings 1650–1700,* 235. This meeting was providential as she became one of the chief leaders of the burgeoning Quaker movement, made Swarthmore Hall the base of operations, and later married Fox.

2   *Apol* 340.

3   Maurice A. Creasey, *"Inward" and "Outward": A Study in Early Quaker Language,* 20.

4   Creasey, *Inward,* 5.

5   Creasey, *Inward,* 12.

6   Creasey, *Inward,* 22.

7   Creasey, *Inward*, 23.

8   Creasey, *Inward*, 23–24.

9   Melvin B. Endy, Jr., *William Penn and Early Quakerism*, 76–77.

10   Endy, *Penn*, 183.

11   Endy, *Penn*, 68–84, 183–189.

12   John Punshon, *Portrait in Grey: A Short History of the Quakers*, 122.

13   Punshon, *Portrait*, 125; see 120–125.

14   Hugh S. Pyper, "Resisting the Inevitable: Universal and Particular Salvation in the Thought of Robert Barclay," 16.

15   Pyper, "Resisting," 17.

16   Pyper, "Resisting," 18.

17   Pyper, "Resisting," 17.

18   Pyper, "Resisting," 18.

19   Pyper, "Resisting," 6–8.

20   Calvin, John. *Institutes of the Christian Religion*. v. I. 35.

21   René Descartes, "Discourse on Method," in *Philosophical Writings*, 119.

22   *Apol* 23.

23   *Apol* 24.

25   See *Apol* 9.

26   *Apol* 335.

27   *Apol* 336.

28   *Apol* 337.

29   *Apol* 335–336.

30   *Apol* 350.

31   *Apol* 337.

32   *Apol* 364.

33   *Apol* 365.

34   *Apol* 336.

35   *Apol* 337.

36   *Apol* 342.

37   See Phyllis Mack, *Visionary Women: Ecstatic Prophecy in Seventeenth-Century England*, 150 153.

38   Robert Barclay, "The Possibility and Necessity of the Inward

& Immediate Revelation of the Spirit of God," in *Truth Triumphant*, v. III, 569.

39   *Apol* 42.
40   *Apol* 43.
41   *Apol* 71; for the same detailing of spiritual senses see Barclay, "Possibility," 574.
42   *Apol* 71.
43   *Apol* 55.
44   *Apol* 43.
45   *Apol* 45.
46   *Apol* 45–46.
47   *Apol* 54.
48   *Apol* 54.
49   *Apol* 69–70.
50   *Apol* 67.
51   *Apol* 68.
52   Pyper, "Resisting," 8.
53   Pyper, "Resisting," 9.
54   Pyper, "Resisting," 10.
55   Pyper, "Resisting," 11–12.
56   *Apol* 144–145.
57   *Apol* 34.
58   *Apol* 132.
59   *Apol* 137.
60   Barclay, "Possibility," 577.
61   *Apol* 137.
62   *Apol* 141–142.
63   *Apol* 138.
64   *Apol* 141.
65   *Apol* 132.
66   *Apol* 121.
67   *Apol* 132.
68   *Apol* 140.
69   *Apol* 172.

70 *Apol* 180.

71 *Apol* 180.

72 *Apol* 161.

73 *Apol* 141.

74 *Apol* 199.

75 *Apol* 141.

76 *Apol* 141–142.

77 *Apol* 147.

78 *Apol* 98.

79 *Apol* 109.

80 *Apol* 199.

81 *Apol* 208.

82 *Apol* 147.

83 *Apol* 137.

84 *Apol* ix.

85 Barclay, "Possibility," 562.

86 Barclay, "Possibility," 565–566.

87 Gotthold Lessing, *Lessing's Theological Writings*, 53 & 55.

88 Barclay, "Possibility," 562–563.

89 Barclay, "Possibility," 570.

90 René Descartes, "The Principles of Philosophy," in *A Discourse on Method and Selected Writings*, 203–204.

91 Barclay, "Possibility," 575.

92 Pyper, "Resisting," 12.

93 Barclay, "Possibility," 577.

94 Barclay, "Possibility," 571.

95 Barclay, "Possibility," 575; cf. Frederick Copleston, S.J., *A History of Philosophy*, v. IV, 93–95.

96 Barclay, "Possibility," 576.

97 Barclay, "Possibility," 575 & 574.

98 Barclay, "Possibility," 577.

99 *Apol* 137.

100 *Apol* 340.

The Growing Up of Principles: Otherness in Robert Barclay's Emergent Thinking

1 *Apol* 199.

2 Martin Buber, *I and Thou*, 127.

3 *Apol* 340.

4 *Apol* 337.

5 *Apol* 350.

6 *Apol* 147.

7 *Apol* 340.

8 *Apol* 340.

9 *Apol* 340.

10 *PI*, par. # 19.

11 *Apol* 38.

12 *Apol* 340.

13 Mircea Eliade, *The Sacred and the Profane: The Nature of Religion*, 9.

14 W.E. Burghardt DuBois, *The Souls of Black Folk*, 23.

15 *Apol* 199.

C. The What, How, and Why of Quaker Theology

The Quaker Vision and the Doing of Theology

1 Frederick B. Tolles, *Meeting House and Counting House: The Quaker Merchants of Colonial Philadelphia, 1682–1763*, 53.

2 Krister Stendahl to William R. Rogers.

3 See Hugh Barbour, ed., *William Penn on Religion and Ethics*; Hugh Barbour and Arthur Roberts, eds., *Early Quaker Writings*; Richard S. Dunn & Mary Maples Dunn, eds., *The Papers of William Penn*. 5 vols; Mary Garman, Judith Applegate, Margaret Benefiel, Dortha Meredith, eds., *Hidden in Plain Sight: Quaker Women's Writings 1650–1700*; T. Canby Jones, ed., *"The Power of the Lord Is Over All": The Pastoral Letters of George Fox*; Isaac Penington, *The Works of Isaac Penington*. 4 vols.

4   *Journal* 30 & 10.

5   William Penn, "A Key Opening a Way to Every Common Understanding," in Hugh S. Barbour, ed., *William Penn on Religion and Ethics: The Emergence of Liberal Quakerism*, 503.

6   Sarah Jones, "This Is Lights Appearance in the Truth," in Garman, et al, eds., *Hidden*, 35.

7   T.C. Jones, *Power ... Fox*, 78.

8   *Journal* 143.

9   IP – "To ... Chalfonts," v. II, 537–38.

10 Penn, "Key," 501.

11 *Journal* 11.

12 *Journal* 282.

13 *Journal* 2.

14 See Margaret Benefiel's discussion of Bathurst and Barclay's systematic theologies in Garman, et al, eds., *Hidden*, 309.

15 *Apol* 340.

16 *Apol* 23.

17 Barclay, "Possibility," 26.

18 Penn, "Key," 501.

19 *Journal* 263.

20 S. Jones, "Lights," in Garman, et al, eds., *Hidden*, 35.

21 John 8:32.

22 IP – "To ... Chalfonts," v. II, 537.

23 *Journal* 28.

24 John Miller, "On Faith," see n. 1 & 3.

25 See R. Melvin Keiser and Elizabeth B. Keiser, "Quaker Principles in the Crucible of Practice."

26 Rupert Read, "On the Nature and Centrality of the Concept of "Practice" among Quakers," 34.

27 See H. Richard Niebuhr, *The Meaning of Revelation*, ch. 2.

28 Read, "Nature," 35.

29 Read, "Nature," 33.

30 Miller, "Faith," 39.

31 1 Corinthians 2:10; RSV.

32 *Journal* 28.

33 Linda Hill Renfer, ed., *Daily Readings from Quaker Writings Ancient & Modern*, 213.

Reflecting Theologically from the Gathered Meeting: The Nature and Origin of Quaker Theology

1 Since a critical moment in my graduate theological formation, this passage from William Langland's *Piers Plowman* (as translated by Elizabeth D. Kirk) has illuminated my quandary:

> But Theology has troubled me ten score times.
> The more I muse on it, the mistier it seems,
> And the deeper I divined, the darker I thought it;
> It's surely no science to argue subtly in;
> If it weren't for the love that lies in it, it would be a lame study.
> But since it allows so much to Love, I love it the better,
> For wherever Love is leader, there's no lack of grace.
> (Passus X, B-Text, l. 183–191)

2 IP – "Way," v. I, 26.

3 IP – "Way," v. I, 27.

4 IP – "Way," v. I, 27–28.

5 See Phillips P. Moulton, ed., *The Journal and Major Essays of John Woolman*, 127.

6 T.C. Jones, *Power … Fox*, 78 & 83.

7 *Journal*, 283–284.

8 John Macmurray, *Persons in Relation*, v. II of *The Form of the Personal*.

III. Quaker Thought as Theopetic: Christ, History, and Biblical Interpretation

1   Stanley Romaine Hopper, *The Way of Transfiguration: Religious Imagination as Theopoiesis.*
2   Stanley Romaine Hopper, "The 'Eclipse of God' and Existential Mistrust," ch. V of *Way*, 169.

Christ in the Mesh of Metaphor

1   *Journal* 2.
2   *Journal* 283–284.
3   Gerard Manley Hopkins, "God's Grandeur," in *Poems and Prose of Gerard Manley Hopkins*, 27.
4   IP – "Babylon the Great Described The City of Confusion In Every Part Whereof AntiChrist Reigns," 148.
5   *Journal* 263.
6   *Journal* 15.
7   *Journal* 27.

Meaning in Historical Existence: Modern and Quaker Perspectives

1   *Quaker History*, 106.1 [Spring 2017]: 1–21.
2   Jeffrey Dudiak, "The Meaning of 'Quaker History,'" 3.
3   Larry Ingle, "One Historian's Reflections on Philosopher Jeffrey Dudiak's Search for the 'Meaning of Quaker History'" and J. William Frost, "Revealed Truth and Quaker History."
4   Frost, "Revealed Truth," 25.
5   See "Relations of Internal and External History," *The Meaning of Revelation*, 81–90.
6   Dudiak, "Meaning," 14.
7   Dudiak, "Meaning," 15.
8   Dudiak, "Meaning," 15.

To See Jesus in Holy Land Travails

1   Mark 12:29–31.
2   Jeremiah 22:3.
3   Leviticus 25:23.

Resurrection for Paul, Mark, and Friends

1   Galations 1:16, RSV.
2   See Robert W. Funk, *Honest To Jesus: Jesus for a New Millennium*, ch. 14.
3   Mark 8:27–33.
4   Matthew 16:17–19.
5   Ezekiel 1: 26; see Walter Wink, *The Human Being: Jesus and the Enigma of the Son of the Man*.
6   Genesis 1:27.
7   Mark 8:31.
8   Mark 14:28.
9   2 Corinthians 3:17.
10 Romans 8:9.
11 Mark 16:8.
12 1 Corinthians 15:44.
13 *Journal*, 346.
14 IP – "Some Directions to the Panting Soul," v. II, 205; *KMLW* 141.

"I Knew Him Not but by Revelation": A Hermeneutics of Inwardness and the Ethics of Same-Sex Love

1   *Journal* 11.
2   *Journal* 11–12; my italics.
3   *Journal* 33.
4   *Journal* 12.
5   *Journal* 13.

6   *Journal* 12.

7   *Journal* 12.

8   *Journal* 11.

9   *Journal* 13.

10   *Journal* 17.

11   *Journal* 13.

12   *Journal* 14–15.

13   *Journal* 14–15.

14   *Journal* 15.

15   *Journal* 10.

16   *Journal* 10.

17   *Journal* 11.

18   *Journal* 11.

19   *Journal* 16.

20   *Journal* 15.

21   *Journal* 16.

22   *Journal* 17.

23   *Journal* 15.

24   *Journal* 16–17.

25   *Journal* 16.

26   *Journal* 19.

27   *Journal* 78.

28   *Journal* 117.

29   *Journal* 55.

30   *Journal* 114.

31   *Journal* 11.

32   *Journal* 75.

33   *Journal* 79.

34   *Journal* 10–11.

35   *Journal* 20–21.

36   *Journal* 10.

37   *Journal* 30.

38   *Journal* 32; my italics.

39   *Journal* 21.

40 *Journal* 17.

41 *Journal* 103.

42 *Journal* 14.

43 *Journal* 19.

44 *Journal* 21.

45 *Journal* 31.

46 *Journal* 31.

47 *Journal* 31.

48 *Journal* 32.

49 *Journal* 32.

50 *Journal* 31.

51 *Journal* 32.

52 *Journal* 32.

53 *Journal* 21.

54 *Journal* 11.

55 *Journal* 11–12.

56 *Journal* 13.

57 *Journal* 14; see 13.

58 *Journal* 10.

59 *Journal* 282.

60 *Journal* 11.

61 *Journal* 281.

62 *Journal* 28.

63 Letty M. Russell, ed., *Feminist Interpretation of the Bible*, 62–63.

64 Russell, ed., *Feminist Interpretation*, 139.

65 Douglas V. Steere, ed., *Quaker Spirituality: Selected Writings*, 96.

66 1 John 4:16.

67 *Journal* 21.

Bibliography

Barbour, Hugh. *The Quakers in Puritan* England. New Haven and London: Yale University Press, 1964.

___Ed. *William Penn on Religion and Ethics: The Emergence of Liberal Quakerism*. Lewiston, Queenston, Lampeter: The Edwin Mellen Press, 1991.

___and Arthur Roberts, eds. *Early Quaker Writings*. Grand Rapids: Eerdmans, 1973.

Barclay, Robert. *An Apology for the True Christian Divinity*. Philadelphia: Friends Books Store, 1908.

___"The Possibility and Necessity of the Inward & Immediate Revelation of the Spirit of God."

Truth Triumphant, v. III. Philadelphia: Benjamin C. Stanton, 1831: 561–585.

___"Quakerism Confirmed: Or a Vindication of the Chief Doctrines and Principles of the People

Called Quakers." *Truth Triumphant*, v. III. Philadelphia: Benjamin C. Stanton, 1831.

___"R.B.'s Apology for the True Christian Divinity Vindicated." *Truth Triumphant*, Vol. III.

Philadelphia: Benjamin C. Stanton, 1831.

Barnett, Walter. *Homosexuality and the Bible: An Interpretation*. Pendle Hill Pamphlet #226.

Wallingford: Pendle Hill, 1979.

Buber, Martin. *I and Thou*. Trans. Walter Kaufmann. New York: Charles Scribner's Sons, 1970.

Calvin, John. *Institutes of the Christian Religion*. v. I. *The Library of Christian Classics*. v. XX. Ed.

John T. McNeill. Trans. Ford Lewis Battles. Philadelphia: The Westminster Press, 1960.

Copleston, Frederick, S.J. *A History of Philosophy*. v. IV. Image Books. New York: Doubleday &

Company, 1963.

Creasey, Maurice A. *"Inward" and "Outward": A Study in Early Quaker Language*. London:

Friends' Historical Society, 1962: 2–24.

Descartes, René. *Descartes: Philosophical Writings. The Modern Library*. Trans. Norman Kemp Smith. The Modern Library. New York: Random House, 1958.

___"Discourse on Method." In *Philosophical Writings*. Trans. Norman Kemp Smith. The Modern

Library. New York: Random House, 1958.

___"The Principles of Philosophy." In *A Discourse on Method and Selected Writings*. Trans. John

Veitch. New York: E.P. Dutton and Company; London: J.M. Dent and Sons, 1951.

DuBois, W.E. Burghardt. *The Souls of Black Folk*. A Fawcett Premier Book. New York: Fawcett

Publications, 1961.

Dudiak, Jeffrey. "The Meaning of 'Quaker History.'" *Quaker History*, 106.1 (Spring 2017).

Dunn, Richard S. and Mary M. Eds. *The Papers of William Penn*. v.1-5. Philadelphia: University of

Pennsylvania Press, 1982–87.

Eliade, Mircea. *The Sacred and the Profane: The Nature of Religion*. Harper Torchbooks. New

York: Harper & Row, 1961.

Eliot, T.S. "East Coker." *Four Quartets*. A Harvest Book. New York: Harcourt, Brace, and World,

1943; 1971.

Endy, Melvin B., Jr. *William Penn and Early Quakerism*. Princeton: Princeton University Press,

1973.

Fell, Margaret. "The Testimony of Margaret Fox Concerning her Late Husband George Fox:

together with a brief Account of some of his Travels, Sufferings,

and Hardships endured for the
Truth's Sake," in Mary Garman, Judith Applegate, Margaret
Benefiel, Dortha Meredith, eds.,
Hidden in Plain Sight: Quaker Women's Writings 1650–1700. Wallingford,
Pennsylvania: Pendle
Hill Publications, 1996.

___*Women's Speaking Justified, Proved and Allowed of By the
Scriptures, All Such as Speak by the Spirit and Power of the Lord
Jesus.* 1666. London. Reprinted Amherst, Massachusetts:
Mosher Book & Tract Committee, New England Yearly
Meeting of Friends, 1980.

Fisher, Samuel. *Rusticus Ad Academicos. or The Rustick's Alarm to
the Rabbies: or The Country*
Correcting the University. London: Robert Wilson, 1660.

Fox, George. *The Journal of George Fox.* Ed. John L. Nickalls.
London: Religious Society of Friends, 1975.

___*"The Power of the Lord Is Over All": The Pastoral Letters of George
Fox.* Ed. T. Canby Jones.
Richmond, IN: Friends United Press, 1989.

Frost, J. William. "Revealed Truth and Quaker History." *Quaker
History*, 106.1 (Spring 2017): 25–27.

Funk, Robert W. *Honest To Jesus: Jesus for a New Millennium.* New
York: HarperCollins, 1996.

Garman, Mary, Judith Applegate, Margaret Benefiel, Dortha
Meredith, eds. *Hidden in Plain Sight:*
Quaker Women's Writings 1650-1700. Wallingford, Pennsylvania:
Pendle Hill Publications, 1996.

Gerona, Carla. *Night Journeys: The Power of Dreams in Transatlantic
Quaker Culture.*
Charlottesville and London: University of Virginia Press, 2004.

Gwyn, Douglas. *Seekers Found: Atonement in Early Quaker
Experience.* Wallingford, Pennsylvania: Pendle Hill
Publications, 2000.

Heidegger, Martin. *An Introduction to Metaphysics.* Trans. Ralph

Manheim. New Haven: Yale University Press, 1959.

Hick, John. *Evil and the God of Love,* The Fontana Library. Thetford, Great Britain: Collins, 1974.

Hill, Christopher. *The World Turned Upside Down: Radical Ideas During the English Revolution.* New York: The Viking Press, 1972.

Hopkins, Gerard Manley. "God's Grandeur." In *Poems and Prose of Gerard Manley Hopkins.* W.H. Gardner, ed. London: Penguin Books, 1985.

Hopper, Stanley Romaine. *The Way of Transfiguration: Religious Imagination as Theopoiesis.* Eds. R. Melvin Keiser and Tony Stoneburner. Louisville, Kentucky: Westminster/John Knox Press, 1992.

___"*Le Cri de Merlin!* or Interpretation and the Metalogical." 1971. *The Way of Transfiguration: Religious Imagination as Theopoiesis.* Eds. R. Melvin Keiser and Tony Stoneburner. Louisville, Kentucky: Westminster/John Knox Press, 1992.

___"The Literary Imagination and the Doing of Theology." 1972. *The Way of Transfiguration: Religious Imagination as Theopoiesis.* Eds. R. Melvin Keiser and Tony Stoneburner. Louisville, Kentucky: Westminster/John Knox Press, 1992.

Ingle, Larry. "One Historian's Reflections on Philosopher Jeffrey Dudiak's Search for the 'Meaning of Quaker History.'" *Quaker History,* 106.1 (Spring 2017): 22–24.

Jones, Sarah. "This Is Lights Appearance in the Truth." Mary Garman, Judith Applegate, Margaret Benefiel, Dortha Meredith, eds. *Hidden in Plain Sight: Quaker Women's Writings 1650–1700.* Wallingford, Pennsylvania: Pendle Hill Publications, 1996.

Keiser, R. Melvin. "From Dark Christian to Fullness of Life: Isaac Penington's Journey from Puritanism to Quakerism." *Guilford Review* 23 (Spring 1986).

___"The Growing Up Of Principles: Otherness Amidst Cartesian Dualism and Emergent Thinking in Robert Barclay." Unpublished paper (longer version) presented to the Quaker Theology Seminar, Woodbrooke, Birmingham, England, 7 April 1999.

___"Inward Light and the New Creation: A Theological Meditation on the Center and Circumference of Quakerism." Wallingford: Pendle Hill, January 1991.

___"The New Creation: Living in Feminist Wisdom." Solicited paper, Conference on George Fox 1624–1691, Lancaster University, 25–28 March 1991.

___"The Quaker Vision and the Doing of Theology." *Quaker Religious Thought* 28.3 (August 1997).

___"Two Lads in Front of a Fire: A Seventeenth-Century Tale." Unpublished.

___"Women Speaking in the New Creation: Margaret Fell's Theological Argument for Sexual Equality." Unpublished.

___and Rosemary Moore, eds. *Knowing the Mystery of Life Within: Selected Writings of Isaac Penington in Their Historical and Theological Context.* London: Quaker Books, 2005.

___and Elizabeth B. Keiser. "Quaker Principles in the Crucible of Practice." *Cross Currents: Journal of ARIL* 43.4 (Winter 1993/94).

Langland, William. *Piers Plowman: The B Version.* Eds. George Kane and E. Talbot Donaldson. New York: Norton Press, 1988.

Lessing, Gotthold. *Lessing's Theological Writings.* Trans. Henry Chadwick. Stanford: Stanford University Press, 1956; rpt. 1967.

Lurting, Thomas. *The Fighting Sailor Turn'd Peaceable Christian.* London: J. Sowle, 1710. Reprinted as appendix to Charles Vipont [Elfrida Vipont Foulds]. *Blow the Man Down.* Oxford: Oxford University Press, 1947.

Mack, Phyllis. *Visionary Women: Ecstatic Prophecy in Seventeenth-Century England.* Berkeley, Los Angeles, Oxford: University of California Press, 1992.

Macmurray, John. *Persons in Relation. v. II of The Form of the*

Personal. London: Faber and Faber Limited, 1961.

Malcolm, Norman. *Ludwig Wittgenstein: A Memoir.* New York: Oxford University Press, 1970.

Merleau-Ponty, Maurice. *Phenomenology of Perception.* Trans. Colin Smith. London: Routledge & Kegan Paul; New York: The Humanities Press, 1962.

Miller, John. "On Faith." *Quaker Religious Thought* 27.4 (December 1995): 39–43.

Nayler, James. 1656. *Love to the Lost. A Collection of Sundry Books.* Cincinnati: B. C. Stanton, 1829.

Niebuhr, H. Richard. *The Kingdom of God in America.* New York: Harper & Brothers, 1937; 1959.

___*The Meaning of Revelation.* New York: The Macmillan Company, 1941.

___*The Responsible Self: An Essay in Christian Moral Philosophy.* New York, Evanston, and London: Harper & Row, 1963.

Niebuhr, Reinhold. *The Nature and Destiny of Man: A Christian Interpretation.* New York: Charles Scribner's Sons, 1949.

Penington, Isaac. *Pre-Quaker Writings by Date of Publication:*

___*The Great and Sole Troubler of the Times.* London: Giles Calvert, 1649.

___*Severall Fresh Inward Openings.* London: Giles Calvert, 1650.

___*Light or Darknesse.* London: John Macock, 1650.

___*Divine Essays or Considerations about Several Things in Religion.* London: John Macock for Giles Calvert, 1654.

___*Expositions with Observations Sometimes on Severall Scriptures.* London: John Macock, 1656.

Penington, Isaac. *Quaker Writings Cited in Works:*

The Works of Isaac Penington: A Minister of the Gospel in the Society of Friends, including His Collected Letters, 4 vols. Glenside, PA: Quaker Heritage Press, 1995–1997.

___"The Way of Life and Death Made Manifest and Set Before Men." 1658. v. I.

___"The Scattered Sheep Sought After." 1659. v. I.

___"Short Catechism for the Sake of the Simple-Hearted." In "The Scattered Sheep Sought After." 1659. v. I.

___"Babylon the Great Described The City of Confusion In Every Part Whereof AntiChrist Reigns." 1659. v. I.

___"The Jew Outward Being A Glass For The Professors Of This Age." 1659. v. I.

___"The Axe Laid To The Root Of The Old Corrupt Tree." 1659. v. I.

___"An Examination Of the Ground Or Causes Which Are Said To Induce the Court of Boston In New England To Make That Order Or Law Of Banishment, Upon Pain Of Death, Against The Quakers." 1660. v. I.

___"Concerning Persecution Which Is The Afflicting Or Punishing That Which is Good, Under The Pretence Of Its Being Evil." 1661. v. II.

___"Some Directions to the Panting Soul." v. II.

___"To All Such As Complain That They Want Power." 1661. v. II.

___"Some Of The Mysteries Of God's Kingdom Glanced At." 1663. v. II.

___"To My Friends at Horton And Thereabouts." 1665. v. II.

___"A True And Faithful Relation, In Brief, Concerning Myself, In Reference To My Spiritual Travails." 1667. v. I.

___"To Friends Of Both The Chalfonts." 1667. v. II.

___"A Question To The Professors Of Christianity Whether They Have The True, Living, Powerful, Saving Knowledge of Christ, Or No." 1667. v. III.

___"Reply To Queries And Animadversions." 1667. v. IV.

___"Life and immortality Brought To Light Through The Gospel Being A True Discovery Of The Nature And Ground Of The Religion And Kingdom Of Christ." 1671. v. IV.

___"To Catharine Pordage." 1671. v. III.

___"A Treatise Concerning God's Teachings, And Christ's Law

With Some Other Things Of Weighty Importance." 1671. v. IV.

___"The Flesh And Blood Of Christ In The Mystery And In The Outward." 1675. v. III.

___ "To___." n.d. v. III.

___"Some Misrepresentations Of Me Concerning Church-Government Cleared And The Power And Authority Of God's Spirit In Governing His Church Testified To." n.d. v. IV.

___"The Seed of God And His Kingdom Treated and Tested Of According To The Scriptures Of Truth And According To True Experience Felt In The Heart From The God Of Truth." n.d. v. IV.

Penington, Mary. *Experiences in the life of Mary Penington (written by herself)*. Ed. Norman Penny. Philadelphia: The Biddle Press; London: Headley Bros., 1911. Rpt. London: Friends Historical Society, 1992.

Penn, William. "A Key Opening a Way to Every Common Understanding." Hugh S. Barbour, ed.

William Penn on Religion and Ethics: The Emergence of Liberal Quakerism. Lewiston,

Queenston, Lampeter: The Edwin Mellen Press, 1991.

___"No Cross, No Crown." 1669. In Frederick B. Tolles, *Meeting House and Counting House: The Quaker Merchants of Colonial Philadelphia 1682–1763*. New York: Norton, 1963.

___*The Papers of William Penn*. v. I–V. Richard S. Dunn & Mary Maples Dunn, eds. Philadelphia: University of Pennsylvania Press, 1981–87.

Polanyi, Michael. *Personal Knowledge: Towards a Post-Critical Philosophy*. London: Routledge and Kegan Paul, 1958.

___*The Tacit Dimension*. Garden City, New York: Doubleday & Company, 1966.

Poteat, William Hardman. *Pascal's Conception of Man and Modern Sensibility*. PhD dissertation, Duke University, 1950.

Punshon, John. *Portrait in Grey: A Short History of the Quakers*.

London: Quaker Home Service, 1984.

Pyper, Hugh S. "Resisting the Inevitable: Universal and Particular Salvation in the Thought of Robert Barclay." *Quaker Religious Thought* 29.1 (August 1998).

Quaker Faith & Practice: The Book of Christian Discipline of the Yearly Meeting of the Religious Society of Friends (Quakers) in Britain. Warwick: The Yearly Meeting of the Religious Society of Friends (Quakers) in Britain, 1995.

Read, Rupert. "On the Nature and Centrality of the Concept of 'Practice' among Quakers." *Quaker Religious Thought* 27.4 (December 1995).

Renfer, Linda Hill. Ed. *Daily Readings from Quaker Writings Ancient & Modern.* Grants Pass, OR: Serenity Press, 1988.

Ricoeur, Paul. *Interpretation Theory: Discourse and the Surplus of Meaning.* Fort Worth: The Texas Christian University Press, 1976.

Ruether, Rosemary Radford. *Sexism and God-Talk: Toward a Feminist Theology.* Boston: Beacon Press, 1983.

Rumi. *The Essential Rumi.* Trans. Coleman Barks with John Moyne. San Francisco: HarperCollins Publishers, 1996.

Russell, Letty M., ed. *Feminist Interpretation of the Bible.* Philadelphia: The Westminster Press, 1985.

Steere, Douglas V., ed. *Quaker Spirituality: Selected Writings.* New York: Paulist Press, 1984.

Tillich, Paul. *Systematic Theology.* v. I–III. Chicago: The University of Chicago Press, 1951–1963.

Tolles, Frederick B. *Meeting House and Counting House: The Quaker Merchants of Colonial Philadelphia, 1682–1763.* Chapel Hill: University of North Carolina Press, 1948.

Wink, Walter. *The Human Being: Jesus and the Enigma of the Son of the Man.* Minneapolis: Fortress Press, 2002.

Wittgenstein, Ludwig. *Philosophical Investigations.* Trans. G.E.M. Anscombe. New York: The Macmillan Company, 1953.

___*Tractatus Logico-Philosophicus*. Trans. D.F. Pears & B.F. McGuinness. London: Routledge & Kegan Paul, 1921 (orig. in German); 1961.

Woolman, John. *The Journal and Major Essays of John Woolman*. Ed. Phillips P. Moulton. New York: Oxford University Press, 1971.

Index

THE NEW OPEN SPACES

Throughout the two thousand years of Christian tradition there
have been, and still are, groups and individuals that exist in
the margins and upon the edge of faith. But in Christianity's
contrapuntal history it has often been these outcasts and
pioneers that have forged contemporary orthodoxy out
of former radicalism as belief evolves to engage with and
encompass the ever-changing social and scientific realities. Real
faith lies not in the comfortable certainties of the Orthodox,
but somewhere in a half-glimpsed hinterland on the dirt track
to Emmaus, where the Death of God meets the Resurrection,
where the supernatural Christ meets the historical Jesus,
and where the revolution liberates both the oppressed and
the oppressors.

Welcome to Christian Alternative... a space at the edge where
the light shines through.
If you have enjoyed this book, why not tell other readers by
posting a review on your preferred book site.
Recent bestsellers from Christian Alternative are:

Bread Not Stones
The Autobiography of An Eventful Life
Una Kroll
The spiritual autobiography of a truly remarkable woman
and a history of the struggle for ordination in the Church of
England.
Paperback: 978-1-78279-804-0 ebook: 978-1-78279-805-7

The Quaker Way

A Rediscovery

Rex Ambler

Although fairly well known, Quakerism is not well understood.
The purpose of this book is to explain how Quakerism works as
a spiritual practice.

Paperback: 978-1-78099-657-8 ebook: 978-1-78099-658-5

Blue Sky God

The Evolution of Science and Christianity

Don MacGregor

Quantum consciousness, morphic fields and blue-sky
thinking about God and Jesus the Christ.

Paperback: 978-1-84694-937-1 ebook: 978-1-84694-938-8

Celtic Wheel of the Year

Tess Ward

An original and inspiring selection of prayers combining
Christian and Celtic Pagan traditions, and interweaving their
calendars into a single pattern of prayer for every morning
and night of the year.

Paperback: 978-1-90504-795-6

Christian Atheist

Belonging without Believing

Brian Mountford

Christian Atheists don't believe in God but miss him: especially
the transcendent beauty of his music, language, ethics, and
community.

Paperback: 978-1-84694-439-0 ebook: 978-1-84694-929-6

Compassion Or Apocalypse?
A Comprehensible Guide to the Thoughts of René Girard
James Warren
How René Girard changes the way we think about God and the
Bible, and its relevance for our apocalypse-threatened world.
Paperback: 978-1-78279-073-0 ebook: 978-1-78279-072-3

Diary Of A Gay Priest
The Tightrope Walker
Rev. Dr. Malcolm Johnson
Full of anecdotes and amusing stories, but the Church is still a
dangerous place for a gay priest.
Paperback: 978-1-78279-002-0 ebook: 978-1-78099-999-9

Do You Need God?
Exploring Different Paths to Spirituality Even For Atheists
Rory J.Q. Barnes
An unbiased guide to the building blocks of spiritual belief.
Paperback: 978-1-78279-380-9 ebook: 978-1-78279-379-3

Readers of ebooks can buy or view any of these bestsellers by
clicking on the live link in the title. Most titles are published
in paperback and as an ebook. Paperbacks are available in
traditional bookshops. Both print and ebook formats are
available online.

Find more titles and sign up to our readers' newsletter at
http://www.johnhuntpublishing.com/christianity
Follow us on Facebook at
https://www.facebook.com/ChristianAlternative